An End to Upside Down Liberty

Also by Mark Gober

AN END TO UPSIDE DOWN THINKING

Dispelling the Myth That the Brain Produces Consciousness, and the Implications for Everyday Life

AN END TO UPSIDE DOWN LIVING

Reorienting Our Consciousness to Live Better and Save the Human Species

An End to Upside Down Liberty

Turning Traditional Political Thinking on Its Head to Break Free from Enslavement

Mark Gober

Waterside Productions
Cardiff-by-the-Sea, California

Copyright © 2021 by Mark Gober
www.markgober.com

All rights reserved. This book or any portion thereof may not be reproduced or used in any manner whatsoever without the express written permission of the publisher, except for the use of brief quotations in articles and book reviews.

Printed in the United States of America
First Printing, 2021

ISBN-13: 978-1-954968-88-2 print edition
ISBN-13: 978-1-954968-89-9 ebook edition
ISBN-13: 979-8-200859-27-6 audiobook edition

Waterside Productions
2055 Oxford Ave.
Cardiff-by-the-Sea, CA 92007
www.waterside.com

To those who want to be free.

"If we look at the black record of mass murder,
exploitation, and tyranny levied on society by
governments over the ages, we need not be loath to
abandon the Leviathan State and...try freedom."

—Murray Rothbard, PhD,
For a New Liberty (1973), p. 290

CONTENTS

PREFACE	CHALLENGING WORLDVIEWS	xi
SECTION I	**HOW DOES GOVERNMENT THREATEN LIBERTY?**	
CHAPTER 1	GOVERNMENT AS ORGANIZED CRIME	3
CHAPTER 2	DANGEROUS PSYCHOLOGY	27
CHAPTER 3	MIND CONTROL	37
SECTION II	**WHAT IS AN ALTERNATIVE TO TRADITIONAL GOVERNMENT?**	
CHAPTER 4	NONAGGRESSION, PRIVATE-PROPERTY RIGHTS, AND TRULY FREE MARKETS	75
CHAPTER 5	PRIVATIZING GOVERNMENT FUNCTIONS	105
SECTION III	**HOW DOES METAPHYSICS RELATE TO POLITICS AND ECONOMICS?**	
CHAPTER 6	THE NATURE OF REALITY	121
CHAPTER 7	MORALITY EMBEDDED IN REALITY	147
CHAPTER 8	METAPHYSICS MEETS POLITICAL AND ECONOMIC THEORY	163
SECTION IV	**WHAT IS THE PATH TO TRUE LIBERTY?**	
CHAPTER 9	A SHIFT IN CONSCIOUSNESS	183

ACKNOWLEDGMENTS 195
GLOSSARY 197
ENDNOTES 207
BIBLIOGRAPHY 233
INDEX 257
ABOUT THE AUTHOR 271

PREFACE

CHALLENGING WORLDVIEWS

Upside down liberty is the mistaken belief that we are free when in fact we are not. Our hidden enslavement occurs on two primary levels: the metaphysical and the physical.

Metaphysically, we are enslaved because of a vast misunderstanding about the nature of reality. Our scientific establishment tells us that we are finite beings living in a random, meaningless universe. As soon as our brain shuts off, we die. Forever. Lights out. However, an abundance of credible scientific evidence—covered extensively in my previous two books and summarized later in this one—suggests otherwise. The evidence flies in the face of mainstream assumptions and instead suggests that we are *infinite* beings who *do not* die when our body does. Furthermore, we're all fundamentally interconnected as part of a unified field of consciousness that our everyday senses simply don't perceive. It's as if we unknowingly live with amnesia under a blindfold.

Our inability to recognize—and live in accordance with—our true nature leads to psychological imprisonment. We become like hamsters running on a wheel that we can't escape, trapped by our narrow perception of only "this body," "this life," and "this dimension," and enslaved by our attachments to worldly desires and fears. Most of us don't even realize we're on a treadmill, effectively going nowhere in spite of seemingly endless efforts and repeated patterns of suffering. The reality is that we can mentally step off at any time once we wake up to the truth.

Physically, we are enslaved—to varying degrees—via the institution of government, but we don't realize it. We all know how much death and destruction governments have caused throughout history during wars, for example. They kill each other's people. But here I'm referring more specifically to the way in which governments can be a threat to their *own* people. That perspective entails viewing government not as a protector of its citizens, but rather as a predator. That makes the citizens prey. Yes, even in "democracies," and yes—I'm sorry to say it—even in America.

The enslavement process can occur gradually over time and can be likened to a frog slowly boiling in a pot of water that doesn't realize what's happened until it's too late. Freedoms are stripped bits at a time. Liberty is eroded under the guise of providing safety. *We're doing this to protect you* is how it's marketed to the masses, but in reality it's death by a thousand cuts. They'll take liberties, and maybe offer a few back to give the appearance of being magnanimous, but they won't give them *all* back. Repeat that process and it's a slippery slope.

Those of us who have never lived under blatantly oppressive regimes like those in North Korea, Nazi Germany, or the Soviet Union under Joseph Stalin, for instance, tend to think that it can't happen to us—and that if it *were* happening to us, we'd recognize the evil and stop it. I'd argue that in today's world, the opposite sentiment is prevalent: some activists, who believe they are doing the right thing, condemn as "dangerous" or "selfish" those who rightfully value freedom.

It's also worth remembering that the Nazis—who came to power within a democratic government—weren't sending Jews to concentration camps on day one of their regime. Erosions to civil liberties always have a starting point and run the risk of transforming into something overtly totalitarian. Therefore, it's best that citizens not rest on their laurels until their government reaches a tyrannical "point of no return."

Now is an especially perilous time because of advances in technology. The potential exists for a surveillance police state in which our every move is tracked by the government. An Orwellian future is no longer fiction. It's within reach, if not already occurring in some places.

If all of this sounds like sensational paranoia, consider what's happening in modern China. As reported in a September 2020 article in *The Atlantic*:

> China already has hundreds of millions of surveillance cameras in place. [President] Xi's government hopes to soon achieve full video coverage of key public areas. Much of the footage collected by China's cameras is parsed by algorithms for security threats of one kind or another. In the near future, every person who enters a public space could be identified, instantly, by [artificial intelligence (AI)] matching them to an ocean of personal data, including their every text communication, and their body's one-of-a-kind protein-construction schema. In time, algorithms will be able to string together data points from a broad range of sources—travel records, friends and associates, reading habits, purchases—to predict political resistance before it happens. China's government could soon achieve an unprecedented political stranglehold on more than 1 billion people....
>
> Artificial intelligence has applications in nearly every human domain, from the instant translation of spoken language to early viral-outbreak detection. But Xi also wants to use AI's awesome analytical powers to push China to the cutting edge of surveillance. He wants to build an all-seeing digital system of social control, patrolled by...algorithms that identify potential dissenters in real time....

> The government might soon have a rich, auto-populating data profile for all of its 1 billion–plus citizens. Each profile would comprise millions of data points, including the person's every appearance in surveilled space, as well as all of her communications and purchases. Her threat risk to the party's power could constantly be updated in real time, with a more granular score than those used in China's pilot "social credit" schemes, which already aim to give every citizen a public social-reputation score based on things like social-media connections and buying habits.[1]

Additionally, in a May 2021 interview, journalist Whitney Webb explained the troubling state of affairs she encountered in Chile:

> I actually lived in Chile for about seven years. I only really recently left, and I reluctantly left.... With the onset of the whole COVID-19 crisis, basically overnight pretty much everything just shut down and things became very rapidly very totalitarian. The situation now in Chile is that if quarantine is declared in the town or community where you live, you are only allowed out of your house twice a week for two hours a pop. So that's a total of four hours per week. And [in] all of that you have to have papers that are provided by police through a new police website, so you basically cannot leave your home without police permission.... Those two-hour permissions include travel time, so if you don't live close to a supermarket or anything like that you have even less time to do essential shopping.... There were cases of people being arrested for having incorrect papers, and this was being enforced by police.... In December [of 2020], it became the military enforcing this stuff. This was going on just between even small cities. I had to go to a small town that was twenty minutes away from where I was living. I would have to pass through what was basically a military checkpoint [and] have the right papers... to go to the next city....

> Chile...is often used as a sort of a test lab by the US and some other western powers....Chileans openly talk about this being reality....Whether that can succeed in a western country really depends on the type of resistance people are willing to show in the face of that type of policy.[2]

Similarly, the state of Victoria, Australia, set up checkpoints in August of 2020, some of which were monitored by the military. A doctor who was often stopped at the checkpoints called it "frightening" and "surreal."[3] In July of 2021, Sydney, Australia, deployed hundreds of soldiers to enforce its lockdown.[4] *The Sydney Morning Herald* reported an additional piece of disturbing news in August of 2021: "Several impounded dogs due to be rescued by a shelter [in the state of New South Wales, Australia] have instead been shot dead...under [a local council's] interpretation of COVID-19 restrictions." The dogs were allegedly killed "to prevent volunteers...from traveling to pick up the animals" in order to "protect employees and the community...from the risk of COVID-19 transmission."[5] And in the same month, the state of Queensland, Australia, announced its plan to build a "new 1000-bed, dedicated quarantine facility."[6]

Along those lines, in March of 2021, Canada's prime minister, Justin Trudeau, announced Canada's COVID-19 travel regulations: "If you're flying back into the country, you'll need to show a negative PCR test result before you board the plane. When you land, you'll need to take another PCR test. You'll then have to wait at an approved hotel, and at your own expense, for your results to come back....If your results come back negative for COVID-19, you'll be able to head home and finish your mandatory quarantine there. If your test results come back positive, you'll need to immediately quarantine in designated government facilities. This is not optional."[7]

***It's for your safety*, we're often told. Maybe it is. On the other hand, maybe in some cases governments are slowly enslaving their people through the weaponization of crisis.** If that were true, they wouldn't openly tell everyone, "We are enslaving you."

Smart criminals wouldn't do that. "We're protecting you" is a much more effective way to do it if a gullible and naive populace—blinded by fear—trusts them.

We might attempt to rationalize the situation by saying to ourselves, *It's okay because we're only giving up freedom temporarily, and then things will go back to normal. It's just to keep us safe, and it's for the common good.* As former US congressman Ron Paul, MD, puts it: **"Sacrificing a little liberty for imaginary safety always ends badly."**[8] [emphasis added]

We often *want* to assume that our political leaders are trustworthy and have good intentions. New Zealand's prime minister, Jacinda Ardern, said this about COVID-19: "We will continue to be your single source of truth....Unless you hear it from us, it is not the truth." She urged citizens to "dismiss anything else."[9] So, the government gets a monopoly on truth? We might think, *It's okay because our elected leaders aren't dishonest; they seem nice and caring on television and should be believed.* Not always so. Robert F. Kennedy Jr., son of former US senator Robert F. Kennedy and nephew of President John F. Kennedy, remarked: "My father told me when I was a child: **people in authority lie**."[10] [emphasis added]

But in America we have a Constitution with a Bill of Rights that protects us from anything really bad, we might be tempted to say. However, during the COVID-19 crisis, the Constitution seemed to have taken a back seat. Rather than presenting information to the public and allowing people to make decisions according to their own risk preferences, many politicians set blanket rules for everyone—in the name of "safety"—regardless of whether such actions were constitutional. In April of 2020, New Jersey's governor, Philip Murphy, was asked what enabled him to arrest fifteen congregants in a New Jersey synagogue who were peacefully assembling. What gave him the authority to ignore the Bill of Rights? Murphy said, "That's above my pay grade" and said he "wasn't thinking of the Bill of Rights when we did this."[11]

What good is a constitution if it's not enforced? It's then just a piece of paper. If it can be ignored in the event of an emergency without penalty, couldn't power-hungry politicians simply weaponize—or even create—an emergency for their own aims? Author Tom Woods reminds us of a fact that is sometimes easy to overlook: "In a free society *people* do not require constitutional authority to act. Government does."[12] [emphasis in original]

In November of 2020, US Supreme Court justice Samuel Alito also commented on this concerning trend: "We have never before seen restrictions as severe, extensive and prolonged as those experienced for most of 2020....The COVID crisis has served as a sort of constitutional stress test and in doing so, it has highlighted disturbing trends that were already present before the virus struck... [including a] dominance of lawmaking by executive fiat rather than legislation."[13] Ron Paul foresaw this back in 2012, stating, "Our Constitution, which was intended to limit government power and abuse, has failed."[14]

Furthermore, in May of 2021, Paul spoke from his personal experience, recalling his past disagreements with other members of Congress while he was in office. He would ask them: "Why are you doing this? You know this is a violation of [the people's] liberties?" **The politicians would reply to Paul, "Yeah but they're so stupid."** [emphasis added] Paul said of the politicians, "They are elitist, they believe they know what's right, and it just happens to fit into their own personal egos and their personal finances.... Some people live for power and some just for money and some just want to be proven right, so they want to be in charge." The "stupidity," according to Paul, is when people become "dependent" on the government.[15]

Cognitive Dissonance

In the absence of a more elaborate discussion (which follows in this book), the ideas discussed so far might sound outlandish. They contradict what we hear in the mainstream press and what our education system teaches us. A natural reaction is to become defensive and resistant. The psychological stress associated with this process of encountering information that contradicts fundamental beliefs is known as *cognitive dissonance*. If not properly identified and managed, it can stifle our development and allow us to become susceptible to evil.

If you're a conventionally trained thinker, this book is likely to cause a great deal of cognitive dissonance. Put another way, as you read, you're apt to say to yourself (often): "No, that can't be true. In fact, the opposite of what's being said here is true." I know this because I've had to deal with it myself. Most of what I've written here comes from my exploration outside of what I learned as an undergraduate at Princeton and beyond my Wall Street and Silicon Valley business experience. I thought my educational and professional background would have given me pretty good insights into how the world works. I was wrong.

In the process of shattering my old reality, I've had to deconstruct cognitive dissonance in my own mind and understand how it unfolds for others. What follows are five psychological hurdles I've identified that will be useful to keep in mind during the remainder of this book:

1. Developing a new worldview is uncomfortable and disorienting. It takes ongoing mental energy to constantly rethink all of one's previous assumptions and consciously formulate new ones.
2. Recognizing the extent of our ignorance crushes the ego—especially if we mistakenly believe we've been well trained. It's difficult to admit, "I was wrong." Sometimes it's even harder to admit, "I was wrong, and you were right."
3. Political belief systems are particularly rigid. For example, a member of one political party might prefer to hold on to an incorrect belief rather than accept that the opposing party is correct.
4. It's difficult to acknowledge that we've been lied to, especially by people we thought were "good." We have to come to grips with the fact that (a) someone we respected and believed to be trustworthy is not, and (b)

we fell for it. As astronomer Carl Sagan put it: "One of the saddest lessons of history is this: If we've been bamboozled long enough, we tend to reject any evidence of the bamboozle. We're no longer interested in finding out the truth. The bamboozle has captured us. It's simply too painful to acknowledge, even to ourselves, that we've been taken. Once you give a charlatan power over you, you almost never get it back."[16]

This mental hurdle is especially challenging with regard to politicians: we are often conditioned to believe that if we elected them as our representatives, they're responsible, honorable servants of the people. This perspective could be accurate in some cases, but it ignores the possibility of being bamboozled by talented actors who simply say what the people want to hear, when in fact all they really care about is power. History teaches us that we shouldn't put political leaders on a pedestal and assume they'll take care of us.

5. Accepting the reality of hidden evil is upsetting. It feels more comfortable to delude ourselves into viewing the world with "rose-colored glasses." That can come back to bite us, however. Ignorance is bliss…until it's not. Carl Raschke, PhD, a professor of religious studies at the University of Denver, summarized this notion: "The American intelligentsia has a tremendous capacity for what psychologists call 'denial.' The trained academic mind has a difficult time accepting that there are people who could willfully do evil for the sake of doing evil."[17] Similarly, author Michael Malice says: "The average person's mechanism for determining a truth claim is simply whether it gives them a positive emotional response."[18] It's often easier to accept comforting ideas than it is to accept disturbing ones.

The intent of this book is not to dwell on darkness, and in fact, many of the metaphysical concepts and accompanying scientific studies are incredibly comforting. Rather, I hope to bring about new ways of looking at the world in an effort to promote a liberated mindset—which, as I see it, is a precursor to a liberated planet. Mere exposure to the forthcoming concepts can be enough to trigger a domino effect leading to a new way of thinking and living.

The process requires discernment, however. Spiritual teacher David Hawkins, MD, PhD, summarized this notion by offering the distinction of "perception versus essence." Perception is what we see on the surface, whereas essence is the truth behind the veil; perception is taking something at face value, whereas essence is reading between the lines. Perception can be a Trojan horse that allows us to fall prey to the "wolf in sheep's clothing."

This is a book about digging into essence rather than perception. It's about identifying where we've been hoodwinked and figuring out how to course-correct. If enough of us can successfully do so, there's no telling how bright our civilization's future can be. So, even if we experience psychological discomfort along the way, I'd say it's worth it. On the other hand, we cannot allow the alternative—full enslavement, both domestically and internationally—to prevail.

SECTION I

HOW DOES GOVERNMENT THREATEN LIBERTY?

CHAPTER 1

GOVERNMENT AS ORGANIZED CRIME

I'm shocked to have written this book on the topic of politics. Previously, I never cared much about the subject one way or the other. I always suspected that the political sphere was full of corruption, but in the end, America's imperfect constitutional republic did enough to make life pretty good for many of us. I was able to go about my life without thinking too much about the government or identifying with political ideologies or parties.

That changed in 2020 when the world went haywire amid the COVID-19 crisis. Suddenly, governmental decisions around the world were impacting everyone's daily lives in a much more direct and visible manner. In spite of the prevalence of illnesses that have burdened society for a long time—such as cancer, heart disease, diabetes, autoimmune conditions, mental ailments, and beyond—governments decided, essentially, that only COVID-19 mattered, and it was enough to shut down the world. Everyone was suddenly assumed to be "sick until proven healthy." Discussions about alternative medical treatments and boosting the body's natural immune system became blasphemy, and fear became a virtue.

Politicians (alongside unelected public health officials) then dictated how physically close people could be to one another; when they could leave their homes; when they could open businesses; which businesses were "essential" and which weren't; whether or not people were allowed to breathe air freely without a mask; when they were allowed to hug one another;[1] when they could sit, in person, with a dying loved one; whether they could sing in places of worship;[2] whether they were allowed to dance at wedding receptions;[3] and so on. **The illness was indeed tragic for many people, but so were the side effects of mandates imposed by governments.**

Furthermore, we started to hear rhetoric suggesting that freedom was something doled out *by* the government *to* the people. For example, in June of 2021, the prime minister of the United Kingdom, Boris Johnson, announced "Freedom Day": the day on which the country's lockdown restrictions would end.[4] Freedom was to be granted only when *the government* said so.

Member of Parliament Graham Brady commented further on the UK's handling of COVID-19 in his July 2021 article published in the *Daily Mail*: "When I asked a Health Minister in the Commons how she could justify banning healthy activities such as golf, tennis or bowls, she actually replied that while those activities were indeed safe, **if we 'let people do those things, they might think they can do other things too.'"** Brady continued: "Many politicians and advisers will admit privately that the policy change compelling people to wear masks was not really about the spread of infection at all but about the psychological effect that they would have. **That real purpose is social control**—to provide a constant reminder to maintain distance from other people. To maintain a state of anxiety that leaves people more likely to comply with the restrictions that might otherwise be resisted or forgotten."[5] [emphasis added]

The French government similarly micromanaged its citizens' lives. In June of 2021, the government suspended its 11 p.m. COVID-19 "curfew" to allow fans to continue watching an all-time classic tennis match at the French Open between Rafael Nadal and

Novak Djokovic—days after having forced fans to leave before the completion of one of the prior matches. In the case of the Nadal-Djokovic match, fans were told: "It is an exception granted given the completely exceptional nature of the circumstances."[6] The crowd "erupted" in cheers upon hearing this news. The government granted fans the freedom to stay past 11 P.M. to continue watching a tennis match.

On a related note, in March of 2021, a visiting professor of health policy and management at George Washington University spoke on CNN about the importance of mass vaccination. In order to convince people to take the COVID-19 vaccine, she contended: "We need to make it clear...that the vaccine is the ticket back to pre-pandemic life. We have a very narrow window to tie reopening policy to vaccination status. Because otherwise if everything is reopened, then what's the 'carrot' going to be? How are we actually going to incentivize people to get the vaccine? So that's why I think the [US government] needs to come out a lot bolder and say, **'If you're vaccinated, you can do all these things, here are all these freedoms that you have.' Because otherwise, people are going to go out and enjoy these freedoms anyway.**"[7] [emphasis added]

This is the sort of language that the state of New South Wales, Australia, used in August of 2021. Its Minister of Health announced that if the state met a vaccination threshold, those "who have received both doses of the COVID-19 vaccine will be allowed more freedoms next month." In some areas, gatherings of "up to five people" would be allowed within five kilometers of one's home. In areas with greater concern about COVID-19, people would be allowed to gather outdoors "for recreation" *for one hour*, which would be "in addition to the one hour allowed for exercise."[8]

I mention these examples neither to debate the efficacy of government policies nor to make a statement about the appropriateness of medical interventions. Rather, the global trends during the COVID-19 crisis introduced fundamental questions for me: *Does the government have the right to micromanage our lives? Does freedom come from the government? Do the answers to these questions change if there is an event dubbed an "emergency"?*

I then started asking even simpler questions: *What is government? What rights do citizens have? When can the government tell us what to do? What is the nature of liberty?*

As I researched, contemplated, and watched the world's events unfold, it became clear that a new paradigm was needed for thinking about the basic nature of politics. That's where we'll begin this journey.

The State

Let's try to forget everything we know about how society is structured and start from scratch. I mean *really* from scratch.

Earth is a planet with lots of people. Billions of them. They all require food and shelter in order to survive. Many of them want to reproduce and care for their offspring. Most, if not all, would like to be happy. Attempting to meet everyone's basic needs comes with inherent challenges. For example, Earth's resources are finite. Weather and wildlife create obstacles. Meanwhile, humans navigate all this through bodies that need to be fueled and cared for.

Complicating matters further is the fact that humans have an innate dark side. History has shown that they will rape and pillage to get what they need. They'll lie, cheat, and steal if necessary. Not everyone abides by the same set of morals. To some, all that matters is their own survival and prosperity, no matter what the cost to others.

A fundamental question then arises: What is the most effective way for people to organize themselves such that their essential human needs are met amid environmental and biological constraints—and compounded with challenges brought forth by human nature?

Political philosophers like Thomas Hobbes (1588–1679) have argued that what's needed is a centralized power structure, which he called the "Leviathan." Without it, the argument goes, we would be living in a state of untenable anarchy and war. As Hobbes stated: "During the time men live without a common Power to keep them in awe, they are in that condition which is called Warre; and such a warre, as is of every man, against every man."[9]

And so modern civilization has consistently employed such a "common power"—also known as "government" or "the State"—as the primary organization method. Simply put, the State is an agency with ultimate decision-making power over a certain territory, while offering services and varying degrees of protection to its citizens.[10] The State is managed by a ruling class of lawmakers who employ law enforcers to ensure the obedience of the citizens (see the illustration below).

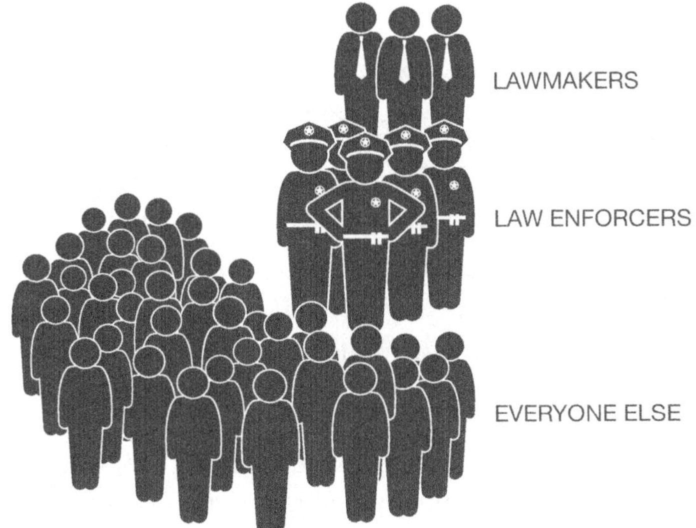

The basic structure of a society managed by the State (adapted from the work of Larken Rose).

The belief that the State should govern society is known as *statism*, the prevailing metaparadigm in contemporary political thinking. It is the idea underlying virtually all theories of politics, whether liberal or conservative. All sides of the statist political spectrum are debating the *role* of the State in governance, and in so doing they presuppose the existence of the State.

In theory, States around the world help their societies run smoothly, and some States do a better job than others. They assist with the building of roads, protect their citizens with police and military forces, house legal systems to resolve disputes, manage the economy through central banking (in America, the Federal Reserve), and provide other regulatory functions as they see fit.

So far, nothing earth-shattering.

However, we'll now turn to a much more exotic and radical idea, which at first probably won't make any sense. Are you ready for this? Cognitive-dissonance alert!

The State's authority is inherently illegitimate. In fact, political philosopher Larken Rose has gone so far to say that the prevailing belief in the legitimacy of the State's authority is "the most dangerous superstition."[11]

From this lens, instead of using polite terms like *government* and *the State*, we could call it *organized crime*[12] or the *Mafia*. It could even be likened to a manipulative religious institution that engages in mystical rituals to deify itself. It's simply dressed up to look righteous: a veritable "wolf in sheep's clothing."

We have to ask ourselves: Should we assume that just because we call it "government" we'll be taken care of? Is it truly possible for a government to remain "limited" in its power before eventually growing into something blatantly authoritarian? Do our elected representatives care more about our interests or *their own*? Or is it idealistic, utopian thinking to believe in the possibility of permanently constrained government, run by politicians who will somehow resist the seduction of power and steer clear of corruption?

We'll be discussing these topics and exploring an alternative to the State—one that respects private-property rights, eliminates sanctioned coercion, endorses voluntary exchanges, and privatizes the government's poorly managed public sector.

If these ideas are new to you, what follows might take a while to sink in. I'll be pointing out problems inherent in the State's fundamental mode of operation. In some instances, there might be a tendency to be accepting (or even welcoming) of those shortcomings, using the following argument: *It's the best we can do. I'm willing to make moral concessions because they're necessary to keep society running smoothly. The system certainly isn't perfect, but it's good enough, and it's the way we've done it for a long time. Many of us have generally enjoyed freedom thanks to our government's protection. We should be grateful rather than critical.*

However, it's essential that we shine a light on the State's foundational defects rather than sweep them under the rug: what start off as seemingly "minor" flaws, could, over time, transform into much more serious transgressions and erosions of civil liberties. And that's precisely what we're seeing with States around the world today—even from States that have traditionally been considered "free" nations.

With this context in mind, we'll now examine the State more closely.

The State Doesn't Eliminate Anarchy

The modern world is full of States governing their respective territorial domains. However, what's often overlooked is the fact that States are not policed by a world government. And even if they were, there would be nothing to police that governing body. While the creation of the State purportedly avoids chaos at one level, it creates a new anarchy: an anarchy of States—which political economist Murray Rothbard, PhD (1926–1995) called "international anarchy."[13] That is, in fact, the condition in which we currently live. The State just kicks the anarchy can down the proverbial road; it doesn't eliminate it, but merely creates a different brand.

The State as a Monopoly

Another basic fact to acknowledge is that the State is inherently monopolistic. Rothbard summed it up well: "Throughout history, groups of men calling themselves 'the government' or 'the State' have attempted—usually successfully—to gain a compulsory monopoly of the commanding heights of the economy and society. In particular, the State has arrogated to itself a compulsory monopoly over police and military services, the provision of law, judicial decision-making, the mint and the power to create money, unused land ('the public domain'), streets and highways, [and] rivers and coastal waters."[14]

Author Tom Woods asks the right question: **"Why do we unthinkingly assume that political monopolies are a good thing, even though we are rightly suspicious of all other sorts of monopoly?"**[15] [emphasis added]

The "Social Contract"

The idea that the State rules in an effectively *compulsory* manner, as Rothbard noted, is worth examining further. In other words, we are born in a certain territory and, as a consequence, we are beholden to the governing State's dictates. *It is not truly voluntary.* We can't stay in a territory and say: "I don't like the government, so I'm going to ignore its rules and consider myself outside of its dominion." In fact, if you do that, the rules will be forced upon you. You can leave the territory (if you're able to do so), but then you'll simply find yourself under the dominion of a different ruler.

Political philosophers such as Hobbes, John Locke (1632–1704), and Jean-Jacques Rousseau (1712–1778) popularized the notion of a *social contract* that is often referenced as a way to justify the legitimacy of the State's authority. The term has come to imply an agreement among citizens to consent to a governmental structure that will protect them, even if it means giving up a little bit of their individual freedoms. Moral and civic duties compel citizens to abide by the social contract.

However, it's difficult to specify what the social contract is... **because it does not exist**. The reality is that the social contract is a mythical, theoretical abstraction. The related political slogan, "consent of the governed," is similarly a myth. There is no true consent by the people to be ruled by a governing body. It's only "implied consent."[16] We don't have an explicit contract with our government.

Alternatively, if there were, in fact, a legitimate, binding contract between citizens and the State, then the organization would cease to be called "the State." **Instead, an organization that performs the same exact functions as the State, but which serves individuals after a contract has been voluntarily signed, is a *service provider*.**[17]

Think about it in this way. When individuals voluntarily subscribe to a service provider in other domains—Netflix, gym memberships, cell-phone services, and so on—they pay in exchange for the service. It's a contractual relationship. The subscriber wants a service, so she signs up and pays money to get what she signed up for. There is a mutually agreed-upon exchange at a mutually agreed-upon price. The subscriber can cancel the subscription and stop paying for the service. And if, within a competitive market, a better service comes along, the subscriber can sign up for that one instead. The same thing is true with employment: the employer hires someone at an agreed-upon price (the wage), the parties have an agreement as to terms of employment, and they can terminate the relationship, as appropriate (through firing and resignation policies). The point is that, in our world, there are many relationships in which parties voluntarily agree to provide a service for a price.

In the instance of the State, citizens pay for services (roads, police, military, courts, and so on) via taxation. The State uses these funds to perform its duties. But the citizens never contractually agreed to this, and the State sets the price.

Hans-Hermann Hoppe, professor emeritus of economics at the University of Nevada, Las Vegas, explains the situation well:

> The State unilaterally fixes the rules of the game—the laws—and can change them by legislation during the game....Imagine a [service provider]...whose offer consisted [of] something like this:..."I will not contractually guarantee you anything. I will not tell you what specific things I will regard as yours to be protected

> property, nor will I tell you what I oblige myself to do if, according to your opinion, I do not fulfill my service to you. But in any case, I reserve the right to unilaterally determine the price that you must pay me for such undefined service."[18]

Is that a compelling offer? Wouldn't it make sense for citizens to have explicit service-provider contracts for government services, like true customers do in other domains?

Taxation and Morality

There's also a moral dilemma embedded in this situation, as often explained by Rose. Imagine for a moment that you see a man on the street with a bag of groceries that he rightfully owns. On the same street, you see a beggar. Consider:

- Would it be morally acceptable for you to take the man's groceries against his will and give them to the beggar?
- Would it be morally acceptable for you to hire someone to take the man's groceries against his will and give them to the beggar?
- What if you and your friends elect a representative who then appoints someone to take the man's groceries and give them to the beggar?
- What if, instead of grabbing the man's groceries, you or your representatives take the man's wallet, which holds money he was just paid for completing a labor-intensive job, and use the money to fund your local police station?

Most non-psychopathic people would say that all of the above examples are objectively immoral. It's not okay to forcibly steal from someone else. It's an act of aggression—in essence, violence. You can't just take someone's private property, including money, without consent.

That same morality applies to everyone—no special privileges. If it's not okay for anyone to take another person's property, then *you're* not off the hook by getting someone else to do it for you.

Ask yourself: *How is this any different from taxation?*

It's not.

Taxation is not truly voluntary; it's a coercive process in which citizens pay the State, under the threat of being locked in a cage (jail) if they don't. As political candidate Jeremy (Spike) Cohen puts it: "Taxes are the price we pay not to be arrested and have our assets and property seized."[19] And yet this sanctioned coercion is the basis of the State's financial lifeblood.

Although some citizens might gladly pay their taxes, others might feel as if they're being extorted. So if we look at taxation objectively, it can be viewed as a form of theft—no matter who receives the stolen funds and no matter how righteous we've been conditioned to believe it is. The political Left might feel better if the funds are distributed to the poor, and the political Right might want the money directed to the police and military. But it's still theft. The only difference is that some people prefer certain types of theft over others, and they'll passionately fight for their candidates to be elected so that they can force their opposition to fund what *they* want. No wonder political debates evoke such hostility!

This exercise raises another moral conundrum: Is it okay to force people to fund an activity that they find morally wrong? Outside the context of government, most of us would probably answer no. For example, it's not morally acceptable to tell a man on the street that he has to give his hard-earned money away to fund abortions, given that his personal belief system is that abortions are immoral. Or alternatively, imagine another man who opposes a government-sponsored war. He knows that the government is killing innocent civilians in a foreign nation, and he morally opposes it. It doesn't matter. He still has to pay taxes that fund the war.[20]

This is taxation in a nutshell. It's not as if the State hands us a list of activities it's considering funding and gives us instructions: "Please check off the causes to which your taxpayer dollars will go. Also, let us know how much you would like to contribute to each cause."

Even more than being coercive theft, taxation illustrates a peculiar feature often highlighted by Rose: It implies that citizens can delegate a right—which they don't have themselves—*to someone else*.[21] What is deemed legal for the government is illegal for the average citizen. Put another way, the thinking is: "I don't have a right to steal from someone, but because people are elected to positions within the government, they have a right to do so. We, the citizens, gave them that right because we voted them into power as our representatives. We're giving them the authority to do something that we don't have the authority to do ourselves. And, most important, we the citizens don't even have an explicit contractual relationship with the government and therefore never formally agreed to this."[22]

Rose makes an even bolder assertion: he says we collectively "hallucinate" that the government has this magical power simply by virtue of its being "government." Sure, it has the ability and means to steal. Anyone *could* steal. But that is distinct from having a moral *right* to steal. The power to do this only exists because we're under a collective spell that trains us not to question the State's legitimacy. Somehow, the State has an **"exemption from morality"** (as Rose phrases it).[23] [emphasis added]

Rose goes so far to say that because the State's power is simply a hallucination, its authority "does not and cannot exist."[24] It *seems* to exist only because the masses, including law enforcement, blindly subscribe to the hallucination, thereby allowing the State's authority to continue largely unquestioned.

Inverting Morality

We're also conditioned to believe the State's aggression is *good*. For example, government officials who enforce tax laws are the good guys and gals who bring to justice those who don't want to pay. The robber is the hero, and the victim is the criminal.[25]

Do you see the inversion here? For any institution other than government, the roles would be reversed. Somehow, it's virtuous to be stolen from and immoral to resist theft.[26]

The State's role in society starts to take on a quasi-religious quality. As Rose puts it: "Like other religions, the gospel of 'government' describes a superhuman, supernatural entity, above mere mortals, which issues commandments to the peasantry, for whom unquestioning obedience is a moral imperative. Disobeying…the commandments ('breaking the law') is viewed as sin."[27] Perhaps all of this is a vestige of a past era of history in which the monarchy's power was established through "the divine right of kings."

I've included Rose's harsh language here because it conveys a perspective that we're not accustomed to considering. We've been so conditioned to describe the State in benign—or even favorable—terms that the more questionable aspects are often obscured. But when we consider what the State is actually doing, without using euphemisms, it becomes clear that its activities are much less wholesome than we initially realized. For example, as Rose notes (again, using severe wording), "Tax collectors" become "professional extortionists," "law enforcers" become "hired thugs," and "laws" become "threats from politicians."[28] Unwinding this conditioning requires true mental energy. (By the way, I just want to acknowledge how much cognitive dissonance you might be experiencing already. This isn't easy!)

Additional Moral Conundrums

Imagine what it must have been like to live in Nazi Germany as a German citizen, recognizing what was going on and being horrified by the civil-rights violations occurring everywhere. The law—the State's determination of "right and wrong"—compelled Germans to do things to Jews and other groups that might have completely contradicted their moral codes. So, would it have been okay for a German to break the "law" in order to obey his or her conscience? Most of us would probably say yes. Of course, this is an extreme example, but think about it in your own life. Can you imagine a situation in which the State passed laws that you would disobey based on your moral principles? Many of us would say, "Yes, I can envision there being at least *some* laws that I wouldn't obey."[29]

The problem, again, is that we're left with an inconsistency. If there are any conditions under which it's okay to break the law, then what is the law, really? If the State's rules can be disobeyed sometimes at will, based on the "arbitrary" morality of the individual, what is the value of having rules at all?

Think about it in another way. If following the law is the moral thing to do under the State's rule, and if a citizen considers aspects of the law to be immoral, then the "morality" inherent in following the law requires that citizen to be immoral. By doing the moral thing, the citizen simultaneously does an immoral thing.[30]

Along those lines, why should it be the State's role to dictate what's moral in the first place? As Murray Rothbard aptly put it, "Placing the [S]tate in charge of moral principles is equivalent to putting the proverbial fox in charge of the chicken coop."[31]

Moreover, if the State can create its own arbitrary standard of morality and force people to do things that they consider immoral, under the threat of imprisonment if they disobey...how does that differ from the concept of slavery? (A point of clarification before proceeding: since the word *slavery* in modern society is often associated with the inhumane treatment of African American slaves, I want to emphasize that the use of that word in this context is different. Here, it refers to the general concept of being under someone else's effective ownership or control against one's will. The conditions of the slavery referenced here are in many cases far less severe than the abhorrent abuse that African American slaves—and many other slaves throughout history—have had to endure. There is a spectrum of severity with regard to slavery, and I don't mean to imply that all forms of slavery are of the same degree, even though they might have the same conceptual basis. **However, the danger of being anywhere on the "slavery"**

spectrum is that things could get worse. That's why I'm suggesting that we pay close attention to any such erosions of liberty and not sugarcoat the situation with language that hides what is objectively happening. Ask yourself: "If I'm not fully free... then what am I? And what could I become?")

Involuntary Servitude

The parallels to slavery—broadly defined—go even further. The State defends its citizens with a military. Some citizens voluntarily sign up, whereas others are forced into service via a "draft" (known as *conscription*). They're sent to war, and some of them die. Those who survive might be permanently injured or traumatized. Some brave individuals welcome this opportunity, while those who resist might face serious penalties.

As Rothbard noted, conscription could be likened to slavery:[32] People are sometimes forced into service against their will.

Here's another, albeit less extreme, example: Rothbard likened compulsory jury service to involuntary servitude. As he stated, "There is little difference in kind, though obviously a great difference in degree, between compulsory jury duty and conscription; both are enslavement, both compel the individual to perform tasks on the State's behalf and at the State's bidding....Furthermore, not only are jurors coerced into attending and serving on juries, but sometimes they are locked behind closed doors for many weeks, and prohibited from reading newspapers."[33]

Our psychological conditioning pushes back on all of this. *Conscription and jury duty are really important functions for society,* we're tempted to say. Many of us might even consider these forms of service to be an honor and a privilege. But that misses the point. The broader question is this: Is it morally acceptable to coerce people into doing things they might not want to do—even if some of us have no issues with the activities themselves?

The discussion here is about *principles* more than anything else. For example, even if you agree with certain government mandates, what's to stop the government from eventually

mandating something that you *wouldn't* want to do? Should the government have this power?

Invasions of Privacy

The State's position of unilateral decision-making authority, and exemption from morality, puts it in a position to become increasingly invasive in our lives. That's where things start to get even more worrisome in the modern era. And advances in technology are helping with that process. For example, involuntary surveillance has become of great concern. What right does the State have to invade or spy on one's private property? Did we grant that right? Apparently, it happens anyway.

In September of 2020, there was a disturbing development in the US, as reported by Reuters: "Seven years after former National Security Agency contractor Edward Snowden blew the whistle on the mass surveillance of Americans' telephone records, an appeals court has found the program was unlawful—and that the U.S. intelligence leaders who publicly defended it were not telling the truth. In a ruling[,]...the U.S. Court of Appeals for the Ninth Circuit said the warrantless telephone dragnet that secretly collected millions of Americans' telephone records violated the Foreign Intelligence Surveillance Act and may well have been unconstitutional."[34]

Furthermore, the US government's response to the 9/11 attacks resulted in immense erosions of civil liberties through the Patriot Act of 2001. Under normal circumstances, the American people might have been outraged, but because of the fear of terrorism, these violations of freedom largely slipped right through. Some of the highlights of the Patriot Act include:

> Allowing law enforcement to use surveillance and wiretapping to investigate terror-related crimes[;] allowing delayed notification search warrants to prevent a terrorist from learning they are a suspect[;] allowing federal agents to seek federal court permission to obtain bank records and business records to aid in national security

> terror investigations and prevent money laundering for terrorism financing[;] allowing search warrants to be obtained in any district where terror-related activity occurs, no matter where the warrant is executed [; and] ending the statute of limitations for certain terror-related crimes.[35]

Also, let's not forget how onerous and intrusive airport security has become since 9/11. To those who fear terrorism, all of these post-9/11 measures might sound like good ideas. But if we look at them with a fresh set of eyes, they sound like invasive provisions from a dictatorship forced upon the masses—even if they originated from leaders who were elected as our representatives. Who gets to decide what constitutes a "terrorist"? What if anyone who disagrees with or opposes the State is declared a "domestic terrorist"?

And perhaps most fundamentally: Do the State's provisions keep its citizens "safe" or, in the very process, do they create totalitarianism?

Sure, humans naturally desire some degree of safety. But at what cost? And what should the government's role be? Ron Paul says it well: "Freedom is not defined by safety....Government cannot create a world without risks, nor would we really wish to live in such a fictional place. Only a totalitarian society would even claim absolute safety as a worthy ideal, because it would require total [S]tate control over its citizens' lives."[36]

Stated another way by Rose: **"In their search for an all-powerful 'good guy' to save the day, statists always end up creating all-powerful bad guys. Over and over again, they build giant, unstoppable 'government' monsters in the hope that they will defend the innocent, only to find that the monsters become a far greater threat to the innocent than the threats they were created to protect against."**[37] [emphasis added]

What Is the State, Really?

So far we've only scratched the surface, and it's already evident that statism is problematic for its citizens—even though some of its advocates might hold ostensibly honorable motives. Yet this flawed structure is the predominant system in which our civilization currently organizes itself.

We've been conditioned to think that elected representatives serve "we the people." But to suggest that the rulers serve the servants in this context is unrealistic and naive.[38] The truth is that the masses involuntarily serve under the government and don't even realize it. The State turns liberty upside down.

Therefore, the fundamental nature of the State needs to be reimagined more precisely for what it has become in the modern era.[39] Rothbard's definition of the State is factually accurate, as difficult as it might be to accept:

> **The State is that organization in society which attempts to maintain a monopoly of the use of force and violence in a given territorial area; in particular, it is the only organization in society that obtains its revenue not by voluntary contribution or payment for services rendered but by coercion. While other individuals or institutions obtain their income by production of goods and services and by the peaceful and voluntary sale of these goods and services to others, the State obtains its revenue by the use of compulsion; that is, by the use and the threat of the jailhouse and the bayonet....One would think that simple observation of all States through history and over the globe would be proof enough of this assertion; but the miasma of myth has lain so long over State activity that elaboration is necessary.**[40] [emphasis added]

Even more than that, the State naturally cares more about its own sustenance than those it allegedly "serves." As Rothbard put it:

> We may test the hypothesis that the State is largely interested in protecting *itself* rather than its subjects by asking: which category of crimes does the State pursue

> and punish most intensely—those against private citizens or those against *itself*? The gravest crimes in the State's lexicon are almost invariably not invasions of private person or property, but dangers to its *own* contentment, for example, treason, desertion of a soldier to the enemy, failure to register for the draft, subversion and subversive conspiracy, assassination of rulers and such economic crimes against the State as counterfeiting its money or evasion of its income tax.... Yet, curiously, the State's openly assigned priority to its own defense against the public strikes few people as inconsistent with its presumed *raison d'etre*.[41] [emphasis in original]

Finally, Ron Paul offered a similar indictment of the State in his farewell address to Congress in 2012:

> Unless one has a criminal mind and no respect for other people and their property, no one claims it's permissible to go into one's neighbor's house and tell them how to behave, what they can eat, smoke and drink or how to spend their money. Yet, rarely is it asked why it is morally acceptable that a stranger with a badge and a gun can do the same thing in the name of law and order. Any resistance is met with brute force, fines, taxes, arrests, and even imprisonment. This is done more frequently every day without a proper search warrant.[42]

Is There an Alternative?

Before we go too far into an analysis of the State, it's worth having in the back of our minds a potential alternative: **a form of libertarian political philosophy known as *voluntaryism*.** It endorses a society in which people can do as they choose—engaging in mutual, voluntary exchanges—**as long as they don't *initiate* aggression upon anyone else or their private property**. But people have the right to self-defense if someone else initiates aggression on them or their private property. *That* is true liberty. And we haven't even discussed the reasons for voluntaryism's benefits from a *metaphysical* lens, which we'll do later.

How does the State fit into voluntaryism? The State is an inherently invasive and coercive institution that constantly violates the precept of not initiating aggression. Therefore, in a voluntarist society, the State wouldn't exist.

But, the functions traditionally held by the State *wouldn't disappear* from society under voluntaryism. Instead, they'd be run by privately held companies in a truly free-market economy—that includes roads, courts, police and defense systems, and so on. The State has an effective monopoly over these functions, meaning that there's no real competition, and therefore there's less of an incentive for the State to perform them well. In a free-market economy, if you perform poorly, you go out of business. No such accountability exists today, and the quality of the government's services suffers as a result. Libertarian Tom Woods sums up this idea well: **"I don't think there's anything the State can do better than the private sector."**[43] [emphasis added]

In a voluntarist society, communities, businesses, and political units would likely still exist, and they would make their own rules. But there would be *voluntary, contractual agreements* between individuals and the private organizations with which they interact; and a legal system with private courts, arbitrators, and mediators to enforce the rules. So, there wouldn't be "implied consent."

In essence, what is now the State would morph into a set of service providers that would have *contracts* with their "subscribers" (in other words, "customers"). Some of these service providers could offer many services "all-in-one," which might *resemble* traditional "government," and others could offer one-off solutions. Citizens would be free to choose service providers based on their individual needs, priorities, and values. The key here is that citizens' relationships with these parties would be fully *voluntary,* and their money would go toward precisely the services that they, themselves, select.

There aren't many historical examples to which we can refer because most societies have operated under some fashion of a

State. Rothbard cited several societies that lived under aspects of voluntaryism, such as Ireland (for roughly one thousand years, until the seventeenth century) and a number of small tribes.[44] In the modern era, there certainly isn't a precedent on a grand scale—although, as we'll discuss later, America was founded upon libertarian ideals that sought to significantly limit the government's power. **Ultimately, because of a lack of contemporary precedent, our discussion about voluntaryism in the modern world will inherently be theoretical.**

One could easily come up with problematic scenarios in a voluntarist society. **But it's worthwhile to keep in mind that those same issues are often problematic for the State and have not been handled so well. Some of the toughest criticisms of voluntaryism end up being the same criticisms of statism.**[45] We're just so conditioned to believe that statism is the only possible way of structuring society that we've grown accustomed to, and overly accepting of, its problems.

Thus, voluntaryism would be *an imperfect solution to an imperfect status quo*. Certain issues will arise regardless of society's structure as a result of human nature. The question is whether voluntaryism could, at some point in the future, be a significant *improvement* over the status quo.

For example, in a voluntarist society, evil and corrupt individuals would still exist. However, without a centralized power structure such as the State, these individuals would arguably do relatively less damage than what can occur under statism. The State's structure naturally grants permission for a few individuals to rule the lives of the masses, whereas voluntaryism inherently decentralizes power.

But the idea of accepting a "less problematic" solution is difficult on the psyche. The challenge here is perhaps psychological as much as anything else: there is a human tendency to reject new prospects in which there will—for sure—be upsetting "losses" (as studied by Nobel Prize–winning psychologist Daniel Kahneman).[46]

Ron Paul addresses this notion in his book *Liberty Defined* (2011):

> We need to become more tolerant of the imperfections that come with freedom, and we need to give up the illusion that somehow putting government in charge of anything is going to improve its workings, much less bring on utopia....We need to come to see government as it is, not as we wish it to be and not as the civics books describe it....We need to give up our dependencies on the [S]tate....Let us understand that it is far better to live in an imperfect world than it is to live in a despotic world ruled by people who lord it over us through force and intimidation.[47]

Is there any way that voluntaryism could work in today's world? Perhaps not immediately on a large scale, but in the long run we might move toward something like it. **Most important, however, this framework serves as a "North Star"[48]—a guiding set of principles—that we can use to steer our aspirations as a civilization and bring us into moral alignment.** Even if pure voluntaryism isn't achieved, a movement toward reducing the government's power and its intrusions upon our lives would represent incremental improvements.

I recognize that at first glance all of this might sound like wishful thinking. And maybe, after all, voluntaryism won't be attainable in a literal, pure form, as contemplated here. We simply don't know how the future will play out. But as you continue reading, I suggest that you reverse this thinking and ask yourself: "Isn't the belief in the State's efficacy and legitimacy—after all the war and destruction that this governing structure has caused throughout history—wishful thinking? Isn't it utopian to believe that society functions best when we hand over unilateral decision-making authority to a monopolistic entity sitting at the center of society—with only 'implied consent' from its citizens?" Former US congressman Thomas B. Reed (1839–1902) said it well: **"One of the greatest delusions in the world is the hope that the evils in this world are to be cured by legislation."**[49] [emphasis added]

As the saying goes, "The definition of insanity is doing the same thing over and over and expecting different results."[50]

What's to Come in This Book

The next chapter explains why—from a psychological standpoint—it's so dangerous to put people in positions of power within the apparatus of the State. We'll then discuss the manner in which the State relies upon mind control to brainwash citizens for its own benefit. This includes an examination of the mainstream media, Hollywood, social media and technology companies, education, secretive government mind-control programs, false-flag operations, and depopulation efforts (chapter 3).

Next, we'll turn to solutions. We'll explore voluntaryism in further detail, including its basic features of nonaggression, private-property rights, and truly free markets. This naturally leads into a discussion of economic matters, including socialism, communism, fascism, the welfare state, capitalism, Keynesian policy, cronyism, monopolies, monetary policy, the nature of money, and the Federal Reserve (chapter 4). That context will allow us to explore the mechanics of privatization through a discussion of police and military-like security, law and dispute resolution, roads, and environmental matters (chapter 5).

Voluntaryism—or really any political theory—needs to be considered within a metaphysical framework. We need to explore why life fundamentally matters in the first place. This is often lacking in political and economic discussions. We will examine scientific evidence that will help us understand the nature of reality, what it truly means to be human, the nature of morality, and why politics is important. The discussion will draw upon research into near-death experiences and other related phenomena. The accumulated evidence suggests that the "Golden Rule"—treating others as we wish to be treated—is fundamentally embedded within the fabric of reality itself (chapters 6 and 7). These notions will allow us to develop a more robust political theory that combines voluntaryism with metaphysics: the State's inherently coercive nature becomes plainly unacceptable in light of metaphysical principles. Therefore, as we'll see, voluntaryism is likely the optimal political theory when considering the nature of reality and the potential meaning of our existence. And furthermore, the implementation of such a political stance becomes more plausible when evaluated within the context of an evolving—rather than a stagnant—human nature. Research on the nature of consciousness supports this notion of collective, metaphysical evolution (chapter 8). Finally, with all of this in mind, we'll chart a path to liberty—metaphysically and physically—and explain why a shift in consciousness is so critical for the future of a free civilization (chapter 9). A glossary of terms is also provided at the end of the book.

CHAPTER 2
DANGEROUS PSYCHOLOGY

While the aforementioned critiques of the State might make sense logically, they're difficult to accept. We're often tempted to believe that we can siphon off a segment of the population—responsible, smart, altruistic, and honorable leaders—who can manage the State, even if it's a morally imperfect system. Our "representatives" in government should be well suited to manage any issues that arise. The thinking goes something like this: Humans ultimately can't be trusted, so we need to create a State to babysit the masses. And since the State will be composed of such trustworthy people, we shouldn't worry about the fact that we have no explicit contractual relationship with it or that it has an effective monopoly of the use of force.

This is flawed—and idealistic—thinking. Larken Rose says it well: "If human beings are so careless, stupid and malicious that they cannot be trusted to do the right thing on their own, how would the situation be improved by taking a *subset* of those very same careless, stupid and malicious human beings and giving them societal *permission* to forcibly control all the others without contractual consent? Why would anyone think that rearranging and reorganizing a group of dangerous beasts would make them civilized?"[1] [emphasis in original]. As Rose aptly says, it's as if we're looking at our fellow citizens, thinking, "I do not trust you to be my neighbor, but I do trust you to be my master."[2]

There is simply a natural human desire to be taken care of, so we *want* to believe in an authority structure that can do this for us. As Rose puts it, people want a "Mommy and Daddy" government.[3] If we call it "government," somehow we're then taken care of. This mentality provides a false sense of security.

I know this is probably causing cognitive dissonance.

But we'll elect good people to be our representatives: since we chose them, they are extensions of what we want, one might argue. This is an enticing sentiment, but it's also faulty. First, it assumes that in a democratic system, the "majority" is able to discern good versus evil essentially based on what it sees on TV and in the media. If the masses can be fooled, this argument falls apart. And if we've already assumed that people are so irresponsible that they need to elect rulers to babysit them, what should make us believe that they're collectively savvy enough to elect the right people into power? We also need to remember that many powerful officials within government agencies are *not* elected by the people. Rather, they're *appointed* within the government. And yet they can remain in positions of high influence indefinitely.

Second, the argument assumes that at least *some* candidates are good. What if an election is held between evil candidates? And even if they're ostensibly good, we often don't know the extent to which politicians are beholden to third parties through covert mechanisms such as blackmail, bribery, and threats. For example, sex trafficker and convicted pedophile Jeffrey Epstein, who hosted many influential people on his private island in the Caribbean, is said to have used hidden cameras on his properties, likely for the purpose of obtaining blackmail material.[4]

Third, the argument assumes that election processes are fair. Elections for positions in the State…are typically run within the general apparatus of the State. So to assume that elections are fair is to assume that the State is capable of honorable, unbiased self-policing rather than action out of self-interest. In fact, following both the 2016 and 2020 US presidential elections, members of the losing political party argued that the winner was illegitimately elected. Neither Democrats nor Republicans seem to have faith in the current election system.

And even if the legal system were to try to resolve legitimate election disputes, it is under the umbrella of the State too. Can we really trust that the State will conduct honest investigations into itself, even if the investigations occur within different "branches"? From this lens, the notion of checks and balances could be considered yet another ruse: There isn't an external body "checking" the power of the State. Those doing the "checking" are *part* of the State. For example, as Murray Rothbard observed, the Supreme Court—part of the US's judicial branch—has "the monopoly of ultimate interpreting power" over the nation's legal matters.[5]

But perhaps most important, the argument that the masses can elect worthy representatives—thus rendering the State the best way to organize society—fails to consider important aspects of *human psychology*:

1. Good people often become evil when placed into positions of power.
2. Authority figures can induce evil behavior in otherwise good people.
3. Positions of power are magnets for psychopathic personalities.

The Stanford Prison Experiment

The infamous Stanford Prison Experiment was conducted in 1971 by Philip Zimbardo, PhD. Twenty-four male college students were divided into roles of prisoners or guards in a mock prison setup. The study was supposed to last for two weeks but had to be stopped after six days because of the cruelty exhibited by the "guards" and the hopelessness experienced by the "prisoners." The guards quickly transformed into abusers: they insulted and threatened the prisoners, forced them to do push-ups and jumping jacks, placed paper bags over their heads and chained them together in a line to walk them to the toilet, forced them into solitary confinement, deprived them of sleep, and sexually humiliated them.[6] In other words, people placed in positions of power morphed into monsters simply by virtue of being in power. As one of the mock prisoners said, "Some guards seemed to really enjoy our agony."[7]

It's difficult to draw too many conclusions from a single study involving such a small number of people, and we don't know whether the results would have been different if aspects of the design had been altered. That said, when we look at historical events such as those in Nazi Germany—in which seemingly normal Germans transformed into bearers of evil—the study's results are plausible.

Zimbardo's book *The Lucifer Effect* (2007) weaves together shocking details of the guard-prisoner dynamic, based upon video recordings and transcripts compiled from the study itself. Reviewing the source material in order to write the book was, in his words, "emotionally painful."[8] Zimbardo summarizes what he calls the "primary simple lesson" of the experiment: *"[S]ituations matter*....Some situations can exert such powerful influence over us that we can be led to behave in ways we would not, could not, predict was possible in advance."[9] [emphasis in original]

He also identifies dehumanization as a key aspect: "Dehumanization is one of the central processes in the transformation of ordinary, normal people into indifferent or even wanton perpetrators of evil. Dehumanization is like a cortical cataract that clouds one's thinking and fosters the perception that other people are less than human. It makes some people come to see those others as enemies deserving of torment, torture, and annihilation."[10] The ideas are reminiscent of Lord Acton's famous saying: **"All power tends to corrupt; absolute power corrupts absolutely."**[11] [emphasis added]

In spite of all this, there's still a human tendency to rationalize our transgressions. As Zimbardo says: "We abdicate responsibility for our actions, blaming them on that role, which we convince ourselves is alien to our nature."[12]

Obedience to Authority

When politicians are corrupted by power, the impact on society is extended far beyond the politicians themselves. Why? **Because there's an innate human instinct to trust authority and acquiesce to its orders, even if the guidance is clearly unethical.** So, unsavory edicts bestowed upon the masses by corrupted representatives might be obeyed anyway. Often people obey simply *because authority says so*, even if they aren't under a threat of punishment for disobedience. People have much less ethical fortitude than we'd like to believe.

This notion was demonstrated viscerally in studies conducted by Stanley Milgram at Yale University in the early 1960s and later replicated elsewhere. The basic version was as follows: Participants enter a psychology laboratory and are told that they'll be partaking in a study about memory and learning. One person in the study is designated as the "teacher" and the other as the "learner." Unbeknownst to the teacher, *the learner is an actor*. The learner is strapped into a chair with an electrode attached to his or her wrist, and the teacher administers electric shocks each time the learner makes an error. The intensity of the shock gradually increases such that at first the learner grunts, but eventually (at elevated voltage levels) the learner's response becomes an "agonized scream." All the while, the authority figure—the experimenter—encourages the teacher to continue.

Milgram summarized the implications in his book *Obedience to Authority* (1974):

> A reader's initial reaction to the experiment may be to wonder why anyone in his right mind would administer even the first shocks. Would he not simply refuse and walk out of the laboratory? **But the fact is that no one ever does**.... [emphasis added]

> Many subjects will obey the experimenter no matter how vehement the pleading of the person being shocked, no matter how painful the shocks seem to be, and no matter how much the victim pleads to be let out. This was seen time and again in our studies and has been observed in several universities where the experiment was repeated. It is the extreme willingness of adults to go to almost any lengths on the command of an authority that constitutes the chief finding of the study....
>
> The ordinary person who shocked the victim did so out of a sense of obligation—a conception of his duties as a subject—and not from any peculiarly aggressive tendencies.
>
> This is, perhaps, the most fundamental lesson of our study: **ordinary people, simply doing their jobs, and without any particular hostility on their part, can become agents in a terrible destructive process.**[13] [emphasis added]

Rose sums up the implications well: "If evil was only committed by evil people, the world would be a far better place than it is today, with basically *good* people constantly committing evil acts, because a perceived authority told them to."[14] [emphasis in original]

Psychopaths

The previous two examples examined how good people can become evil based on situational variables. Now we will turn to people who need no conversion to evil: psychopaths.[15] This personality type is naturally drawn to positions of power. Therefore, the State becomes an even more dangerous political structure if such individuals find their way into the political system and can successfully fool an unsuspecting electorate.

Psychopathy is a well-known psychological condition, and yet a psychopath's behavior makes no sense to most people. **A potential challenge in examining this phenomenon is that most people are generally good, and they might struggle to imagine what it**

would be like to be so evil. Likewise, perhaps there's a tendency to overestimate our ability to *detect* such evil.

Robert Hare, PhD, a professor emeritus of psychology at the University of British Columbia, has studied criminal psychology and wrote the book *Without Conscience: The Disturbing World of the Psychopaths Among Us* (1999). Hare summarizes the psychopath concisely: "Their hallmark is a stunning lack of conscience; their game is self-gratification at the other person's expense.[16]... [They have] a deeply disturbing inability to care about the pain and suffering experienced by others—in short, a complete lack of empathy, the prerequisite for love."[17] One psychopath who was in prison for committing rape, robbery, and fraud was asked if he had any weaknesses, to which he responded: "I don't have any weaknesses, except maybe I'm too caring."[18]

Hare notes, "Psychopaths don't feel they have psychological or emotional problems, and they see no reason to change their behavior to conform to societal standards with which they do not agree....They perceive themselves as superior beings in a hostile, dog-eat-dog world in which others are competitors for power and resources."[19] They also "have a strong need for psychological and physical control over others. They must be in charge, and they will use charm, intimidation, and violence to assure their authority."[20] And their lack of empathy can lead to unspeakable behaviors: "For example, they can torture and mutilate their victims with about the same concern that we feel when we carve a turkey for Thanksgiving dinner."[21]

The phenomenon is not rare, either. At the time he wrote the book in the 1990s, Hare conservatively estimated that there were roughly two million psychopaths in North America alone. What's perhaps even more disturbing is that not all psychopaths are easy-to-spot criminals who commit grisly murders. Many are chameleon-like. Hare contends that "many psychopaths never go to prison or any other facility. They appear to function reasonably well—as lawyers, doctors, psychiatrists, academics, mercenaries, police officers, cult leaders, military personnel, businesspeople, writers, artists, entertainers, and so forth—without breaking the law, or at least without being caught and convicted. These individuals are every bit as egocentric, callous, and manipulative as the average criminal psychopath; however, their intelligence, family background, social skills, and circumstances permit them to construct a facade of normalcy and to get what they want with relative impunity."[22]

The phenomenon of the psychopath demonstrates that evil can be well hidden. And once embedded within the political apparatus that controls law enforcement, psychopaths have an easier time covering their tracks. As a result, many unsuspecting citizens might tend to dismiss the possibility that authority figures could be psychopathic, so they see the world in an overly idealistic (and inaccurate) manner.

Author William March said it well:

> [G]ood people are rarely suspicious: they cannot imagine others doing the things they themselves are incapable of doing; usually they accept the undramatic solution as the correct one, and let matters rest there. Then too, the normal are inclined to visualize the [psychopath] as one who's as monstrous in appearance as he is in mind, which is about as far from the truth as one could well get....These monsters of real life usually looked and behaved in a more normal manner than their actually normal brothers and sisters; they presented a more convincing picture of virtue than virtue presented of itself.[23]

It's also important to keep in mind that only a small number of psychopaths in positions of power is sufficient to do immense damage. If there is enough obedience, lots of evil can follow. Rose puts this another way: **"A few evil rulers + many obedient subjects = widespread injustice and oppression."**[24] [emphasis added]

So far, I've focused exclusively on negative possibilities with regard to politicians. I don't mean to imply that every single politician is automatically evil. It's certainly possible that some legitimately good people exist in power. However, the discussion here is not about specific individuals but rather the overarching apparatus of the State and its general tendencies. The State, for the reasons mentioned, is naturally a hub for insidiousness. We cannot simply assume that our apparent ability to elect representatives makes everything okay.

With our eyes wide open, we'll now move to an examination of how the State often implements evil from its position of centralized power—particularly though its ability to manipulate the psychology of its citizens.

CHAPTER 3

MIND CONTROL

South African anti-apartheid activist Steve Biko (1946–1977) stated: **"The most potent weapon in the hands of the oppressor is the mind of the oppressed."**[1] [emphasis added] Mind control (such as brainwashing) is therefore of the utmost importance to the State and its power-hungry representatives. In fact, one could even argue that mind control is *required* for the State's survival. It logically follows that understanding mind control is of utmost importance to *us*, as potential victims. Sometimes simply knowing that something exists is sufficient to defuse its manipulative capacity.

We're conditioned to think that these things happen elsewhere, like in North Korea. Thus, we overlook the possibility that those of us in the "free" world are being deceived—regularly—and falling for it. The whole point of brainwashing is that you don't realize it's happening to you. It's psychological warfare.

In this chapter, we'll examine the use of mind control through multiple vehicles:

- The mainstream media
- Hollywood

- ❍ Social media and technology companies
- ❍ Education
- ❍ Government-sponsored mind-control programs
- ❍ False-flag operations
- ❍ Depopulation

But before diving into each of these areas, it's worthwhile to acknowledge the inherently conspiratorial nature of the subject matter. The term *conspiracy theory* has begun to carry so much baggage that it's necessary to first examine it, along with the corresponding secrecy that underlies it.

Conspiracy Theories

People sometimes conspire. This is simply a fact of human history and a tendency of human nature. Yet, the term *conspiracy theory* is typically used to dismiss something as automatically crazy and false. It is now so widely used that it can apply to any belief that isn't shared by the mainstream media. Or as comedian JP Sears puts it: **"Today's most popular conspiracy theory: Believing that people who think differently than you are conspiracy theorists."**[2] [emphasis added]

And even more than that, what constitutes a conspiracy theory seems to change rapidly. For instance, the theory that COVID-19 leaked from the Wuhan Institute of Virology was blasted as conspiracy nonsense at the start of the pandemic in 2020. Suddenly, it became a mainstream, credible discussion topic in 2021. Facebook had been actively censoring articles that made such claims, and then changed its stance nearly a year later.[3] All too often, yesterday's "wacky idea" becomes today's "norm." As nineteenth-century German philosopher Arthur Schopenhauer said: "All truth goes through three stages. First it is ridiculed. Then it is violently opposed. Finally it is accepted as self-evident."[4]

It's likely that the public's negative view of conspiracy theories is itself a product of mind control. In a 1967 CIA memo now publicly available, titled "Countering Criticism of the Warren Report,"[5] the CIA expressed concern that 46 percent of Americans did not think that Lee Harvey Oswald acted alone in the assassination of former president John F. Kennedy. The memo talks about ways of "countering and discrediting the claims of the conspiracy theorists." Moreover, one of the talking points suggests saying to "friendly elite contacts (especially politicians and editors)" that "parts of the conspiracy talk appear to be deliberately generated by Communist propagandists." The memo then states: "Urge [friendly elite contacts] to use their influence to discourage unfounded and irresponsible claims."

So, the CIA wanted to discredit people who questioned the official narrative about the JFK assassination back in 1967. However, now, the "summary of findings" at the official National Archives, JFK Assassination Records website states: **"The committee believes, on the basis of the evidence available to it, that President John F. Kennedy was probably assassinated as a result of a conspiracy."**[6] [emphasis added]

Along these lines, in his essay *Anatomy of the State* (original edition circa 1965), Murray Rothbard noted that the State intentionally diverts public interest *away* from conspiracy theories to protect itself:

> It is...important for the State to inculcate in its subjects an aversion to any "conspiracy theory of history"; for a search for "conspiracies" means a search for motives and an attribution of responsibility for historical misdeeds. If, however, any tyranny imposed by the State, or venality, or aggressive war, was caused not by the State rulers but by mysterious and arcane "social forces," or by the imperfect state of the world or, if in some way, everyone was responsible ("We Are All Murderers," proclaims one slogan), then there is no point to the people becoming indignant or rising up against such misdeeds. Furthermore, an attack on "conspiracy theories" means that the subjects will become more gullible in believing the "general welfare" reasons that are always

> put forth by the State for engaging in any of its despotic actions. A "conspiracy theory" can unsettle the system by causing the public to doubt the State's ideological propaganda.[7]

So when we hear comments such as the following from the former deputy White House press secretary, we shouldn't be surprised: "Organizations or individuals who traffic in conspiracy theories, propaganda and lies to spread disinformation will not be tolerated"[8] (January 2021).

The point here is that the State, and any accomplices, have an incentive for the masses *not to* seriously consider conspiracies. An unquestioning populace is much easier to control than one that engages in independent, critical thinking. In fact, the State might even attack those trying to expose conspiracies. Whistleblower Kevin Annett uses a simple phrase to describe the way in which conspirators sweep damaging stories under the rug: **Deny, Discredit, and Distract**.[9] When the media, technology companies, and government dictate what "truth" is and want to shut down alternative opinions, our antennae ought to go up.

Am I suggesting that we should therefore accept every conspiracy theory we hear? Absolutely not. I'm simply suggesting that we remain open to alternative narratives.

Secret Influence

Implicit in the notion of conspiracy is secrecy: groups of people—potentially even members of secret societies—are quietly working behind the scenes to orchestrate devious plans. From this lens, politicians might just be puppets of special-interest groups. **Furthermore, the State—as a centralized, monopolistic power structure—is a mechanism through which any such conspiratorial plans can be enacted on a massive scale.** To be clear, I'm not asserting that the elimination of the State would eliminate conspiracies. Rather, I'm theorizing that the absence of the traditional State structure would make the enactment of large-scale conspiracies relatively more difficult. The State provides a pathway to influence large populations: conspirators would need to control a few key decision makers within the State's power hierarchy, and then they'd have effective access to policies governing the masses.

Many researchers point to the formation of the Illuminati secret society in Europe (1776) as an historical example of an influential conspiratorial group. Some even believe that its lineage still exerts influence today. John Robison, a professor of natural philosophy and secretary to the Royal Society of Edinburgh, wrote the book *Proofs of a Conspiracy* (1798), calling the Illuminati a "detestable Association."[10] He wrote that their methods were "for the express purpose of breaking all the bands of society...solely in order that the leaders might rule the world with uncontrollable power, while all the rest...will be...employed as mere tools of the ambition of their unknown superiors."[11] While he claimed the Illuminati was abolished in 1786, it was "revived immediately after, under another name, and in a different form, all over Germany. It was again detected, and seemingly broken up; but it had by this time taken so deep root that it still subsists without being detected, and has spread into all the countries of Europe."[12]

Additionally, prominent individuals in more contemporary times have implicated secret groups who wield their influence over government:

- President Woodrow Wilson wrote in *The New Freedom* in 1913:

  Since I entered politics, I have chiefly had men's views confided to me privately. Some of the biggest men in the United States, in the field of commerce and manufacture, are afraid of somebody, are afraid of something. They know that there is a power somewhere so organized, so subtle, so watchful, so interlocked, so complete, so pervasive, that they had better not speak above their breath when they speak in condemnation of it....There has come over the land that un-American set of conditions which enables a small number of men who control the government to get favors from the government; by those favors to exclude their fellows from equal business opportunity; by those favors to extend a network of control that will presently dominate every industry in the country.[13]

- In his 1922 autobiography, former mayor of New York John Francis Hylan mentioned "the invisible government, which reaches into the inner congressional and legislative halls of every section."[14]
- Senator William E. Jenner said in a 1954 speech: "Today the path to total dictatorship in the U.S. can be laid by strictly legal means, unseen and unheard by Congress, the President, or the people. Outwardly we have a Constitutional government. We have operating within our government and political system…a well-organized political-action group in this country, determined to destroy our Constitution and establish a one-party state. The important point to remember about this group is not its ideology but its organization….It operates secretly, silently, continuously to transform our Government. This group...is answerable neither to the President, the Congress, nor the courts. It is practically irremovable."[15]
- FBI director J. Edgar Hoover spoke of the Communist threat in 1956: "The individual is handicapped by coming face-to-face with a conspiracy so monstrous he cannot believe it exists. The American mind simply has not come to a realization of the evil which has been introduced into our midst. It rejects even the assumption that human creatures could espouse a philosophy which must ultimately destroy all that is good and decent."[16]
- In President Dwight Eisenhower's farewell speech in 1961, he warned of secret influence arising from what he called *the military-industrial complex*: "In the councils of government, we must guard against the

acquisition of unwarranted influence, whether sought or unsought, by the military-industrial complex. The potential for the disastrous rise of misplaced power exists and will persist. We must never let the weight of this combination endanger our liberties or democratic processes. We should take nothing for granted. Only an alert and knowledgeable citizenry can compel the proper meshing of the huge industrial and military machinery of defense with our peaceful methods and goals, so that security and liberty may prosper together."[17]

- Carroll Quigley, a Georgetown University professor, wrote in his 1966 book *Tragedy & Hope: A History of the World in Our Time*: "There does exist, and has existed for a generation, an international Anglophile network....[T]his network...has no aversion to cooperating with the Communists, or any other groups, and frequently does so. I know of the operations of this network because I have studied it for twenty years and was permitted for two years, in the early 1960's, to examine its papers and secret records."[18]

- Former Hawaii senator Daniel K. Inouye spoke on visions of government at the end of the Iran-Contra hearings (1987) and warned of "a shadowy government with its own Air Force, its own Navy, its own fundraising mechanism, and the ability to pursue its own ideas of the national interest, free from all checks and balances, and free from the law itself. It is an elitist vision of government that trusts no one, not the people, not the Congress, and not the cabinet. It is a vision of a government operated by persons convinced they have a monopoly on truth."[19]

The point is, there's probably a lot going on that the public knows very little about. The fact that we can't always pinpoint the exact individuals involved doesn't mean they don't exist. So while we can't see the inner mechanics of power structures, we can see—and feel—their effects. We see bits and pieces of evidence, but we don't know what's happening beneath the surface, who is involved, or in what capacity. It's similar to seeing the tip of an iceberg that has a significant unseen mass. We don't know what we don't know.

The general public isn't necessarily privy to the way in which the world actually functions.

As we'll see next, mind control is essential for the "powers that be."

The Mainstream Media

In the foreword to the 1946 edition of his 1932 book *Brave New World*, Aldous Huxley wrote: "A really efficient totalitarian state would be one in which the all-powerful executive of political bosses and their army of managers control a population of slaves who do not have to be coerced, because they love their servitude. To make them love it is the task assigned, in present-day totalitarian states, to ministries of propaganda, newspaper editors and school teachers....The greatest triumphs of propaganda have been accomplished, not by doing something, but by refraining from doing. Great is truth, but still greater, from a practical point of view, is silence about truth."[20]

Huxley's prophetic words apply directly to what is happening in today's world. One of the vehicles for the silencing of truth is the mainstream media, which often serves as the public's primary source for learning about what's happening in the world. Since each individual cannot personally experience every world event, we have no choice but to rely on other people's accounts.

The way in which we view current events is therefore dramatically shaped by what the media tells us. The unfortunate reality for the masses—and the fortunate reality for the State and any related conspirators—is that the mainstream media can be used to manipulate mass perception for its own purposes: it can present the news it wants us to see and purposely suppress stories that it doesn't want us to see.

The United States media has consolidated significantly, and much of it is owned by a small handful of companies (for example, AT&T/Time Warner, Comcast, Disney, News Corporation, Viacom, and CBS).[21] Such a high concentration of media ownership is problematic for the masses because it can dictate so much of what people learn about the world—unless they proactively seek out alternative media sources. This can lead to a dangerous sentiment in which people believe: "If it's not on the news, then it's not real."

The State uses this to its advantage. For example, as shown in a 2017 C-SPAN video clip, House Minority Leader Nancy Pelosi explained how the media can be used to amplify the State's lies. She described a political "diversionary tactic" in which "you demonize," called "the wrap-up smear." In her words: "You smear somebody with falsehoods and all the rest and then you merchandise it. And then you write it, and they'll say 'see, it's reported in the press.' So they have that validation that the press reported the smear, and then it's called 'the wrap-up smear.' Now I'm going to merchandise the press's report on the smear that we made....It's a tactic."[22]

The press's manipulative capacity is further exemplified in undercover footage of a technical director at CNN, released by the journalism enterprise Project Veritas in April of 2021. In this publicly available footage, the technical director spoke candidly about CNN's operations while on dates with an undercover female journalist. **He said explicitly that CNN engages in "propaganda"; "fear sells"; there is "an art to manipulation"; "you can shape an entire people's perception about anything…just by forcing a story"; and "there's no such thing as unbiased news" because "there's too many agendas." He said the way in which they "manipulate people" is "enough to change the world."** [emphasis added]

Much of what CNN's technical director said shouldn't be surprising to anyone who watches the news, but to see the level of deception in explicit terms is striking and important. For this reason, I've included many examples from the undercover footage.[23] (Warning: for some readers this will cause a great deal of cognitive dissonance.)

- CNN's technical director commented on what COVID-19 meant for the network: "COVID? Gangbusters with ratings, right? Which is why we constantly have the [COVID-19] death toll on the side [of the television screen]….I've even looked at it and be like, 'Let's make [the death toll] higher, like why isn't it high enough today?...It would make our point better if it was higher.'…That's a problem that we're doing that." He talked about being told by the head of the network: "'There's nothing that you're doing right now that makes me want to stick. Put the [COVID-19] numbers back up, because that's the most enticing thing that we had.'…Things like that are constantly talked about." He admitted, "Fear really drives numbers" and "The happiest days in news, people, I would imagine, turn it off and then they go with their family. They don't stay glued to it, unless there's something that's uniting them….Fear is the thing that keeps you tuned in." He added, "If you can get someone impassioned, that does really well with ratings. Sad news back-to-back-to-back, doesn't do well unless it affects them directly."

- When asked by the undercover journalist why CNN doesn't show statistics about people who had COVID-19 *and recovered*, he said they don't show it "because that's not scary. I would imagine, that's why they don't do it....If it bleeds it leads....I think no one ever says those things out loud, but it's obvious based on...the amount of stories that we do."
- In regard to the 2020 presidential election between Donald Trump and Joe Biden, he said: "Look at what we did, we got Trump out. I am a hundred percent going to say it. And I a hundred percent believe it that if it wasn't for CNN, I don't know that Trump would have got voted out....I came to CNN because I wanted to be a part of that."
- He stated that CNN made up a story about former president Donald Trump's health: "Trump, we did it...when Trump was, I don't know...his hand was shaking....We brought in...so many medical people to....all tell a story....It was all speculation, that he was...neurologically damaged, that he was losing it. He's unfit, to, you know, whatever....We were creating a story there that we didn't know anything about....I think that's propaganda. We had nothing else to run with at that time. We were...just taking shots off the bow just hoping something would hit."
- On the other hand, he commented on the network's attempts to diminish concerns about Joe Biden's health: "The whole thing of him running during the entire...like run for the campaign, showing [Biden] jogging was obviously a deflection of his age and they're trying to make it like, 'Oh, I'm healthy.' We would always show shots of him jogging...and him in his aviator shades....You paint him as a young geriatric."

- He talked about CNN's overall weaponization of fear around the time of the COVID-19 crisis: "I think there's just like a COVID fatigue. So...whenever a new story comes up they're going to latch onto it. They've already announced in our office that once the public... will be open to it, we're going to start focusing mainly on climate....Climate, like global warming, and that's going to be our next...focus. Like our focus was to get Trump out of office, right? Without saying it, that's what it was, right? So our next thing is going to be climate change awareness." He said it will be like the next "pandemic-like story, that we'll beat to death, but that one's got longevity." When asked about whether the stories would be related to fear about the climate he said, "Yeah. Fear sells."

- He spoke openly about bias in the media: "There's no such thing as unbiased news. It just doesn't exist. There's too many agendas. There's too many people that have jobs, that need to feed their families for it to be unbiased. It's impossible. The most unbiased news is grassroots, out of people's basements with podcasts....And unfortunately the trend is that when you could actually start making money off of it, you start to inherently destroy the thing that you love." He thinks CNN has done that, and said, "I don't think CNN's any different than FOX. I think it's on the different side of it."

- He spoke about the way in which interviewees on CNN are questioned by the reporters: "Listen to the way they ask questions. Because they're not actually asking questions....What they're actually doing is they're telling the person what to say. It's an art form in there....We've led [the interviewees] to talk about how we want them to talk about it. It's always leading them in a direction before they even open their mouths. And the only people that we will let on the

> air, for the most part, are people that have a proven track record of taking the bait."

Journalist Bari Weiss echoes claims of biased reporting in the mainstream press. Apparently, the problems were severe enough to make her leave her role at the *New York Times*. In her June 2020 resignation letter, she explains why she left:

> [L]essons about the importance of understanding other Americans, the necessity of resisting tribalism, and the centrality of the free exchange of ideas to a democratic society—have not been learned. Instead, a new consensus has emerged in the press, but perhaps especially at this paper: that truth isn't a process of collective discovery, but an orthodoxy already known to an enlightened few whose job is to inform everyone else.

Her letter continues:

> Stories [at the *New York Times*] are chosen and told in a way to satisfy the narrowest of audiences, rather than to allow a curious public to read about the world and then draw their own conclusions. I was always taught that journalists were charged with writing the first rough draft of history. Now, history itself is one more ephemeral thing molded to fit the needs of a predetermined narrative....
>
> Part of me wishes I could say that my experience was unique. But the truth is that intellectual curiosity—let alone risk-taking—is now a liability at The Times....
>
> What rules that remain at The Times are applied with extreme selectivity. If a person's ideology is in keeping with the new orthodoxy, they and their work remain unscrutinized. Everyone else lives in fear of the digital thunderdome. Online venom is excused so long as it is directed at the proper targets.[24]

The government's role in all of this shouldn't be understated either. For example, investigative journalist Tareq Haddad resigned from his position at *Newsweek* in December of 2019 and conveyed what he saw: "The US government, in an ugly alliance with those [that] profit the most from war, has its tentacles in every part of the media—imposters, with ties to the US State Department, sit in newsrooms all over the world. Editors, with no apparent connections to the member's club, have done nothing to resist. Together, they filter out what can or cannot be reported. Inconvenient stories are completely blocked. As a result, journalism is quickly dying. America is regressing because it lacks the truth."[25]

In fact, this sort of behavior isn't new. For instance, information about the government's involvement in the media was revealed in an April 1976 US Senate report titled "Final Report of the Select Committee to Study Government Operations with Respect to Intelligence Activities":

> The CIA currently maintains a network of several hundred foreign individuals around the world who provide intelligence for the CIA and at times attempt to influence opinion through the use of covert propaganda. These individuals provide the CIA with direct access to a large number of newspapers and periodicals, scores of press services and news agencies, radio and television stations, commercial book publishers, and other foreign media outlets....
>
> The Committee is concerned that the use of American journalists and media organizations for clandestine operations is a threat to the integrity of the press. All American journalists...may be suspects when they are engaged in covert activities.[26]

Hollywood

Along those lines, Hollywood can be used to steer our perception of the world, and US intelligence and military agencies seem to be involved there as well. The CIA even established an Entertainment Liaison Office (1996)[27] that was led by CIA veterans.[28] A former CIA agent told *The Guardian* in 2008: "All these people that run the studios—they go to Washington, they hang around with senators, they hang around with CIA directors, and everybody's on board."[29] For instance, the head of foreign and domestic censorship for Paramount in the 1950s was working for the CIA.[30]

The intelligence community's influence can come in the form of money,[31] but also in direct assistance with scripts. As reported in *Wired* (2011), the CIA pitches scripts to Hollywood. Furthermore, the Department of Defense sometimes alters scripts. The deputy director of the Defense Department's Entertainment Liaison Office said: "The scripts we get are only the writer's idea of how the Department of Defense operates....We make sure the Department and facilities and people are portrayed in the most accurate and positive light possible."[32] The article also reports: "Standard procedure is to review the script, make notes on what the Defense Department would like changed, and kick it back to the producer. If the changes are made, the military will provide whatever help they can—declassified information, equipment, personnel, etc.—for a price. If an agreement can't be reached, the project is either scrapped or made without Pentagon help."[33]

In some cases, the entertainment industry's impact on culture and public perception is quite clear. For example, the movie *Top Gun* boosted military sign-ups.[34] And the popular show *24* normalized torture.[35]

Social Media and Technology Companies

Similarly, we are highly influenced by social media and technology companies, and they seem to have affiliations with government. For example, the CIA's effective investment arm, In-Q-Tel, funds important and innovative technology companies. Of note, it invested in Keyhole, which was acquired by Google in 2004 and has been used to develop Google Earth.[36] Additionally, CBS News reported in 2011 that Google actively collaborates with the government by providing it with information or wiping information from the web. In a sense, that is a version of writing and rewriting history.[37] In a similar vein, *Newsweek* discusses a 2019 report revealing that a Twitter executive with editorial responsibility "is also a reservist officer of the British Army's psychological warfare and propaganda unit."[38] Ostensibly, the intent is to stop the spread of what the company regards as "disinformation."

Social media companies also have the power to delete or restrict individuals' accounts such that their messages won't be seen. As confirmed by videotaped footage obtained by Project Veritas, a Twitter senior engineer in 2018 attests to the fact that the company engages in "shadow banning." The engineer states, **"The idea of a shadow ban is that you ban someone but they don't know they've been banned, because they keep posting and no one sees their content. So they just think that no one is engaging with their content, when in reality, no one is seeing it."**[39] [emphasis added]

Project Veritas also obtained internal documents from Facebook employees related to the social media company's policy regarding COVID-19 vaccines. The documents reveal that Facebook had plans to curb "vaccine hesitancy" among its users by "drastically reducing user exposure" to such comments on the social media platform. In other words, Facebook intentionally manipulates the information its users see. Even if users post information that represents "true events or facts" about vaccination concerns, such posts can be demoted and hidden from users. As one of the Facebook insiders puts it, **"They're trying to control this content before it even makes it onto your page, before you even see it."**[40] [emphasis added]

Furthermore, emails between Facebook's CEO, Mark Zuckerberg, and the director of the US National Institute of Allergy and Infectious Diseases, Dr. Anthony Fauci, were made public in June of 2021. The emails were from March of 2020, at the beginning of the COVID-19 crisis. They clearly demonstrate that Facebook was coordinating with the government's health officials with regard to its planned "Coronavirus Information Hub" that would contain "authoritative" information about the pandemic. Thus, there exists a direct line of communication between social media and government agencies—and an ability to alter the public's worldview.[41]

This became even more evident in July of 2021 when the White House announced, "We're flagging problematic posts for Facebook that spread disinformation."[42] [emphasis added] So, the State—in partnership with social media—gets to decide what information is acceptable for its citizens to see.

Facebook has also become involved in trying to curb what it calls "extremism." In July of 2021, users began seeing pop-up messages saying: "Are you concerned that someone you know is becoming an extremist? We care about preventing extremism on Facebook. Others in your situation have received confidential support."[43] Additional messages asked users to "report" anyone they know who is becoming an extremist.[44] Facebook called its new messaging a "test."[45]

In the same month, large technology companies—including Facebook, Microsoft, Twitter, and Google-owned YouTube—decided to crack down on "extremist content." As reported by Reuters, the technology companies are sharing this content in a "database."[46] Also in July of 2021, PayPal announced its plan to uncover and disrupt financial pipelines that support "extremist" movements.[47] **What if "extremism" became synonymous with "political opponents"? How could the State work with technology companies to weaponize this form of effective surveillance, under the guise of "keeping its citizens safe"?**

Technology platforms have also been regularly deleting videos and posts. In May of 2021, Facebook said that it had removed more than 18 million posts, including those on Instagram, which violate its COVID-19 "misinformation policy."[48] Similarly, a May 2021 article in the *BMJ* (formerly known as the *British Medical Journal*) reported that YouTube has deleted more than 850,000 videos for "dangerous or misleading covid-19 medical information."[49]

Additionally, there are many examples in which users have been banned and links have been blocked. This sort of censorship occurs most often among everyday people who challenge mainstream narratives, but there are some high-profile examples. For instance, in October of 2020, Twitter locked the *New York Post*'s account for sharing an article about Joe Biden's son and even blocked links related to the material.[50] In February of 2021, Instagram banned Robert F. Kennedy Jr.'s account because of information he shared about COVID-19 and vaccines.[51] In April of 2021, Twitter permanently suspended James O'Keefe, the founder of Project Veritas, after sharing the commentary made by CNN's technical director.[52] In June of 2021, YouTube suspended US senator Ron Johnson for a week for uploading a video about alternative COVID-19 treatments. The video was removed as well.[53] Former adviser to Bill Clinton and renowned feminist author Dr. Naomi Wolf was banned from Twitter in June of 2021 for questioning the mainstream narrative about COVID-19 and vaccines.[54] She also warned that the US is becoming a "totalitarian state before our eyes."[55] Additionally, YouTube deleted a video recording of a North Carolina county's board of commissioners meeting in June of 2021 because the video included a discussion about vaccines that violated YouTube's policies.[56] In July of 2021, Twitter suspended accounts that had been posting updates about Arizona's 2020 election audit.[57] And perhaps the most widely discussed case of censorship has been the suspension of Donald Trump's accounts from Facebook, Twitter, and YouTube in 2021, while he was still the sitting president.[58]

Even Amazon has begun censoring its content. In February of 2021, it removed—without explanation—a documentary about US Supreme Court justice Clarence Thomas titled "Created Equal."[59] In March of 2021, Amazon began banning books that contain what it deems "offensive content" such as "hate speech" (which it did not define).[60] As the German poet Heinrich Heine (1797–1856) famously put it: "Where they burn books, they will also ultimately burn people."[61]

Finally, the online "encyclopedia" *Wikipedia* appears to be restricting information. In a July 2021 interview, *Wikipedia*'s cofounder, Larry Sanger, explained that the platform is now "propaganda." He is no longer with the company and feels that it has changed drastically since its launch in 2001. Rather than allowing all sides of an idea to be heard in *Wikipedia*'s entries, Sanger said, "You can't cite the *Daily Mail* at all. You can't cite *Fox News* on socio-political issues either....It's banned. So what does that mean? It means that if a controversy does not appear in the mainstream center-left media, then it's not going to appear on *Wikipedia*." Additionally, with regard to COVID-19, Sanger says, "If you look at the articles that *Wikipedia* has, you can just see how they are simply mouthing the view of the...World Economic Forum, and the World Health Organization, the CDC and various other establishment mouthpieces....There's a global enforcement of a certain point of view...which is amazing to me." He says: **"If only one version of the facts is allowed, that then gives a huge incentive to wealthy and powerful people to seize control of things like *Wikipedia* in order to shore up their power. And they do that."**[62] [bold added]

Although the cases discussed here represent only a brief sampling, they make clear that technology platforms are tools for controlling and manipulating what the public knows about the world. As private companies, they have the right to do so, and users have a right to switch to other platforms if they disagree with a company's policies. But the greatest danger exists when the State collaborates with (or takes a significant ownership stake in) these powerful organizations—and all other facets of media—in order to mold public perception in the ways *it* sees fit. **It can thus steer the public toward certain perspectives and away from others, while silencing voices along the way and intentionally sowing division (a "divide-and-conquer" tactic).** Allowing the State to dictate what ideas are "acceptable"—while having the ability to track and surveille citizens using data from technology platforms—is a recipe for disaster.

Education

Manipulating a population's youth is another essential brainwashing tactic to consider. All forms of media can serve this function, but State-sponsored programs, including public schools, represent additional outlets for mind control. The Nazis, for example, were able to propagandize via the Hitler Youth program. Although it's sometimes tempting to say, "Obviously the bad guys would brainwash their youth, but in the free world, that would never happen," we should be carefully examining our own institutions with this context in mind.

Moreover, the role of intellectual leaders in society needs to be considered. Murray Rothbard noted, "In all societies, public opinion is determined by the intellectual classes, the opinion moulders [*sic*] of society. For most people neither originate nor disseminate ideas and concepts; on the contrary, they tend to adopt those ideas promulgated by the professional intellectual classes, the professional dealers in ideas." Intellectuals can thus be weaponized by the State to indoctrinate the masses. In Rothbard's words: "Ruling elites of States have had far more need of the services of intellectuals than have peaceful citizens in a free society."[63]

Until relatively recently, the "intellectual class" had essentially been members of the Church. After the more widespread separation of Church and State, the State needed a new alliance, which is where the intellectuals fit in. Eventually "science" became the new "religion." Rothbard commented, "Now it was science that allegedly required the rule of the economy and of society by technocratic 'experts.' In exchange for spreading this message to the public, the new breed of intellectuals was rewarded with jobs and prestige."[64]

This symbiotic relationship between the State and its new "partners" has bled into the realm of education. Rothbard explained:

> To insure the dominance of the new statism over public opinion, to insure that the public's consent would be engineered, the governments of the Western world in the late nineteenth and early twentieth centuries moved to seize control over education, the minds of men: over the universities, and over general education through compulsory school attendance laws and a network of public schools. **The public schools were consciously used to inculcate obedience to the State as well as other civic virtues among their young charges**. Furthermore, this statizing of education insured that one of the biggest vested interests in expanding statism would

> be the nation's teachers and professional educationists.[65] [emphasis added]

I can say from personal experience—arguably having been academically and professionally bred within the "intellectual class" (but without having any explicit ties to government)—it has been particularly difficult to overcome statist programming. I notice it in my own thinking and in that of many others I know who have similar backgrounds. There is simply a natural, knee-jerk reaction against ideas that challenge the consensus opinions of the "experts." Breaking that conditioning is almost like weight training that requires continual practice in order to build muscles that have atrophied. In fact, I've observed that individuals who have the most difficult time thinking "outside the box" are sometimes the most well educated: they all too often reject the possibility that what they learned in school was incomplete or simply wrong.

Government-Sponsored Mind-Control Programs

Potentially underlying the aforementioned brainwashing tactics is a dark history of mind-control experimentation, which has now been widely validated but is often underdiscussed. The history here illuminates the level of sophistication—and secrecy—in play. What follows is an elaboration.

Operation Paperclip

Around the end of World War II, the United States began recruiting scientists from Germany and Japan in order to keep them and their valuable knowledge base "out of Soviet hands."[66] For example, former Nazi Kurt Blome was one such scientist. As author Stephen Kinzer notes in his book *Poisoner in Chief* (2019), Blome worked out of a complex in Germany that had, among other things, "laboratories devoted to virology, pharmacology, radiology, and bacteriology; [and] a 'tumor farm' where malignant viruses were cultivated. Blome developed aerosol delivery systems for nerve gas, to be tested on inmates at the Auschwitz concentration camp....His complex was officially known as the Central Cancer Institute."[67]

Blome came to work for the United States, as did renowned Japanese torturer Shirō Ishii. In fact, the United States had a formal program, initiated by President Harry Truman in 1946, in which it recruited Nazi scientists: Operation Paperclip.[68] Paperclip was a secret program through which Nazi scientists' biographies were strategically falsified, and where government officials were allowed to issue visas "in the interest of national security." However, Truman's order was supposed to exclude any individual who had been "a member of the Nazi Party and more than a nominal participant in its activities, or an active supporter of Nazi militarism."[69] Those in charge of Operation Paperclip ignored Truman's stipulation, ultimately bringing on more than fifteen hundred Nazi scientists (including Wernher von Braun, who founded NASA).[70]

US Mind-Control Programs

The existence of Operation Paperclip demonstrates that Nazism did not die when the Germans lost the war. To the contrary, Nazi ideology quietly infiltrated the United States decades ago. Who knows how much of that lineage continues within government agencies today?

The history of the Nazi-influenced mind-control programs within the US tells a harrowing story. For example, unethical human experimentation existed *under US supervision*—such as a US Army–operated base in Germany called Camp King in which it held ex-Nazis. CIA director Allen Dulles utilized Camp King and other secret prisons for the "Operation Bluebird" mind-control program, operating beyond the reach of US law because it was in West Germany. As Kinzer states: "At these secret prisons, Bluebird interrogators worked without any outside supervision. This set a precedent that marked a breakthrough for the CIA."[71] The CIA duplicated this process in Japan as well.[72]

In 1951, Dulles assigned chemist Sidney Gottlieb to a new project called Operation Artichoke, which expanded on the work of Operation Bluebird. A CIA memo offers insight into the program's intent and the mindset of this government-sponsored program:

> Specific research should be undertaken to develop new chemicals or drugs, or to improve known elements for use in Artichoke work.
>
> An exhaustive study should be made of various gases and aerosols....Gas guns, jets, or sprays, both concealed [and] open, should be studied. In addition, the problem of permanent brain injury and amnesia following lack of oxygen or exposure to other gases should be studied.
>
> The effects of high and low pressures on individuals should be examined.
>
> A considerable amount of research could profitably be expended in the field of sound. This research would include the effect on human beings of various types of vibrations, monotonous sounds, concussion, ultra-high frequency, ultra-sonics, the effect of constantly repeated words, sounds, continuous suggestion, non-rhythmic sounds, whispering, etc.
>
> Bacteria, plant cultures, fungi, poisons of various types... are capable of producing illnesses which in turn would produce high fevers, delirium, etc.
>
> The removal of certain basic food elements such as sugar, starch, calcium, vitamins, protein, etc. from the food of an individual over a certain period of time will produce psychological and physical reactions in an individual. A study should be made to determine whether or not the removal of certain food elements from the diet of prisoners over a given period of time will materially condition them for Artichoke work.
>
> Whether an individual will reveal information as a result of electroshock, or while in an electroshock coma, has not yet been demonstrated....Whether electroshock can produce controlled amnesias does not appear to be established.

> If an electronically induced sleep could be obtained, and that sleep is used as a means of gaining hypnotic control of an individual, this apparatus might be of extreme value to the Artichoke work.
>
> The Agency under no circumstances would consider [lobotomy and brain surgery] as an operative measure. However, it is felt that the subject could be examined.
>
> Special research should be conducted to determine the effect of long and continuous exposure of individuals to infra-red and ultra-violet light.
>
> There are a great many psychological techniques that could be used in connection with the Artichoke work [including] moving or vibrating rooms; distorted rooms; the deliberate creation on an anxiety condition; the creation of panic, fear, or the exploitation of established phobias, etc.; the effects of heat and cold; the effect of dampness dryness or saturated or dry air; the general problem of disorientation; [and] completely soundproof areas.
>
> It would be a great advantage if a small, effective hypospray device should be designed along the lines of a fountain pen. This, of course, would necessarily have to include some effective chemical or drug that could be used in this connection. This would be a very valuable weapon.[73]

Gottlieb's work continued into the more well-known MK-ULTRA project beginning in 1953, in which he experimented on human subjects with substances such as LSD, often without their knowledge. For example, as stated in his obituary published by *The Independent*, "Prostitutes would slip drugs to their customers, and the results would be observed by agency officials through two-way mirrors."[74] Kinzer reports that during Gottlieb's tenure, "hundreds of people were tormented and many minds were permanently shattered."[75] He retired in 1972 but faced lawsuits from people who suspected that they were victims. In the end, Gottlieb "revealed almost nothing beyond the fact that before leaving the CIA he had destroyed all records of what he did. He was never convicted of a crime."[76] *The Independent*'s obituary asserted that Gottlieb "was living vindication...that there is nothing, however evil, pointless or even lunatic, that unaccountable intelligence agencies will not get up to in the pursuit of their secret wars."[77]

The Universality of Mind-Control Reports

It's worth noting that the mind-control phenomenon does not appear unique to the United States: counselors have heard reports from their clients about mind-control programming in Canada, the United Kingdom, the Netherlands, Germany, Norway, Sweden, New Zealand, Australia, South Africa, France, Israel, Russia, Tibet, Afghanistan, India, Lebanon, Italy, China, Belgium, and Japan.[78]

Additionally, psychologist D. Corydon Hammond, PhD, commented on the uniformity of the stories told by survivors of mind-control abuse and also cult abuse (1992): "When you start to find the same highly esoteric information in different states and different countries, from Florida to California, you start to get an idea that there is something going on that is very large, very well coordinated with a great deal of communication and systematicness [*sic*] to what is happening."[79]

Case Study: Candy Jones

To provide a greater sense of how mind control works, it's worthwhile to review a well-examined case from many decades ago: that of Candy Jones. The activities here are sinister, but perhaps just as striking is the fact that mind-control victims can be so well hidden. We're left to wonder how much more sophisticated the mind-control "technology" is today and who might be secretly programmed in a similar manner. Along those lines, the notion of a brainwashed "Manchurian candidate" who carries out secret government plans—as described in the 1962 novel and subsequent films—becomes plausible as a real phenomenon rather than fiction.

Candy Jones was a famous American model in the 1940s whose face was featured on eleven magazine covers within one month in 1943. What is less well known is that she was later subjected to CIA mind-control programs to carry out specific tasks. Donald Bain's book on this subject, titled *The Control of Candy Jones* (1976), was written *before* the CIA released its "behavior modification files." As Bain wrote, "As I read the [CIA] documents, I catch my breath at times. Candy could not have known those things unless she lived them....The odds of her hallucinating these documented events are a trillion to one now."[80]

Jones's second husband was Long John Nebel, New York's most successful radio talk-show host. They'd been dating for just twenty-eight days before they married in 1972, and at the wedding, Nebel noted, "Something happened that I really can't put into words. You'd have to have known Candy as I did to notice the change in her. She developed an expression on her face that wasn't Candy, at least not the Candy I'd come to love. I'd never seen that expression before—tense, angry, concerned, I asked her if anything was wrong and she gave me a curt 'No.' I couldn't believe it was the same woman."[81] He recalled that Jones again transformed after the wedding, in their hotel room: "She said something to me in an entirely different voice. I don't recall her words, but I do remember her voice was bitter, biting. It was frightening."[82]

During the first several months of their marriage, Nebel noted that Jones's mood would occasionally shift, but not enough to cause major problems in their relationship. She did develop insomnia, however, and Nebel offered to try hypnosis on her as a remedy. While he had not previously performed hypnosis on anyone, he had read extensively about the subject and had friends in the medical field who practiced hypnosis (one of whom ultimately wrote the foreword to Bain's book).[83] In Nebel's first attempt to hypnotize his wife, he was successful—she entered a relaxed state and was finally able to sleep well. However, in future hypnosis sessions, she began to spontaneously age-regress, meaning that she began reliving events from her past.[84]

Bain's process of writing the book involved listening to more than two hundred hours of taped hypnosis sessions, in addition to sixty hours of interviews with Nebel and Jones. The tapes revealed that Jones was used as a messenger by the CIA under an alternate personality, "Arlene Grant," for twelve years. In other words, this personality was distinct from Jones but operated through her, during which time the real Jones was mentally absent. This alternate personality was apparently created artificially.

Dr. Gilbert Jensen appears to have been the man who did this. He met with Jones in 1960 and offered her a position in the CIA. Her first visit to his office, as uncovered under hypnosis, revealed that she filled out a simple form with personal information. Jensen then began hypnotizing Jones using a variety of techniques including a pendulum, a candle, lights, and sounds, and eventually gave her IV fluids that made her more suggestible (telling her they were "vitamins"). Jones had no memory of the visits with Jensen unless she was under hypnosis. As Bain explained, "The major difficulty in dredging up this material is that Candy Jones was programmed by Jensen *not* to remember, and this programming proved frighteningly effective."[85] [emphasis in original]

Apparently, Jensen was able to secretly program Jones's new personality, who carried out special missions for the CIA. For instance, as Jones revealed under Nebel's hypnosis, she traveled to Taiwan to deliver an envelope to a specific man. He then tortured her with electric shocks in an attempt to extract additional information, which she didn't have.[86]

Based on the information that arose under hypnosis, Jensen had programmed Jones with what Bain called "hate training": racism toward various ethnic groups. Jensen also taught her how to fire pistols; and he abused her sexually at a meeting in Langley, Virginia, with his colleagues and seven other human subjects.[87]

At times, Arlene Grant (Jones's alternate personality) would emerge around Nebel without warning, as it apparently did on the day of their wedding. In one instance, flickering candles in a restaurant caused Arlene to emerge unprompted, and afterward, Jones told Nebel that she had no recollection of what had happened just moments before.[88] Another time, she spontaneously transformed into Arlene and began strangling Nebel. He said, "I don't think I'd ever been as frightened in my life....She had turned into a monster, a woman with strength I didn't know she had, and whose face had taken on a mean, vicious expression like something you'd see in a horror movie."[89] After Arlene calmed down, Jones's "real self" seemed to emerge, and she denied that the attack happened, claiming she wasn't even aware of it. Later, under hypnosis, Arlene emerged and said, "They weren't *her* hands" that tried to strangle Nebel (referring to Jones). When Nebel asked whose hands they were, she replied, "Mine."[90]

Hypnosis also revealed a secret plan for Jones to commit suicide in the Bahamas. She said, "[Jensen] wanted me to go down there and jump off the rock."[91] The plan was for Jensen to book her a first-class ticket to the Bahamas, at which point he would call her and trigger Arlene to emerge, who would then fall to her death from an elevated location. Under hypnosis, Jones said, "[Jensen's] not going to do anything unless he can make it look accidental.... He wouldn't do it yet because it could be traced to him."[92]

Bain's book includes a signed letter from Jones's attorney, addressed to Jones, which lends credibility to this story. The letter explicitly said: "You told me...were you to die or disappear under unusual circumstances, particularly if you died under a different name, I should carefully check out the facts of your case. In addition, I received numerous flight insurance statements during the 1960's from your many trips around the country, including your trips to the Caribbean, particularly the Bahamas."[93]

Also supporting the credibility of Jones's case was the testimony of psychiatrist Herbert Spiegel, MD. He wrote the book's foreword and concluded that Jones was among a group of no more than 10 percent of the population that is "extremely hypnotizable," which was confirmed independently by two other psychiatrists. In Spiegel's words: "This high hypnotizability makes plausible her capacity to regress to earlier times in her life and to act as though she were in the present. It is also consistent with her global amnesia—that is, her complete 'forgetting' of many events in her life."[94]

Bain also spoke of more widespread government-sponsored mind control. After the publication of his book, he wrote: "Many letters arrived from those who claimed to have also been tampered with by the CIA. Candy Jones was, after all, only one of thousands of well-meaning and patriotic citizens who were deliberately injured by our intelligence community in the interest of proving that the perfect spy, the perfect courier could be *manufactured*."[95] [emphasis in original]

Not all allegations of mind control are as well documented as that of Candy Jones, but other high-profile cases have been widely speculated. One often-alleged example is that of Sirhan Sirhan, who was convicted for the 1968 murder of Senator Robert Kennedy. In 2011, his attorneys wrote in a court filing, "[Sirhan] was an involuntary participant in the crimes being committed because he was subjected to sophisticated hypno-programming and memory implantation techniques which rendered him unable to consciously control his thoughts and actions at the time the crimes were being committed."[96] He was deemed suitable for parole in 2021. Additionally, journalist Tom O'Neill's book *CHAOS: Charles Manson, the CIA, and the Secret History of the Sixties* (2019) investigates potential links between murderer Charles Manson and MK-ULTRA mind-control programming.

False-Flag Operations

Mind-control operations are clearly sophisticated. There's no telling to what extent governments might use related psychological techniques to covertly influence public perception. "False-flag" operations might be one such category of calculated manipulation. These are planned catastrophes that enable governments to steer narratives in a desired direction.

This process is often known as "Problem-Reaction-Solution."[97] The steps are: (1) The State creates a *problem*, (2) which generates a predictable *reaction* by the masses to that problem, (3) which then allows the State to swoop in as the savior by giving a *solution*...to the problem it intentionally created. And the solution is the thing the State wanted in the first place.

The purpose of a false flag could be to induce immense fear in the public psyche. When fear is amplified through the media's repetition (that is, through mind control), the public demands any solution to make the fear go away. That solution often involves the sacrifice of individual liberties in exchange for perceived safety. In this regard, the State can take freedoms and enact its will much more seamlessly. Without the impetus of a false flag, the State might otherwise have to impose its will more forcefully, thereby bringing about resistance.

The Burning of the Reichstag

It is perhaps not surprising that many believe the Nazis employed false flags to achieve their objectives. One such example was setting on fire the home of Germany's parliament, the Reichstag building, in 1933.[98] **While some historians debate the cause of the fire, many argue that the Nazis themselves intentionally caused it but lied and blamed it on Communist terrorists.** That enabled them to enact a sweeping decree as "defense" against such terrorism. As summarized by the United States Holocaust Memorial Museum, the decree "suspended individual rights and due process of law. [It] permitted the regime to arrest and incarcerate political opponents without specific charge, dissolve political organizations, and to suppress publications. It also gave the central government the authority to overrule state and local laws and overthrow state and local governments. The decree was a key step in the establishment of the Nazi dictatorship. Germany became a police state in which citizens enjoyed no guaranteed basic rights."[99]

Historians seem to agree that a man was found inside the Reichstag who eventually confessed to starting the fire, but some argue that in the subsequent court sessions, he exhibited symptoms of mind control. We know from our earlier discussion that the Nazis were experts in mind control, so this hypothesis is worthy of consideration.

Operation Northwoods

Maybe it's believable that the Nazis would enact such evil, but it's harder for us to imagine that the United States government would. However, let's remember that through Operation Paperclip, many Nazis were brought into high-level US organizations.

In fact, a Joint Chiefs of Staff document from 1962 was declassified in 2001 and is suggestive of a detailed false-flag plan. This was known as Operation Northwoods (related to Operation Mongoose). The plan was created as a proposal to make Cuba look like a dangerous aggressor but was not enacted. The fact that such a plan was even contemplated in detail is significant, however: it demonstrates what the government is capable of and how it sometimes thinks.

According to the publicly available document, the United States would stage an attack—for example, "Blow up a US ship," *and then blame it on the Cubans.* The document went as far as suggesting that they would "conduct funerals for mock-victims" in addition to starting rumors and riots. The efforts would "provide adequate justification for US military intervention. Such a plan would enable a logical buildup of incidents to be combined with other seemingly unrelated events to camouflage the ultimate objective." The desired outcome would be "to place the United States in the apparent position of suffering defensible grievances from a rash and irresponsible government of Cuba and to develop an international image of a Cuban threat to peace in the Western Hemisphere."[100]

I will not speculate here as to the possibility that other major events in US (and world) history have been false flags. However, our knowledge about this brand of manipulation should make us question catastrophes we see on the news. We cannot automatically assume that they happened in the way the media tells us they did.

A useful exercise in this regard is to identify the outcomes of a given event, examine which parties benefited most, what rights were taken away from citizens as a result (if any), and whether any or all of those rights were eventually given back. Also, it's important to examine who benefited financially.

Depopulation

Perhaps the most direct method of mind control is population reduction, which means that the State doesn't have as many minds to control. For most of us, it's difficult to imagine thinking in this way. But for psychopaths who lack empathy and crave power, it's easy. And we can't forget the innate tendency of normal, good people to obey authority, thereby extending the reach of evil.

The most obvious example of depopulation comes from war. Under the premise of "defending our nation," war can be used to justify the fact that States are simply committing mass murder.[101] In a similar vein, genocide has been an all-too-commonly employed tactic. The Nazis even endorsed "eugenics": the desire to selectively breed by allowing those with "preferred" genetics to live, while experimenting on, and murdering and segregating, those deemed less desirable.

We might hope that citizens in the "free world" would see warning signs before anything so severe could happen today. But history has shown repeatedly that genocide can rear its ugly head, particularly when a population has been psychologically manipulated through mind control.

Dr. Gregory Stanton, a former professor at George Mason University and the president of Genocide Watch, laid out ten stages commonly found in genocidal situations (1996). We should be asking ourselves whether any of these early stages are happening in the world around us—whether related to race, political ideology, religious beliefs, vaccination or health status, and so on. Awareness of historical patterns can help us nip potential horrors in the bud. What follows are Stanton's ten stages with abbreviated explanations:[102]

1. *Classification:* Divide people into "us and them."
2. *Symbolization:* Give "them" a classification and force them to identify themselves. For example, in Nazi

Germany, Jews were forced to wear a yellow Star of David on their clothing in public (inscribed with the word *Jew*, written in German language or the local language).[103]

3. *Discrimination:* Use law, custom, or political power to exclude "them" and deny basic rights.
4. *Dehumanization:* Categorize "them" as subhuman, equating them with "animals, vermin, insects, or diseases," which serves to "overcome the normal human revulsion against murder." The dominant group is "indoctrinated to believe that 'we are better off without them.'"
5. *Organization:* Organize and train for genocidal killings, through militias or army units, for example.
6. *Polarization:* Drive a deep wedge between "us" and "them" with propaganda, potentially forbidding intermarriage, disarming "them," and intimidating moderates.
7. *Preparation:* Plan genocide (such as the Final Solution in Nazi Germany), using euphemisms to "cloak" true intentions, while amplifying fear of "them" through intensified propaganda: "Leaders often claim that 'if we don't kill them, they will kill us,' disguising genocide as self-defense."
8. *Persecution:* Begin the violation of basic human rights, create "death lists," deprive "them" of basic resources such as food and water, expropriate their property, take children from their parents, deport "them" to concentration camps, prevent procreation though forced sterilization and abortion, and so on.
9. *Extermination:* Begin mass killings: "It is 'extermination' to the killers because they do not believe their victims to be fully human."
10. *Denial:* Cover up evidence by digging mass graves, burning the bodies, blocking investigations into the crimes, intimidating witnesses, and so on.

There are noteworthy examples of such depopulation tactics in the modern era, including forced abortion and sterilization. Gruesome reports have come from China and elsewhere, for instance.[104] Along these lines, in 2012, a judge ruled that HIV-positive women in Namibia, Africa, were sterilized without informed consent.[105] Similarly, a 2015 report by the Population Research Institute stated that "over one in three women in India between the ages of 15 and 45 have been sterilized....Among women who have been sterilized, one in three say that they weren't informed that the procedure was permanent."[106]

In the United States, the infamous Tuskegee Experiment could be regarded in a similar manner. As summarized by Colin A. Ross, MD, in his book *The CIA Doctors: Human Rights Violations by American Psychiatrists* (2006):

> In 1932, 399 illiterate poor rural black men with syphilis were recruited as subjects, along with 201 controls without syphilis. The purpose of the Study was to make sure the 399 men never got treatment. They were followed for decades to see how the syphilis affected them....
>
> The subjects and their families had no idea what the Study was all about. They weren't told they had syphilis and didn't know it was treatable....The cure for syphilis, penicillin, was introduced in the early 1940's. It was withheld from the Tuskegee men for thirty years....The published results of the Study showed, as expected, that the men with untreated syphilis were sicker and died younger than controls. This is only part of the problem. How many acts of unprotected sexual intercourse did these 399 men engage in over forty years?[107]

(Note: The men who participated were awarded a certificate in 1958 for their service and $25, one dollar for each year of participation. The study was terminated in 1972 when a journalist caught wind of it, but there was no indication that it would have been shut down otherwise. A class-action lawsuit was filed in 1973, and there was eventually an out-of-court settlement of $10 million. In 1997, President Bill Clinton apologized to the Tuskegee subjects and their families.[108])

Ross also describes radiation experiments that were perpetrated upon the American public without meaningful informed consent. In one instance, "clouds of radioactive material were released into the atmosphere and tracked as they moved downwind, often through populated areas." These were conducted at specific sites in Utah, Tennessee, New Mexico, and the state of Washington from 1948 to 1952. An experiment with the code name "GREEN RUN" involved the release of radioactive iodine-131 in Washington, and the cloud "contained hundreds and perhaps thousands as times [*sic*] as much radiation as was released accidentally at Three Mile Island in 1979."[109]

The existence of such disturbing programs can be concealed for many years before the general public finds out about them, and perhaps some programs will remain hidden forever. So while a number of the discussed case studies occurred long ago, they are noteworthy because they provide insights into the State's devious potential. We have to wonder what could be happening today under our noses. Therefore, it's sensible for citizens to demand transparency in the event of government-sponsored biological interventions of any kind. The State's dark history certainly does not lend itself to automatic trust from the populace.

SECTION II

WHAT IS AN ALTERNATIVE TO TRADITIONAL GOVERNMENT?

CHAPTER 4

NONAGGRESSION, PRIVATE-PROPERTY RIGHTS, AND TRULY FREE MARKETS

By now it's abundantly clear that the State can be a danger to its own people. Such a centralized power structure amplifies the effects of evil. Yet we are so accustomed to having that structure in place to run society that alternatives are simply difficult to fathom. The stickiness is almost religious in nature. We *want* to believe that a superhuman, all-knowing political entity can magically take care of society's problems for us, and that its representatives are trustworthy and altruistic.

Perhaps we collectively have Stockholm syndrome, whereby, as longtime prisoners, we've developed a psychological attachment to our abusers. In fact, this sort of mentality occurred among African American slaves, as reported by Frederick Douglass in his memoir about escaping from slavery (1845):

> [S]laves…imbibe prejudices quite common to others. They think their own better than that of others. Many, under the influence of this prejudice, think their own masters are better than the masters of other slaves; and this, too, in some cases, when the very reverse is true.

> Indeed, it is not uncommon for slaves even to fall out and quarrel among themselves about the relative goodness of their masters, each contending for the superior goodness of his own over that of the others....They seemed to think that the greatness of their masters was transferable to themselves. It was considered as being bad enough to be a slave; but to be a poor man's slave was deemed a disgrace indeed![1]

This is strikingly similar to what happens in modern society: People argue over which political leaders are better, and they take pride as followers. It's as if they're arguing, "My ruler is better than yours." And, indeed, sometimes political leaders are nicer and more effective than others. But that doesn't change the fact that they're rulers.[2]

It's time to consider an alternative.

Libertarianism and Its Influence in Early America

For the remainder of this chapter, we will revisit the political philosophy mentioned in chapter 1, known as "voluntaryism." This is a form of libertarianism arguing that there shouldn't be a State, although the functions classically held by the State would be offered by privately owned service providers. People would pay—voluntarily—for the services they want (and can afford). They would become true customers. **Moreover, citizens would have contractual arrangements with the service providers they choose, whereas under statism, there isn't an explicit contract between citizens and the State.** Although this philosophy doesn't claim to provide a perfect solution, it is arguably better than the status quo of statism. Additionally, and perhaps most important, voluntaryism is superior to statism from a metaphysical lens (as we'll discuss in section III).

Even though voluntaryism is a form of libertarianism, not all libertarians would subscribe to the former philosophy. **Libertarians generally believe in individual rights and limited government,**

while the voluntarist brand of libertarianism posits *no* government (that is, the government's functions are replaced by service providers).

It's also worth keeping in mind that the general ideas here are not new, and in fact, skepticism about the State has a long history in America. The early Americans were particularly influenced by "Cato's Letters"—a series of newspaper articles published in the 1720s in London—which were often reprinted by the American colonists and warned about the corrupting influence of power. For example, "It is the Nature of Power to be ever encroaching, and converting every extraordinary Power, granted at particular Times, upon particular occasions, into an ordinary Power, to be used at all Times, when there is no Occasion....Alas! Power encroaches daily upon Liberty, with a Success too evident....Tyranny has engrossed almost the whole Earth."[3]

The American revolutionaries embodied this mentality, as noted by former Harvard University historian Bernard Bailyn in 1973: "**American leaders moved swiftly and with little social disruption to implement systematically the outermost possibilities of the whole range of radically libertarian ideas**....The first is the belief that power is evil...that it is infinitely corrupting; and that it must be controlled, limited, restricted, in every way compatible with a minimum of civil order. Written constitutions; the separation of powers; bills of rights; limitations on executives, on legislatures, and courts; restrictions on the right to coerce and wage war **all express the profound distrust of power that lies at the ideological heart of the American Revolution**."[4] [emphasis added]

This libertarian impulse continued in the nineteenth century, as summarized by Murray Rothbard:

> The Jeffersonian and Jacksonian movements...explicitly strived for the virtual elimination of government from American life. It was to be a government without a standing army or navy; a government without debt and with no direct federal or excise taxes and virtually no

> import tariffs—that is, with negligible levels of taxation and expenditures; a government that does not engage in public works or internal improvements; a government that does not control or regulate; a government that leaves money and banking free, hard, and uninflated; in short, in the words of H.L. Mencken's ideal, "a government that barely escapes being no government at all."[5]

"Barely" is not the same as "fully," however. The truth is that America couldn't totally escape "being no government at all." It was still a State. And over the years, the notion of limited government has eroded to the point that we're now dealing with a behemoth that has its tentacles in so many aspects of our lives, including our finances.

Although America has no doubt enabled freedoms unseen in many other parts of the world—and we should not forget that—its history teaches us an important lesson about the State: Even in an *initially* "limited" form, it cannot *remain* limited in the long run. It always grows and grows. In other words, the notion of permanent "small government" is a myth. Or, as Rothbard said, **"The idea of a strictly limited government has proved to be utopian."**[6] [emphasis added]

Furthermore, Rothbard commented, "Advocates of a limited government often hold up the ideal of a government above the fray, refraining from taking sides or throwing its weight around, an 'umpire' arbitrating impartially between contending factions in society. Yet why *should* the government do so? Given the unchecked power of the State, the State and its rulers will act to maximize their power and wealth....[T]here are no institutional mechanisms to *keep* the State limited."[7] [emphasis in original]

Larken Rose echoes these sentiments: "Perhaps the most valuable thing the 'Great American Experiment' accomplished was to demonstrate that 'limited government' is impossible. There cannot be a master who answers to his slaves. There cannot be a lord who serves his subjects. There cannot be a ruler who is both above the people and subordinate to them."[8]

Therefore, it's worth revisiting the philosophy behind America's early libertarian ideals—but this time going all the way by removing traditional government from the picture altogether. We'll now give voluntaryism a fair hearing.

Voluntaryism

In a voluntarist, Stateless society, citizens would have the liberty to live as they choose, as long as they do not *initiate* any form of aggression upon another's private property—**whether it be theft, coercion, physical violence, fraud, extortion, and so on**. Aggression in self-defense—which could include assistance from others—is acceptable because it is *in response* to another party's actions. Acts of aggression simply can't be initiated (this is known as the *nonaggression principle*). Private courts, arbitrators, and mediators would manage violations of private property and related contract disputes (more on this in chapter 5).

This philosophy sometimes goes by names other than "voluntaryism," so it's worth clarifying the terminology before proceeding. A common alternative to the term *voluntaryism* is *anarcho-capitalism*. Voluntaryism is a gentler way of describing it. On the contrary, the equivalent term *anarcho-capitalism* is much more inflammatory and has the potential to upset basically everyone: *anarcho* conjures up images of a lawless society, which the political Right tends to dislike; and *capitalism* is sometimes aversive to those on the political Left. But the term *anarchism* tends to be misunderstood: in this context it refers to a society without *rulers* rather than a society without rules. The society we'll be contemplating would absolutely have rules: individuals, communities, and political units would set guidelines for their private property, and formal engagements between parties would involve contracts. This means that people can live in whatever type of society they want—with whatever rules and regulations they so choose. But in order to abide by the nonaggression principle, the engagements need to be explicitly consensual and voluntary rather than compulsory.

Therefore, by definition, the State cannot exist in such a society. Why? Because the State is inherently an invasive, coercive aggressor: it *forces* itself upon citizens' private property (for example, via taxation) without their explicit consent. As Rothbard put it, "The State provides a legal, orderly, systematic channel for the predation of private property."[9]

Rothbard thus provided a simple definition of a voluntarist society: "One where there is no *legal* possibility for coercive aggression against the person or property of any individual."[10] [emphasis added]

Private Property

Since private property is central to voluntaryism, we need to define it more precisely. We can start with the easy part: An individual's body is private property. You naturally own your body.[11]

But of course it's possible to own things other than your body, like pencils, forks, cars, homes, money, land, and so on. And that's where things get a little more complicated. How do we define rightful ownership of such nonbodily property?[12] Walter Block, PhD, a professor of economics at Loyola University New Orleans, summarizes the libertarian perspective concisely. It was initially adapted from John Locke and involves "mixing your labor with the land or other unowned parts of nature."[13] This process is known as "homesteading."

With regard to land, Block suggests that the homesteading process required to claim ownership could be as simple as "clearing away dead branches, creating paths and building bathroom facilities, etc., so that the land may be more readily enjoyed."[14] That would enable private landownership while preserving nature. Owners would also have the option to develop the land more extensively.

Moreover, Rothbard gives an example of homesteading of non-land property: a sculptor who molds clay into a unique form. After creating the art, the sculptor becomes the owner. Through his energy and effort, the sculptor used a natural material (clay) and mixed his "labor" with it, which, in Rothbard's words, then became "a veritable *extension* of his own personality."[15] [emphasis in original]

As Block comments, once you own something through this method of homesteading—land or other material objects—you can then transfer it to someone else "through any voluntary non-fraudulent means: sale, gift, barter, trade, gambling, inheritance."[16]

So the process is: People use natural resources and mix in their labor, which becomes their private property. They can then keep that property, or they can transfer ownership to someone else. If anyone initiates aggression upon that private property, the owner has a right to self-defense. The same applies to one's body since it's also private property. This is voluntaryism in a nutshell. It is a clean, simple, and free way of living.

Rothbard said it well: "Freedom is a condition in which a person's ownership rights in his own body and his legitimate material property are *not* invaded, are not aggressed against....Slavery—the opposite of freedom—is a condition in which the slave has little or no right of self-ownership; his person and his produce are systematically expropriated by his masters by the use of violence."[17] [emphasis in original]

Socialism and Communism

From this lens, the philosophies of socialism and communism—both of which enthusiastically advocate the State's aggression upon citizens' private property—can be seen to promote the opposite of liberty. For example, under socialism, the means of production and the distribution of goods are controlled by the State, which serves as the central planner and manager of the economy. Advocates of this system might speak to the hypothetical benefits of such an anticapitalist strategy: the State can balance inequalities and provide for "free" what citizens need. Economics professor Thomas DiLorenzo, PhD, calls it: "Government as Santa Claus."[18]

DiLorenzo gives an example to illustrate how socialism works: "I joke with my Principles of Economics classes, and the first day I tell them, 'Here's what we're gonna do: I'm gonna give seven exams during the course of the fourteen-week semester.... When I get all the grades, those of you who get the low grades, I'm gonna take points away from the good students who got the high grades and...give you some of their points so that everybody gets a C.' And I tell them, 'Well, that's academic socialism.'"[19] When this sort of thinking is applied to society-at-large, major problems arise with regard to private-property rights.

Rothbard explained it in another way. In his framing, the socialistic perspective tends to advocate freedom over one's own body but often denies private ownership of things people produce. So, socialism divides private property into separate categories, advocating one but not the other. Another way of saying it is that the socialist advocates "human rights" but condemns "external" property rights; you own yourself but not what you produce.

Paradoxically, socialists commonly regard freedom of speech as a human right, yet they overlook the fact that one cannot transmit speech without a platform. The platform could be within a business property, in a newspaper, on social media, in someone's home, and so on. So free speech takes place *within private property*. By extension, without private property, free speech is in big trouble.

Because private property can be controlled and owned by the government under socialism, Rothbard asked, "If, for example, the government owns all the newsprint and all the printing shops, how is the right to a free press to be exercised? If the government owns all the newsprint, it, then, necessarily has the right and the power to allocate that newsprint, and someone's 'right to a free press' becomes a mockery if the government decides not to allocate newsprint in his direction. And since the government must allocate scarce newsprint in *some* way, the right to a free press of, say, minorities, or 'subversive' antisocialists will get short shrift indeed."[20] [emphasis added] The individual's rights are therefore *dependent* upon the State. That is not freedom. In fact, becoming dependent on the government in any fashion creates a clear path to enslavement.

Other types of human-rights violations are possible under socialism as well. Rothbard stated, "For example, if the government of

Soviet Russia, being atheistic, decides not to allocate many scarce resources to the production of matzohs [unleavened bread eaten by Jews during the Passover holiday], for Orthodox Jews the 'freedom of religion' becomes a mockery; but again, the Soviet government can always rebut that Orthodox Jews are a small minority and that capital equipment should not be diverted to matzoh production."[21]

If the State—a dangerous entity to begin with—is allowed to control private property and therefore dictate who gets what, basic human rights are at risk. As Rothbard summed it up, "There *are no* human rights that are separable from property rights."[22] [emphasis in original] This is an unresolvable contradiction for the socialist.

Perhaps there's a reason why the clear problems of socialism are so often overlooked, even among well-educated communities. Rothbard noted in his historical analysis that socialist philosophy was one of the ideologies used by the intellectual class to infiltrate youthful minds via the education system.[23] Essentially, it's been used to brainwash the public into advocating for the State's interventionist activities, whereby aggressions upon private property are regarded as necessary and virtuous. Through mind control, the State is able to perpetuate itself more easily by creating in the populace a "mental block" toward opposing ideologies.

A related political philosophy, communism, shares similar flaws with socialism. In some respects, socialism and communism could be considered the same, but communism is typically characterized by granting even more power to a central planner (the State). *The Communist Manifesto* (1848), written by Karl Marx and Frederick Engels, explicitly advocated for the "abolition" of private property.[24] Furthermore, as Rothbard explained, communism can involve forcing citizens to have an "equal quotal share of everyone else."[25] Rothbard elaborated: "Every man is entitled to own a part of everyone else, yet is not entitled *to own himself*....We can picture the viability of such a world: a world in which *no* man is free to take *any* action whatever without prior approval or indeed command by *everyone* else in society."[26] [emphasis in original] Again, this is the opposite of freedom.

Communism has been catastrophic for its citizens. *The Black Book of Communism*, written by Stephane Courtois et al., and published by Harvard University Press in 1999, gives an historical perspective on the atrocities committed under communist rule:

> These crimes tend to fit a recognizable pattern even if the practices vary to some extent by regime. The pattern includes execution by various means, such as firing squads, hanging, drowning, battering, and, in certain cases, gassing, poisoning, or "car accidents"; destruction of the population by starvation, through man-made famine, the withholding of food, or both; deportation, through which death can occur in transit (either through physical exhaustion or through confinement in an enclosed space), at one's place of residence, or through forced labor (exhaustion, illness, hunger, cold).[27]

The book provided an unofficial estimate of the resulting death toll at the hands of communist regimes, which approached 100 million:[28]

China: 65 million deaths

USSR: 20 million deaths

North Korea: 2 million deaths

Cambodia: 2 million deaths

Africa: 1.7 million deaths

Afghanistan: 1.5 million deaths

Eastern Europe: 1 million deaths

Vietnam: 1 million deaths

Latin America: 150,000 deaths

Fascism

Although the previous figures focus on communism—rather than fascism—we shouldn't ignore fascist regimes in this discussion. They've been incredibly destructive, as well. For instance, Nazi Germany was responsible for an estimated 11 million deaths.[29]

Fascism, in fact, shares elements of communism and socialism. I recognize how counterintuitive that might sound. Because these terms have emotionally charged connotations in modern society, their similarities are often overlooked. Most significant, like communism and socialism, fascism involves a central planner. As author Lew Rockwell defines it, "Fascism is the system of government that cartelizes the private sector, centrally plans the economy to subsidize producers, exalts the police state as the source of order, denies fundamental rights and liberties to individuals, and makes the executive state the unlimited master of society."[30] **So whether we call a regime communist, socialist, or fascist, the essence of domineering government, with substantial control over private property,[31] remains.**

Additionally, there exists historical precedent showing the overlap between these dictatorial philosophies. Italy is one such example. Benito Mussolini rose to power in 1922 via a democratic election, and he adopted fascism. However, as Rockwell notes, "Socialists crossed over to join the fascists *en masse*" because they "realized that their anticapitalistic agenda could best be achieved within the framework of the authoritarian, planning state."[32] Similarly, the Nazi party was officially the National *Socialist* German Workers' Party. As DiLorenzo summarizes the situation: "The Russians called themselves International Socialists, the German socialists called themselves National Socialists, but they were all socialists, just a different variety."[33] Nobel Prize–winning economist F. A. Hayek made a similar point in his book *The Road to Serfdom* (1944), in which he devoted a full chapter to "The Socialist Roots of Nazism."[34] He stated in summary: "Few are ready to recognise that the rise of Fascism and Nazism was not a reaction against the socialist trends of the preceding period, but a necessary outcome of those tendencies."[35]

But, as noted by former UC Berkeley Russian history professor Martin Malia (1924–2004), because of the flagrant and unacceptable racism associated with Nazi fascism, it sometimes carries a worse reputation in the Western psyche than communism does. As a result, communism seems to hold a "permanent qualitative advantage...over Nazism in any evaluation of their quantitative atrocities. For the Communist project, in origin, claimed commitment to universalistic and egalitarian goals, whereas the Nazi project offered only unabashed national egoism. Small matter, then, that their practices were comparable; their moral auras were antithetical, and it is the latter feature that counts in Western, domestic politics."[36] As we've seen, however, the "morality" in communism (and socialism) is just a facade for systems proven to be destructive in practice.

In conclusion, we've seen why allowing the State to have control over private property—while playing the role of a central planner—is a recipe for disaster. In principle, it might sound benign, virtuous, and cooperative. But it's not. On the other hand, voluntaryism avoids many of these problems by eliminating a compulsory central planner (the State).

The Welfare State

A concept related to socialism and communism is the modern "welfare state," wherein the central-planning government redistributes wealth in order to provide for the less fortunate. "Redistribution of wealth" is a euphemism for theft of private property. It simply means taking citizens' money—whether they like it or not—and distributing that money to third parties as the State sees fit. **Yes, the State provides a "safety net" for its citizens and might appear virtuous for doing so. But it's easy to overlook the fact that the safety net itself only exists because of the State's aggression toward private property. And that's not so virtuous.**

Under voluntaryism, the State-sponsored safety net would disappear. How, then, does the voluntarist perspective think about helping the underprivileged? First, it's worth remembering that in a voluntarist society, charitable organizations would still exist.

In fact, they might even become more prominent. Without a formal State, much more responsibility would be placed on citizens (rather than assuming that the government will take care of everything for us). Along those lines, it's possible that some people would unite within communities or political units requiring contributions that would go toward helping the poor. New technologies might emerge to enable this process.[37] Furthermore, *voluntary* socialism or communism would be acceptable if that's what certain people want to do: it's only problematic, from a voluntarist's perspective, when these systems are *forced upon unwilling participants* (a point often emphasized by Block).

To some economists, the welfare state itself is inherently problematic because it can lead people to become dependent on the State, thereby diminishing their motivation to work and become self-sufficient (for example, see the paper *Welfare Harms Its Ostensible Beneficiaries* [2017] by Fast et al.).[38] In fact, in 1766, Benjamin Franklin made this argument as well.[39]

But regardless of one's views on that nuanced topic, the elimination of the State would actually confer some immediate benefits to the underprivileged. For example, such individuals would be able to retain more money in a voluntarist society because their tax burden would go away.

Also, without the State, there wouldn't be minimum-wage laws. Although the concept of a minimum wage sounds nice because it forbids businesses from paying employees below a certain amount, this restriction *can create* unemployment. For example, let's say minimum-wage laws prohibit salaries below $15 per hour, but some businesses can't afford to pay all of their employees that much. Those businesses might then be forced to fire workers simply because of the State's law. And consequently, the people being fired would be the lowest-wage workers—*likely the ones who are the most underprivileged and who might have the most difficulty finding new jobs*. Even if employers really, really wanted to hire certain people at rates below the minimum-wage level, the government's edict would make it illegal to do so.

Finally, in a voluntarist society, there likely wouldn't be a central bank.[40] Central banks have an ability to *cause* inflation through the creation of new money, for example.[41] Inflation means that the purchasing power of money goes down: the underprivileged (and citizens more broadly) are able to buy less with the money they have. In effect, inflation makes people poorer.

The overarching point is this: The voluntarist society wouldn't have a State-sponsored welfare system because there wouldn't be a State. However, individuals, communities, and charities could fund their own creative support systems. This would be critical. As we'll discuss in section III, a more charitable collective mindset is conceivable in humanity's future if consciousness evolves to a more mature level. Also, the elimination of the State might confer net benefits to the underprivileged relative to the status quo. It's certainly an imperfect solution to an ever-present challenge, but arguably it's a *less imperfect* solution than what's typically provided by the State.

True Capitalism and the Austrian School of Economics

Unlike socialism and other statist systems, voluntaryism entails a *completely* free market economy—true laissez-faire capitalism. This means that the State would in no way intervene in the economy—which is by definition the case because under voluntaryism, the State wouldn't exist. We tend to think of America's current economy as a capitalistic system, when in reality it only has *elements* of capitalism. In the same way that "a little bit of government" implies statism and not voluntaryism, "a little bit of government in the economy" is not true capitalism. In fact, the truth today is that we're facing more than "a little bit of government in the economy."

A truly free-market, capitalistic system is compatible with the teachings of the **"Austrian School" of economics**, modeled after the work of Carl Menger (1840–1921); Eugen von Böhm-Bawerk (1851–1914); Ludwig von Mises (1881–1973); Henry Hazlitt (1894–1993); Nobel laureate F. A. Hayek (1899–1992); Murray

Rothbard (1926–1995), and others; and continues today at the Mises Institute in Auburn, Alabama.[42] (Note: Not all Austrian economists are voluntarists, and not all voluntarists subscribe to Austrian economics, per se. There exists a diversity of opinion on various matters *within* these schools of economic and political thinking. For the purposes of this book, I emphasize the Austrian economic principles that align with both voluntaryism and the metaphysical framing discussed in chapter 8.)[43]

As summarized concisely by former US congressman Ron Paul, an advocate of Austrian economics, Menger believed that "**economic value extends from the human mind alone** and is not something that exists as an inherent part of goods and services; valuation changes according to social needs and circumstances."[44] [emphasis added]

Let's break that down. This basically means that the entire economy starts with consumer demand—in other words, what people want to buy. That's why economic value stems from the "human mind." For example, let's say that Sally is about to throw a party and, based on her personal preference, she decides to buy a dozen cupcakes. She could have chosen any food for the party, but she made the decision to go with cupcakes. *Based on that demand for cupcakes*—and the demand of other consumers—the bakery knows what to produce to meet consumers' needs, such as the number of workers and which supplies are needed (cupcake ingredients, ovens, and so on). So the bakery then becomes a consumer of its own in the market for workers, food supplies, and even real estate (so that it has a place to make desserts). Now that the bakery is a consumer in the market, it stimulates the production of the things it needs, and the cycle continues. Production ripples throughout the economy as a result.

It's worth noting here that complex production can occur simply based upon the consumer-producer dynamic. No coercion or intervention from the government is needed to make this happen. The government doesn't supervise every step of the cupcake-making process by explaining to the bakery how to make its food in order to meet consumer preferences. The free market itself handles the process naturally—producers have a financial incentive to perform well. **In other words, the desire for profits and the aversion toward losses compels producers to do a good job for consumers.**[45] Or, as von Mises put it, "The market process is an interaction...deliberately striving after the best possible removal of dissatisfaction."[46]

Additionally, we learn from the example that lots of economic activity flowed from Sally's (and other consumers') preference to buy cupcakes. This highlights an important feature of the Austrian School's perspective: Consumers' needs are inherently *subjective*—or as von Mises phrased it, consumers employ "a subjective judgment of value, colored by the individual's personality. Different people and the same people at different times value the same objective facts in a different way."[47] Put another way: People want different things, and the things people want *change*. And since the things people want tend to influence the entire economy, this is a very significant point. It also makes economic analysis more complex than many mainstream economists might like to admit.

In some types of analysis, we don't need to worry about subjective, changing preferences. For instance, we know that 10 is greater than 4, and 4 is greater than 2. Based on the transitive property, we know that 10 is greater than 2. No surprises there. But human preferences—which are much more subjective—begin to complicate matters and make economic planning a challenge. Let's say that Tim ranks his preferences for ice-cream flavors: he likes chocolate more than vanilla, and he likes vanilla more than strawberry. Classical economists might use the transitive property to say that it must be the case that Tim likes chocolate more than strawberry. Using more mathematical notation:

> chocolate > vanilla; vanilla > strawberry; therefore,
> chocolate > strawberry

Why *can't* we assume that this is true, as we could in the previous example with numbers? Because, as economists Walter Block and William Barnett note, "These three separate and independent events occur at entirely different times."[48] In other words, people's preferences *change*. At one time they like one thing, but later they change their minds. For example, Tim might have once loved vanilla ice cream, but one day he got tired of it inexplicably, and he started enjoying strawberry ice cream much more. **Preferences can change in an *unpredictable* manner.**

Therefore—and much to the chagrin of many traditional economists—mathematical models are unlikely to be able to account for the full range of human behaviors. That throws a wrench into trying to predict the economy with certainty.

Moreover, by extension, the State cannot truly know what is best for the economy, no matter how wise it believes itself to be, and no matter how many economic "experts" with PhDs it employs. To intervene in the economy unilaterally, and without the consent of all parties involved, risks disaster and lacks humility. Human behavior is simply too unpredictable for a third party to know what is optimal for each and every individual in a complex economy.

Furthermore, the free-market interactions between consumers' preferences and producers' production naturally result in a system of *pricing* within the economy. If Rick buys a chair from Lisa for $100, that means he values that chair more than $100, and Lisa values $100 more than the chair.[49] Pricing is thus driven by subjective preferences, which can differ depending on the individual and change over time. So, accurate pricing is best established in a free market in which there isn't outside, involuntary intervention—such as the State's regulations—which can interrupt the natural exchanges between consumers and producers. As Ron Paul puts it, "We need markets to *reveal to us* the valuations of consumers and producers in the form of the price system that works within a market setting."[50] [emphasis added]

(Note: From the Austrian perspective, as formulated by von Mises, this is another reason why purely socialistic State planning cannot ultimately work. If the State owns the means of production, it will not be able to know how to manage its own production processes because it will necessarily lack the accurate price system normally offered by a free market. Since the State theoretically becomes the only producer in such a society, the system will inherently lack the free-exchange process needed to establish accurate pricing. Thus, it won't be able to efficiently allocate resources and make goods and services for its citizens in an economically sustainable manner. This means that the people will suffer. Economist Jonathan Newman, PhD, concisely summed up the Austrian position against socialism: "Without ownership, there is no exchange. Without exchange, there are no prices. Without prices, there is no economic calculation. Without economic calculation, production decisions are made in the dark. When that happens, basic needs go unmet."[51])

Even in the absence of pure socialism, however, problems associated with the State's economic interventions are evident. For example, consider taxation. Taxation essentially requires that consumers give some of their money to the government instead of using that money for their own subjective preferences. That *distorts* the would-be production system. The market will never know what the consumer *would have done* with that money. Instead, the government moves an individual's money into the causes that *it* wants. It's not as if every citizen gives the government money and says, "You must give my money to these causes that I want to fund."

In fact, any government regulation you can think of has a similarly distortive effect—it forces consumers and producers to allocate their resources based on the government's rules, rather than subjective consumer preferences, thereby taking away from the natural intelligence of the free market.[52] Moreover, when the government intervenes by extracting money (taxation) or altering competitive dynamics, it diminishes financial *incentives* within the economy.

By contrast, free-market systems are beneficial because they provide incentives for new companies to enter the market: if they can make stuff that people like, they'll make money. This entails *competition*. Sometimes that word is vilified, but in fact for consumers and society, it's a great thing. It means that producers are trying their hardest to create the best products they can. If a competitor is working really hard to build an improved product, that means everyone else in that industry needs to work hard just to keep up.

Competition encourages innovation. Innovation requires entrepreneurship. And entrepreneurship entails risk-taking because there's no guarantee that a new venture will succeed. The free-market system—which financially rewards strong producers and risk-takers—thus thrives on competition and entrepreneurship. The consumers—*and society as a whole*—benefit from the resultant innovation.

This incentive to innovate is lacking in highly socialistic systems because competitive dynamics are taken away. If people don't see a reward at the end of the tunnel, they'll be less likely to go the extra mile to produce and innovate, and they'll be less likely to take entrepreneurial risk. Innovation-at-large then suffers. Consequently, societal progress—including technological and medical advancements, for example—will be stifled. And that hurts people of *all income classes.*

In summary, Rothbard explained how and why free-market systems work so well:

> Superficially, it looks to many people as if the free market is a chaotic and anarchic place, while government intervention imposes order and community values upon this anarchy. Actually...the truth is quite the reverse. We may divide our analysis into the direct, or palpable, effects, and the indirect, hidden effects of the two principles. Directly, voluntary action—free exchange—leads to the mutual benefit of both parties to the exchange. Indirectly...the network of these free exchanges in society—known as the "free market"—creates a delicate and even awe-inspiring mechanism of harmony, adjustment, and precision in allocating productive resources, deciding upon prices, and gently but swiftly guiding the economic system toward the greatest possible satisfaction of the desires of all the consumers. In short, not only does the free market directly benefit all parties and

> leave them free and uncoerced; it also creates a mighty and efficient instrument of social order.[53]

When the State intervenes in the economy, which is currently what happens all too often, the entire process becomes unnatural. How could the government possibly have the intelligence to know what will work, given the seemingly infinite number of variables and consumer preferences within the economy? The government can't know each person's subjective value for every product at every point in time.

As DiLorenzo further explains: "It's unthinkable that a human mind or even a hundred human minds working with the most powerful computer in the world could possibly possess and utilize all of the information that the millions of workers and consumers and business managers and investors and on and on have, that they use in their daily lives."[54] Hayek, in his 1974 Nobel Prize lecture, called this the "pretense of knowledge."[55] Simply put, it's a big mistake to believe that a group of government officials knows what's best for a system as complex as an entire economy. The government isn't superhuman and all-knowing.

As Rockwell explains, "If anything should be clear to those who care about evidence, it's that the market economy is superior to all forms of economic planning. **Even minimal amounts of government intervention produce sector-specific stagnation. Compare Fed-Ex, for example, to the post office, or public schools to private schools, or the unregulated high-tech sector with the highly regulated and unionized steel industry.**"[56] [emphasis added]

Free markets can also lead to tremendous profits for some and not others. And for that reason, they are often disparaged. While this claim is certainly accurate, it's important to remember that businesses provide things that people need, and it's therefore reasonable to be compensated for that service through voluntary exchanges. Rothbard noted that the psychology underlying this common objection to capitalism might in fact be influenced by the State's propaganda. Perhaps the State and its politicians deflect their own greed by pointing the finger elsewhere:

> [A] tried and true method for bending subjects to one's will is the infusion of guilt. Any increase in private well-being can be attacked as "unconscionable greed," "materialism," or "excessive affluence."...Somehow the conclusion always drawn is that more resources should be expropriated from the private sector and siphoned into the parasitic "public," or State, sector. Often the call upon the public to yield more resources is couched in a stern call by the ruling elite for more "sacrifices."... Somehow, however, while the public is supposed to sacrifice and curtail its "materialistic greed," the sacrifices are always one way. The *State* does not sacrifice; the State eagerly grabs more and more of the public's material resources. Indeed, it is a useful rule of thumb: when your ruler calls aloud for "sacrifices," look to your own life and pocketbook!
>
> This sort of argumentation reflects a general double standard of morality that is always applied to State rulers but not anyone else. No one, for example, is surprised or horrified to learn that businessmen are seeking higher profits. No one is horrified if workers leave lower-paying for higher-paying jobs. All this is considered proper and normal behavior. But if anyone should dare assert that politicians and bureaucrats are motivated by the desire to maximize *their* incomes, the hue and cry of "conspiracy theorist"...spreads throughout the land. The general opinion—carefully cultivated, of course, by the State itself—is that men enter politics or government purely out of devoted concern for the common good.[57] [emphasis in original]

Keynesian Economics and the Great Depression

In light of all the above, it seems wise to both understand and become suspicious of the way in which governments steer the economy. One way in which it intervenes is through Keynesian policy (influenced heavily by John Maynard Keynes's *The General Theory of Employment, Interest, and Money*, published in 1936).

Keynesian policy fundamentally relies on government planning for economic growth.[58] In particular, it encourages government spending (and borrowing) in the event of economic downturns. On the other hand, proponents of Austrian free-market economics encourage savings and production as a mechanism for a strong economy.[59] Ron Paul comments on the danger of excessive borrowing in the Keynesian model: "This myth perpetuates the notion that a government and its citizens can live beyond their means."[60]

Keynesian, interventionist policies are often credited for getting the US out of the Great Depression. As Rothbard explained: "The common opinion—among economists and the lay public alike—holds that 'Unreconstructed Capitalism' prevailed during the 1920s, and that the tragic depression shows that old-fashioned laissez-faire can work no longer."[61] Therefore, an interventionist approach is typically viewed as necessary to escape economic downturns. **Put another way, people point to the Great Depression as evidence that the State is *required* to help the economy.**

One might wonder: In the absence of government support, can the economy rebound on its own? The free-market Austrian perspective is that, indeed, any such downturns will be managed naturally by the innate intelligence of the market. The economy could get ugly for a period of time—that's simply a part of life that we have to accept—but the free-market forces will even things out on their own. And that will occur *more efficiently* than if the government were to intervene, without the consent of all market participants, and with its inherently limited knowledge.

While President Herbert Hoover is widely believed to have taken a laissez-faire, free-market stance that allegedly prolonged the Great Depression, an alternative view of history suggests that Hoover *did* in fact intervene a great deal. Rothbard noted that his activities included "bolstering of wage rates and prices, expansion of credit, propping up of weak firms, and increased government spending (e.g., subsidies to unemployment and public works)."[62] These interventionist activities are even referred to as the "Hoover New Deal."

The Austrian School's argument is that government intervention not only worsened the Great Depression but also contributed to its occurrence in the first place via the Federal Reserve.[63] In Rothbard's book *America's Great Depression* (1963), he examined this underdiscussed history in detail. As he concisely summarizes: "Economic theory demonstrates that only governmental inflation can generate a boom-and-bust cycle, and that **the depression will be prolonged and aggravated by inflationist and other interventionary measures**. In contrast to the myth of laissez-faire... government intervention generated the unsound boom of the 1920s, and...Hoover's new departure aggravated the Great Depression by massive measures of interference. **The guilt for the Great Depression must, at long last, be lifted from the shoulders of the free-market economy, and placed where it properly belongs: at the doors of politicians, bureaucrats, and the mass of 'enlightened' economists.**"[64] [emphasis added]

Cronyism

The State's ability to unilaterally intervene in the economy from its monopolistic position of authority likewise gives it an ability to support some parties more than others. As economist Joseph Salerno, PhD, notes, this can occur through the preferential "bailing out" of failing companies and through other support, such as subsidies and contracts.[65] Thus, the State can help whichever parties serve *its own* interests—not the general public's. Salerno calls this "government plundering": taking money from producers in society via taxation and giving to others as the State sees fit.[66] Thus, it makes sense to want to be on the plunderer's good side. And this means that those who want to ensure their interests are taken care of will be incentivized to buy off politicians. As journalist P. J. O'Rourke said, **"When buying and selling are controlled by legislation, the first things to be bought and sold are legislators."** [emphasis added]

This phenomenon is broadly known as *cronyism*.[67] Corporations and wealthy individuals cozy up to the government, and in return, the government helps those parties with its economic policies and regulations. They scratch each other's backs. And, in fact, it is rational for both parties to do so—they're enabling each other and utilizing the system to their advantage. Perhaps the problem with this situation is not the actors so much as it is the system itself: statism.

With that backdrop, we can begin to see that the term *crony-capitalism*, often used to deride capitalism, is really a misnomer. Corporations and wealthy individuals are able to get special treatment from the government...because the government exists. Cronyism couldn't happen in this manner in a *truly* free market. There would be no government with which to collude.

Does that mean in a voluntarist, Stateless society all corruption would magically disappear? Of course not. It's an inevitability. The argument here, however, is that corruption *is much worse* when a centralized power such as the State exists.

Monopolies

With this thinking in mind, it's worthwhile to consider monopolies (dominant market players). Typically, our instinct might be to think that the State is *necessary* to break up monopolies so that consumers don't get hurt. But, embedded in that argument is a major contradiction. Think about it: The government itself is a political monopoly at the center of society. If one wanted to be logically consistent, the thinking here must be as follows: "Monopolies are dangerous, so let's enable a monopoly (the State) to break up all the other monopolies." That doesn't make sense. **An aversion toward monopolies inherently implies an aversion toward the State. You can't have one without the other.**

But even if we ignore that glaring problem, defining a monopoly in business is difficult to begin with. If a monopoly is a dominant producer of a good, then monopolies are everywhere. For example, as economist Jeffrey Herbener, PhD, points out, we could say that

Ford has a monopoly on Ford Trucks. Moreover, each individual has a monopoly on him- or herself.

To illustrate this point, Herbener uses a hypothetical situation involving podcast host Tom Woods. Woods is the only version of himself, and because of that, he has a monopolistic position in terms of giving lectures, writing books, conducting podcast interviews, and so on. Because he's the only Tom Woods, he can charge whatever price he wants for his products and services. And furthermore, since there's only one Tom Woods, he's restricting the supply of himself, thereby depriving the market.[68] Clearly this line of reasoning is nonsensical when applied outside the typical context of a large, dominant business.

This example raises a critical issue, though: Where does one draw the line for a monopoly? What is a monopoly versus a non-monopolistic, but successful, business? The answer is that it's arbitrary. And typically that arbitrary decision-making power is given to the State, with all of its allegedly superhuman wisdom.

In fact, Rothbard's (nontraditional) definition of a monopoly *includes* collusion with the State itself: "Monopoly is a grant of special privilege by the State, reserving a certain area of production to one particular individual or group. Entry into the field is prohibited to others, and this prohibition is enforced by the gendarmes of the State."[69] Without the State, these issues—by definition—would not arise.

In a free market, companies' success can persist without government obstruction: their prosperity indicates that they're providing value to consumers, and the market naturally modulates pricing. If companies set their prices too high, that's an opportunity for entrepreneurs to jump in and develop competitive products that sell for a lower price. If companies set their prices too low, that's better for consumers who are now paying less.

Of course, negative outcomes are still possible here. Dominant companies could become powerful and corrupt. The system wouldn't be perfect. But the idea, again, is that the free market will ultimately do a better job than whatever would occur under a system in which a monopolistic and coercive entity—the State—pulls the levers for the economy.

Monetary Policy and Central Banks

Another way in which the government can influence the economy on behalf of its benefactors is through monetary policy. This involves creating new money and setting interest rates, and these functions can be accomplished through central banks (such as the Federal Reserve [the Fed]).

The Austrian perspective is critical of this sort of intervention. Here, we'll focus specifically on problems associated with the creation of new money. **As Rothbard said, the State "acquired the monopoly power to counterfeit and calls it increasing the supply of dollars."**[70] [emphasis added] That naturally makes the State less inclined to think about careful spending. And the system opens up the possibility of giving money to preferred partners. As Ron Paul says in his book *End the Fed* (2011): "The fact that the Fed can create trillions of dollars and distribute them to its cronies without congressional oversight should shock us all."[71] Creating new money can also cause inflation such that people are able to buy less with the money they have. It's really a form of backdoor taxation, without calling it taxation: citizens effectively become poorer as a result of the government's monetary intervention.

Unfortunately, a lack of transparency hides the Fed's full range of activities. As Rothbard noted in his book *The Case Against the Fed* (1994): "It is little known…that there is a federal agency that tops the others in secrecy by a country mile. The Federal Reserve System is accountable to no one; it has no budget; it is subject to no audit; and no Congressional committee knows of, or can truly supervise, its operations. The Federal Reserve, virtually in total control of the nation's vital monetary system, is accountable to nobody—and this strange situation, if acknowledged at all, is invariably trumpeted as a virtue."[72]

But the free-market voluntarist doesn't see a need for the Fed or any central bank, for that matter. One might then wonder how currency would work without a central bank to create money. The voluntarist perspective is that, just like with any product, currencies should be competitive, and consumers should choose based on their subjective preferences. Consumers would want the currency of their choosing to have some inherent value. Since 1971 in the US economy, however, the dollar has become just a piece of paper, whereas, in the past, a dollar could be converted into a corresponding amount of gold (a metal with inherent value).

In order to understand this more fully, it's worth examining what money truly is. Imagine a time in which there was no "money," but rather, two people who were looking to make a barter exchange. Kim had an orange that Jon wanted. Jon needed to give her something that she found valuable in exchange. Let's say she would have accepted an apple as fair payment. Then she stopped herself. She realized that she wanted to buy a pen from someone else, but she wasn't sure if sellers of pens would accept an apple as a form of payment. Kim ideally would have wanted to accept a form of payment from Jon that other people would have found valuable so that she could more easily buy what she needed from others.

Gold is considered a precious metal and therefore has more universal value. If Jon gave Kim a small piece of gold, and in return she gave him the orange he wanted, she would then have a form of payment she could use to buy things from other people more easily—because gold would have a much broader appeal. But if everyone started trading gold in high quantities, it might start to become physically unwieldy to carry around heavy pieces of metal. It might also become challenging to measure exact amounts of gold for each transaction. Some might prefer to trade pieces of paper, for example, that *represent* a certain amount of gold. People could trade the pieces of paper while keeping the valuable asset—the precious metals—in safe locations.

Since 1971, when the US fully ended its backing of the dollar with gold, the currency literally became pieces of paper. By contrast, in a society that wouldn't rely on a central bank, individuals would want to come up with forms of currency that give them confidence in their value. Currencies would need to have some feature that is likely to be universally desired—whether it's a precious metal or otherwise. And it would be up to the entrepreneurial creativity of market participants to develop solutions, just like they do for all other products.

Cryptocurrencies have become popular alternative currencies in this regard, although whether they'll be successful in the long run is still uncertain. Since they aren't connected to central banks, they've gained traction—at least in concept—within libertarian communities and elsewhere.[73] Other alternative currencies may arise in the future as well.

As Ron Paul says: "I would like to see competitive currencies on the market and be permitted to thrive....Paper money is a drug and Washington is addicted."[74] The "addiction" relates to the fact that money can be printed and used carelessly for whatever causes the State wishes, such as "warfare and welfare."[75] As noted by economist Mark Thornton, PhD, the seemingly unrestricted ability to print money often results in "reckless" government spending. He concisely summarizes the Austrian perspective here: "The gold standard...was the ultimate check on government folly."[76]

In summary, we've discussed a number of ways in which the government intervenes in the economy: through taxation, bailouts, subsidies, contracts, the creation of money, cozying up with corporations and wealthy individuals—and that doesn't even include the countless other rules and regulations it places on businesses. Whatever the form of government intervention might be, it interrupts the free flow of voluntary exchanges in the marketplace and undermines the natural intelligence of the system.

Government intervention thus infringes upon citizens' freedom to use their money the way *they* want. That's an attack on individual liberty. For instance, if you can't buy what you want simply because the government has distorted your finances and artificially modified the marketplace, are you fully free?

The economy is just one more vital avenue through which the State can—and does—erode citizens' liberties through its forceful and coercive intrusion. By contrast, a voluntarist, truly free-market society would enable greater economic liberty.

CHAPTER 5

PRIVATIZING GOVERNMENT FUNCTIONS

We've now outlined the basic features of voluntaryism, including its nonaggression principle in accordance with private-property rights. By extension, we've examined the mechanics of a Stateless, free-market economy.

Eliminating the State would impact society in another significant way: **the State-run "public sector" would disappear**. Instead, the services currently under the State's purview would be managed by privately owned companies that are financially incentivized to perform well. They would have true accountability.

As Tom DiLorenzo says:

> In government, you don't have the free-market feedback mechanism that rewards with profits efficient behavior and penalizes with losses bad behavior. In fact, it's just the opposite: in any government program...failure is success. The worse you do at teaching the kids in school, the more money we give to the public schools. The worse poverty becomes, the more money we give the poverty bureaucracy, and on and on and on. So the

> worse you do, the more money you get—just the opposite of the market....People always spend other people's money less carefully than they spend their own money, don't they?[1]

With this context in mind, in this chapter we'll be discussing the following domains that would be handled within a voluntarist, Stateless society:

- Police
- Military-like security
- Law and dispute resolution
- Roads
- Environmental matters

However, just as we discussed with new currencies, there aren't specific solutions that anyone can give categorically. We can't know exactly how any function would be run by private organizations. There are simply too many variables to make predictions with absolute certainty. Free markets will always determine the solution ultimately adopted: subjective consumer preferences will drive demand for creative entrepreneurs to produce and innovate. For example, fifty years ago, we might have had a difficult time conceptualizing Amazon and its novel and evolving business model. It takes creative, financially incentivized innovators to most effectively generate products that people like.

Murray Rothbard summed up how to think about innovative solutions in this context:

> [T]he advocate of a free market in *anything* cannot provide a "constructive" blueprint of such a market in advance. The essence and the glory of the free market is that individual firms and businesses, competing on the market, provide an ever-changing orchestration of efficient and progressive goods and services: continually improving products and markets, advancing technology,

> cutting costs, and meeting changing consumer demands as swiftly and as efficiently as possible. The libertarian economist can try to offer a few guidelines as to how markets *might* develop where they are now prevented or restricted from developing; but he can do little more than point the way toward freedom, to call for government to get out of the way of the productive and ever-inventive energies of the public as expressed in voluntary market activity. No one can predict the number of firms, the size of each firm, the pricing policies, etc., of any future market in any service or commodity.... [A] free market will do the job infinitely better than the compulsory monopoly of bureaucratic government.[2] [emphasis in original]

For this reason, as mentioned in chapter 1, libertarian Tom Woods says, **"I don't think there's anything the State can do better than the private sector."**[3] [emphasis added]

DiLorenzo adds: "The argument that...governments always make about efficiency is, 'Well, we're gonna make government more business-like....We're gonna hire some retired CEO to run [a government operation]'....But that then begs the argument: if you think being business-like is such a good idea, why not privatize it and let a real business operate [it]? Why are you 'playing' business?"[4]

But this line of thinking goes against statist programming, which tells us that the government is somehow *uniquely qualified* to take care of certain things. Larken Rose notes that we're conditioned to believe governments have a mythical "master plan,"[5] which serves as a psychological parachute for statism and a barrier to creative, free-market thinking.

There exists a natural temptation to believe that the privatization of all government functions is too idealistic and that certain functions cannot work without the State. That's our deeply engrained conditioning. What I'm suggesting is that we expend mental energy to challenge this fundamental belief—which we're likely not used to doing in this domain—and ask ourselves whether the State really does such a good job. We tend to overlook the State's flaws in its operations because we're so accustomed to them. But we shouldn't be so accepting. The argument here is that the private sector could do a *relatively* better job, even though it would have problems of its own. The issues that would be challenging in a voluntarist society are also challenging under the rule of the State.

What follows are discussions—rough ideas rather than definitive prescriptions—that abandon the delusion of government "master plans" and consider the privatization of exemplary government functions. The intent is to lay out a general framework for the future *with the acknowledgment that modern-day society is far away from what's contemplated here.* The material is presented in a question-and-answer format and aims to address topics that often arise.

Without the State's police force, how would people stay safe?

The notion of "police" is so intertwined with the State that it's nearly impossible to imagine another way of protecting people within society. However, as economist Hans-Hermann Hoppe points out, since citizens have no contractual relationship with the State, its security "services" are undefined. We're guaranteed nothing by the State's police: no guarantee of accountability, no promises, and potentially no penalty if it mistreats citizens.[6]

On the contrary, Rothbard explained why a free market for police—meaning private, competing police companies—would be better for society:

> Consumers would pay for whatever degree of protection they wish to purchase. The consumers who just want to see a policeman once in a while would pay less than those who want continuous patrolling, and far less than those who demand 24-hour bodyguard service. On the free market, protection would be supplied in proportion and in whatever way that the consumers wish to pay for it. A drive for efficiency would be insured, as always is

> on the free market, by the compulsion to make profits and avoid losses, thereby to keep costs low and serve the highest demands of the consumers. Any police firm that suffers from gross inefficiency would soon go bankrupt and disappear....Free-market police have a strong incentive to be courteous and refrain from brutality.[7]

Police services might also be supplied by landowners to ensure security within the bounds of their property. Theoretically, there wouldn't be any "public property" in a Stateless society, so each property owner would be responsible for providing security as required.

Insurance companies might also play a role here. For example, they would have an incentive to keep crime rates low so that they wouldn't have to make substantial payments to customers who are victimized by crime. That means they'd want to find creative ways to ensure security—or even penalize customers who are too risky—which benefits society as a whole.[8]

Without the State's police force, who would protect the poor?

First, it's worth keeping in mind that in a voluntarist society, individuals would have the right to personally own weapons for self-defense. The types of weapons permitted and banned might vary depending upon the rules set by various private-property owners. So in some cases, individuals of all income classes might be able to protect themselves without paying for external support.

But, for the purposes of this discussion, let's assume that an underprivileged person can't afford—or prefers not to own—a weapon for self-defense. Who would protect that individual?

The answer is similar to what we discussed with regard to the welfare state (and we could apply this to other areas like personal health care). For instance, individuals, communities, and charities would need to play an important role. They would "intervene" in the economy based upon their voluntary desire to give their own money and resources to parties that are willing to accept them. Similarly, voluntary communities might form in which one's membership would be contingent upon making charitable contributions. **These ideas are distinct from government intervention, which is much more unilateral and comes from an inherently monopolistic entity whose funds are obtained through sanctioned coercion (taxation).**

Additionally, we should remember that police services under the State aren't actually free—they exist because of taxpayer money, which includes tax dollars *from the lower economic classes*. So, as Rothbard noted, the underprivileged are already paying for the police.[9] In a voluntarist society, they could theoretically apply some of those tax savings to private security (or other basic needs).

Private police companies would also have a financial incentive to make mass-market services available at affordable prices. Rothbard noted that "with the economies of such a large-scale market, police protection would undoubtedly be much cheaper. No police company would wish to price itself out of a large chunk of its market."[10]

And we can't ignore the possibility that Good Samaritans exist—in some cases, officers might help someone for free if an emergency were to arise nearby, and there could be pro bono work to serve underprivileged clients (just like we see now with law firms).[11]

Without the State, would private police or security companies provide enough protection against a large and well-armed gang? Or, let's say a traditional State with a substantial military coexisted with a nearby voluntarist society—would that State attack and conquer the voluntarists?

Military emergencies could indeed present problems for a voluntarist society. But the same is true today within a statist society. History is full of examples of military violence between armed nations. However, even in modern society, it's not as if *all* neighboring countries around the world are constantly at war with one another.

Before diving into hypotheticals, it's worth acknowledging that these questions might be top-of-mind because of indoctrination: we're constantly being told—by the State—to worry about external military threats. As Rothbard said: "[A]ny alternative to the existing State is encased in an aura of fear. Neglecting its own monopoly of theft and predation, the State raises the spectre among its subjects of the chaos that would supposedly ensue if the State should disappear. The people on their own, it is maintained, could not possibly supply their own protection....Furthermore, each State has been particularly successful over the centuries in instilling fear among its subjects of *other* State rulers."[12] [emphasis in original]

But let's assume here that there would indeed be legitimate military threats in a voluntarist society. This is certainly an inevitability, even if the perceived risk is sometimes exaggerated.

"State-like" communities with political units and large-scale defense might form. Any such political units would simply be "service providers" that have contractual relationships with their voluntary subscribers. These large, voluntarist communities—which would *resemble* "nations"—might be able to afford private "militaries" because of their significant membership size. In other words, paying for this type of defense could be part of one's "membership dues." And the same mechanism could be used to fund nonmilitary catastrophes and emergencies. (Note: This arrangement differs from our current association with the State in which we do not have an explicit contractual relationship: we're not truly "customers" of the State.)

A voluntarist society would likely have smaller, decentralized communities as well. Paradoxically, they might present unique challenges for violent aggressors. As an example, Rothbard described England's challenges in conquering Ireland. Until the seventeenth century, Ireland had lived in a manner resembling voluntaryism: "[P]erhaps the major reason it took the English centuries to conquer ancient Ireland is that the Irish had no State, and that there was therefore no ruling governmental structure to keep treaties, transmit orders, etc. It is for this reason that the English kept denouncing the 'wild' and 'uncivilized' Irish as 'faithless,' because they would not keep treaties with the English conquerors. The English could never understand that, lacking any sort of State, the Irish warriors who concluded treaties with the English could *only* speak for themselves; they could never commit any other group of the Irish population."[13] [emphasis in original]

Rothbard mentioned a similar dynamic with regard to Britain's conquest of West Africa: "[T]hey found it extremely difficult to govern the Ibo tribe (later to form Biafra) because that tribe was essentially libertarian, and had no ruling government of tribal chiefs to transmit orders to the natives."[14]

Additionally, citizens could use their own weapons to defend themselves against intruders, if absolutely needed, via guerilla warfare. We should remember that the United States, with all its military might, struggled greatly against guerilla warfare during the Vietnam War.[15]

It is, of course, difficult to draw too many conclusions from just a few historical examples. However, the overarching theme is evident: decentralized communities can sometimes withstand military aggression surprisingly well. And we should keep in mind that the potential exists for technological advancements that could change the playing field (for both defenders and aggressors).

Without the State, would there be laws? How would disputes be resolved?

In the absence of State-run courts and State-created laws, a voluntarist society would have its own rules, regulations, and methods of managing disputes. Societies have figured this out in the past. As Rothbard noted, legal systems were successfully developed—without a State—in medieval England among merchants, in admiralty law (the law of the sea), and in Ireland (prior to the English conquest in the seventeenth century).[16]

Within a voluntarist society, a core aspect of rule-making would be private contracts: they would serve as a form of mutually agreed-upon "law" between parties. Similarly, communities could set their own rules.[17] **People who like the rules of a certain community might voluntarily become subscribers, whereas those who don't would simply need to look elsewhere.**

Any disputes that arise would be managed by private bodies that specialize in dispute management—private courts, arbitrators, or mediators. It's worth noting that even within our current statist society, parties sometimes use methods outside the State's system to resolve disputes. As indicated by Georgetown University law professor John Hansas, studies suggest that mediation often works *better* than traditional State-run litigation: it has led to higher satisfaction among participants (both in terms of the process and results), resolved cases more quickly and at a much lower cost, and had more voluntary compliance at the end of the case.[18]

Mediation has been successful historically as well. Hansas notes that in Europe, before the rise of nation-states, matters were "mediated by the members of a local community in an effort to reestablish a harmonious relationship. Essentially, public pressure was brought upon the parties to settle their disputes peacefully through negotiation and compromise. The incentives of this ancient system favored cooperation and conciliation rather than defeating one's opponent."[19]

Furthermore, Rothbard noted that in the Middle Ages, people simply ostracized those who were clearly evading the law. If, for example, a merchant refused "to submit to arbitration or ignore a decision, the other merchants would publish this fact in the trade, and would refuse to deal with the recalcitrant merchant, bringing him quickly to heel."[20] He even cites modern examples of similar behavior.[21]

But in spite of these examples, there's a natural tendency to be skeptical about solutions outside the State's courts. We're conditioned to believe that the State provides a robust, objective, and impersonal "rule of law." However, Hansas calls this a "myth." He comments: "The law is an amalgam of contradictory rules and counter-rules expressed in inherently vague language that can yield a legitimate argument for any desired conclusion. For this reason, as long as the law remains a state monopoly, it will always reflect the political ideology of those invested with decision-making power."[22] Possibilities for biased, unfair, and corrupt decisions abound.

If citizens notice such legal injustice in State-run courts, there's not much they can do. They can protest all they want, but the State's court system isn't going anywhere. And it has little incentive to change because of its monopolistic position. Taxpayers fund it, no matter what.

On the contrary, if these services were offered in a free market by competitive, private dispute-resolution companies, there would be a financial incentive to make predictably reasonable legal decisions. The companies that do their jobs well would be more likely to be hired in the future, whereas the ones that do a bad job would risk losing future customers and going out of business. Our current legal system lacks this corrective mechanism.

Without the State, who would take care of roads?

Roads would be owned and maintained by private individuals and companies rather than the State. They could be bought and sold just like any other private property.

One might wonder if this structure implies that we'd all be stopping at tollbooths every five minutes as we go from road to road (assuming ownership would be fragmented, although it might not be). Fortunately, thanks to modern technology, it's more likely that sensors would allow drivers to be charged for their use of roads electronically so as to allow for smoother, uninterrupted drives. Increases in road usage would translate into more revenue to the road owners.

Road owners could alter prices throughout the day based on the amount of traffic. For example, during periods of high congestion, fewer cars would pass through the owned road, which would translate into less revenue. Road owners could then increase prices during these busier times, which would motivate people to drive on a given road at more varied times so as to avoid the high prices. One could envision technologies that would show drivers road prices in real time based on traffic patterns so that they would be able to plan their drives accordingly. This could translate into less traffic overall within society.

Additionally, road owners would have a strong incentive to make sure that roads are safe and properly maintained. For example, when there are many potholes and accidents, that means more congestion and fewer cars driving on the roads. That also means less revenue to the road owners. The free market would therefore incentivize road owners to minimize car accidents. The State's management lacks this financial impetus.

Road owners would have to be concerned about pollution as well: if it negatively affected nearby landowners, road owners could be sued for aggression against their private property. So, for example, road owners could charge more to drivers whose cars don't meet certain manufacturing standards. That would incentivize drivers to buy cleaner cars, which would imply that car manufacturers would be incentivized to make cars with improved innovations in this regard.

There are countless other ways in which privatized roads could be managed. Walter Block's book *The Privatization of Roads & Highways* (2009) provides an extensive analysis, of which I have only given a few brief examples here.[23]

Without the State to regulate corporate behavior, would businesses destroy the environment?

The example regarding roads is just one illustration of the way in which a free-market economy would naturally handle environmental problems (known in economics as negative "externalities"). The basic idea is this: damage to the environment will, in turn, damage private property, which will lead to a cascade of economic or legal actions that will incentivize the polluter to do something about it. So, the capitalistic quest for profit maximization might actually result in a *cleaner* environment than what we experience under the State's rule.

For example, if a company is polluting the air and making people sick, that is an act of aggression against private property (many harmed bodies). The polluter could then be subject to class-action litigation that would include the complaints of all injured people and would give the polluter a reason to fix the problem quickly. Otherwise, the legal bills would eat away at profitability. Similarly, excessive noise could be considered a violation of private property; therefore, the same dynamic could apply. Companies that engage in such reckless behavior might also face boycotts, which would further incentivize them to be more considerate.[24]

Under the State's dominion, large corporations can use their influence to sway policy in their favor, whereas without a State they'd lose this advantage. As Rothbard put it: "When we peel away the confusions and the unsound philosophy of modern ecologists... the case turns out to be not against capitalism, private property, growth, or technology per se. It is a case against the failure of government to allow and to defend the rights of private property against invasion."[25]

With regard to natural resources such as bodies of water, private ownership could be environmentally beneficial. For example, a hypothetical river owner who sells the river's fish would be incentivized to ensure the cleanliness of the water and the health of its fish. Walter Block and engineer Peter Nelson, coauthors of *Water Capitalism: The Case for Privatizing Oceans, Rivers, Lakes, and Aquifers* (2016), summarize the broader implications of privatization in this context:

> [W]hile land is privately owned, water is unowned (with the exception of a few small lakes and ponds),

> or governmentally owned (rivers, large lakes). This gives rise to the tragedy of the commons: **when something is unowned, people have less of an incentive to care for it, preserve it, and protect it, than when they own it.** [emphasis added] As a result we have oil spills, depletion of fish stocks, threatened extinction of some species (e.g. whales), shark attacks, polluted and dried-up rivers, misallocated water, unsafe boating, piracy, and other indices of economic disarray which, if they had occurred on the land, would have been more easily identified as the result of the tragedy of the commons and/or government ownership and mismanagement.... In the tragic example of the Soviet Union, the 97% of the land owned by the [S]tate accounted for 75% of the crops. On the 3% of the land privately owned, 25% of the crops were grown.[26]

However, some might worry that natural resources would become depleted if the State didn't exist to preserve them. Rothbard countered that concern by pointing to the mining of copper. Additionally, it's widely acknowledged that farmers and oil companies engage in similar activities.

As Rothbard noted, copper ore could have been exhausted long ago, but because of market forces, the owners limited how much they mined each year. If they overproduced in any given year, they would have reduced what they could have sold in future years. And that would have decreased the overall value of the mine. Also, in the event of a predicted future market shortage, the mine owner would be incentivized to withhold mining activities until the future year. That way the owner could sell at higher prices.[27]

As these examples demonstrate, free markets—and the associated motivation to maximize profits—can naturally create a form of self-regulation. But if consumers decide they need more protection, it's possible that private "regulation" companies would emerge to provide additional transparency. This could apply not only to environmental matters, but to all other sectors of the economy (including health care, finance, food, and beyond). For example, a private regulator might sell a gold-standard "test" or "protocol," which, when satisfactorily met by producers, would send a positive signal to potential consumers. Producers would be financially incentivized to meet any such standards because reassured consumers would be more likely to buy their products and services.

The overarching point here is that the State is neither necessary nor uniquely qualified to provide services. One could envision superior private-market solutions for *any* potential issues that arise within society.

SECTION III

HOW DOES METAPHYSICS RELATE TO POLITICS AND ECONOMICS?

CHAPTER 6
THE NATURE OF REALITY

So far, our discussion has focused on political theory and related economic matters. Clearly, statism is a problematic manner of structuring society, and a theoretical case can be made for voluntaryism as a relative improvement.

We're now about to switch gears (in a big way) and turn on a different part of our brain. This next analysis delves into metaphysics, science, consciousness, and the nature of reality.

We've largely talked about politics and economics in a vacuum. What do I mean by that? Well, we haven't explained why any of it fundamentally matters. Is there real meaning in life; or are we just random, meaningless specks on a tiny planet? What happens when we die? What does it mean to be a human being? Is morality built into the universe? Do our actions have metaphysical consequences? Is it metaphysically problematic to structure society around an organization that relies upon coercive aggression for its survival (that is, the State)? If the whole planet becomes fully enslaved, is there cosmic significance? Or does it not really matter, since we're all going to die anyway?

I would argue that any political and economic theories are woefully incomplete without an understanding of these issues. Because the theorists themselves are so focused on their individual domains, discussions of the metaphysical underpinnings are often simplistic in nature. One might make the assumption that "God exists" or "there is no God," and leave it there, saying, "There's a lot we don't know and can't prove."

Over the next two chapters, we will examine these metaphysical subjects more systematically, and then in chapter 8 we'll blend them with the notions of statism and voluntaryism. That will enable us to create a more metaphysically complete theory of governance.

But this entails examining subject matter that, at first, might seem unrelated to what we've discussed. For instance, you might wonder as you read: *What does the nature of consciousness have to do with politics and economics? Why do we need to know about the brain, near-death experiences, and quantum physics?* As we'll soon see, delving into these topics (and others) is a critical and unavoidable excursion if we really want to get to the heart of political and economic theory. Ultimately, this metaphysical discussion will provide a more comprehensive perspective on morality, purpose, and how to optimally structure society.

These topics served as the basis of my previous two books (*An End to Upside Down Thinking* [2018] and *An End to Upside Down Living* [2020]); and my podcast (*Where Is My Mind?* [2019]), which provide extensive detail into subjects that are merely summarized in this book.

If you're new to this, *I'll give you a major cognitive dissonance alert*: the implications are life-changing—and I can say this with confidence because my own life radically changed several years ago once I became aware of these ideas and the associated scientific evidence. This could take a while to sink in.

Radical Humility

We're about to get into some abstract subjects, and first, it's important to remind ourselves of our innate limitations. There's so much that we simply cannot comprehend with our intellect. For instance, even though we know that "infinity" is a mathematical reality, our minds are incapable of fully grasping it.

Also, our bodily sense organs are limited. Our eyes are able to see only a small fraction of light on the electromagnetic spectrum (see the illustration below), our ears can only hear certain types of sound waves, and so on.

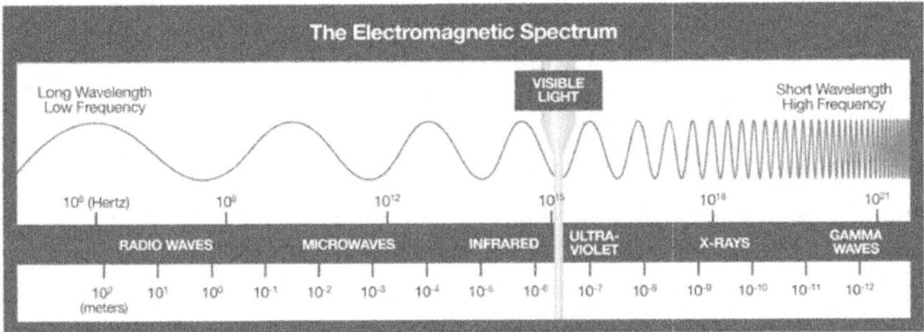

Visible light is only a tiny fraction of the electromagnetic spectrum. Most of the spectrum exists beyond what our ordinary vision can detect. Our eyes show us only a sliver of reality.[1]

Furthermore, our science is primitive, even though we'd like to think we have it mostly figured out. Scientists admit that roughly 96 percent of the universe is comprised of "dark matter" and "dark energy," about which we know very little. Who knows what else exists that we could never comprehend or perceive? We should assume that whatever we "know" at this moment is a largely incomplete picture of reality. Over and over again in science, new paradigms replace old ways of thinking. It would be foolish to believe that we've reached the pinnacle of scientific understanding. Therefore, it's wise to remain *radically humble* in pursuits to understand the nature of reality.[2]

The Metaphysical Metaparadigm

With that in mind, let's "start from scratch" with metaphysics in the same way we "started from scratch" in chapter 1 with regard to political theory. Much of modern science, and everyday thinking, holds a view of reality called **"physicalism,"** also known as "scientific materialism." It says that reality emerges from physical material called "matter": There was a "Big Bang" roughly 13.8 billion years ago that filled the universe with tiny units of matter ("atoms"), which over time bumped into each other ("chemistry") in a random fashion. After enough of these random chemical reactions occurred, self-replicating molecules formed—such as DNA—which led to the development of biological organisms like human beings. As the human evolved, so did the brain, and from the brain, "consciousness" emerged.

Consciousness is our sense of experiencing life. It is the awareness required for us to have the capacity to know that we are alive. Without consciousness, we wouldn't even be able to contemplate our existence (let alone ponder political and economic theory). Put another way, consciousness is the part of us that experiences, or "listens to," our thoughts. Thoughts emerge *within* consciousness. Consciousness is the backdrop in which all experience is registered. **In summary, physicalism says that this essential aspect of our existence—consciousness—comes from our brain.**

The figure that follows illustrates the basic idea of the physicalist perspective (adapted from the work of Dean Radin, PhD[3]). This could be considered the metaparadigm of modern science. As we'll soon see, it has serious scientific and philosophical flaws.

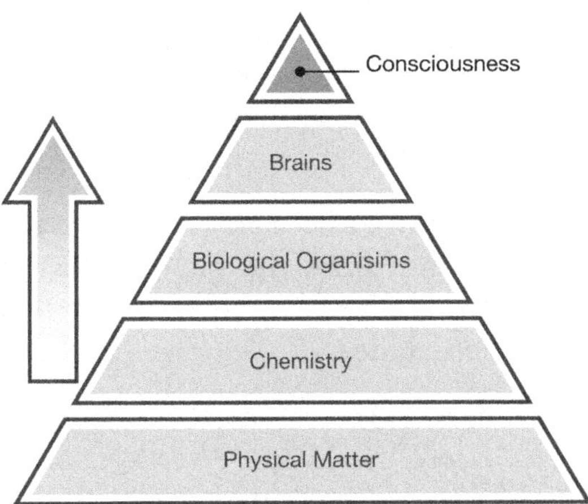

Physicalism (also sometimes called *scientific materialism*): The interactions of units of matter (via chemistry) create biological organisms like human beings, which develop brains, out of which consciousness arises. The physicalist framework thus implies that consciousness is a by-product of random, evolutionary processes. It also supports atheism.

Embedded within the physicalist worldview is necessarily a bleak outlook on life: Life is random, and when your body dies, your consciousness dies. You can try to "create" temporary meaning while you're alive, but ultimately you're just rationalizing—because once you die, your memories, thoughts, and feelings are all gone. Under this premise, notions of an afterlife, the paranormal, and "God" are mere fiction. There is no true meaning built into the universe. I know this well because it used to be my outlook on life: I accepted physicalism as scientific truth and understood the nihilistic perspective it innately promoted (whether I liked it or not).

Without intrinsic meaning, morality is inherently subjective. "Good" and "evil" are whatever you want them to be. There is no "moral imperative" built into the fabric of reality. If we only exist because of a random evolutionary process, our lives are all about "survival of the fittest." Physicalists who think really, really hard about this would realize that there are no rules, and they can do whatever they want as long as no one catches them. There are no "metaphysical" consequences to anyone's actions. This line of thinking is incredibly insidious. Immense selfishness can sometimes follow. And given the prevalence of physicalism in modern society, many of the world's problems—including those related to politics and economics—start to make more sense.

But this worldview is flawed because it relies on the assumption that consciousness comes from the brain. What I've argued in my previous books and will argue again here is that we need to rethink this fundamental idea.

You might be wondering, *Wait a minute. Isn't there an entire field of neuroscience that clearly shows how important the brain is to our consciousness?* Indeed, there *is* ample evidence that the brain *has a relationship to consciousness*: We know that changes to the brain result in changes to one's experience of the world. For example, damaging the part of the brain responsible for vision can affect a person's eyesight. **But just because two things are related does not always mean that one *causes* the other: there could be another explanation.** The potential error here is often stated as "correlation does not imply causation." It tells us that we need to at least consider other possibilities.

What if, instead of creating consciousness, the brain is more like an antenna-receiver-transmitter of consciousness—almost like a cell phone that is tapping into the "cloud"? A rough analogy: Imagine that you have a TV set with a damaged antenna. You might not be able to watch your favorite show because you need a functional antenna to process the wireless signal carrying the program's information. When the antenna breaks, all that you see on your screen is a fuzzy, blurry picture. But even when the antenna is broken, the signal itself is untouched. All that's affected is the apparatus for *processing* the signal.[4] Analogously, when the brain stops working, the signal that it normally receives (consciousness) is still present, and it is undamaged. This analogy doesn't imply that the brain is insignificant, however. In fact, the biological configuration of each of our brains informs the way in which we uniquely pick up the "signal" of consciousness and experience life.

A slightly different, and more precise, way of looking at this would be to consider the brain as a filter or blindfold of consciousness, presenting us with only a limited sliver of a much bigger reality. **An analogy: consciousness is like the sun that is always shining, but our brain can create "clouds" that block the rays.**[5]

In other words, what if consciousness exists independently of the body, and the brain simply processes and filters it? If that were true, then by getting the brain out of the way, one should experience a purer version of consciousness. When the blindfold is removed, reality is revealed more fully. When we get the clouds out of the way, more of the sun's rays shine through.

In fact, there is real scientific evidence for this idea. We see this pattern in the near-death experience (NDE) phenomenon: A person endures bodily trauma, and the brain is either completely turned "off" or it is barely functioning (for example, during cardiac arrest). Yet many individuals report a remarkable clarity of consciousness during the time of little or no brain function, sometimes giving *accurate reports* of what happened in the room while they were "dead" or "unconscious." So, by definition, those cases are not hallucinations (see *The Self Does Not Die* [2016] for more than one hundred well-documented cases, and we'll discuss additional examples soon). As NDE researcher Bruce Greyson, MD, from the University of Virginia puts it: **"We're left with this paradox that at a time when the brain isn't functioning, the mind is functioning better than ever."**[6] [emphasis added]

A similar pattern is found in emerging psychedelics research in which an enriched consciousness during the "trip" is associated with certain reductions in brain functioning.[7] It also occurs in cases of "terminal lucidity," in which a person with a damaged brain somehow experiences clear consciousness near the time of death. For example, someone with Alzheimer's disease, who has had severe memory problems, sometimes snaps back into mental clarity shortly before dying.[8] Similarly, individuals with savant syndrome often have severe brain impairments and yet possess extraordinary memories or mathematical abilities, for instance.[9] This pattern of **"less brain, more consciousness"** is found in many phenomena, as detailed by philosopher Bernardo Kastrup, PhD, in his *Scientific American* article "Transcending the Brain" (2017).[10]

Less brain, *more* consciousness—that's the opposite of what we'd expect under the mainstream idea of physicalism. If the brain creates consciousness, as physicalism says, shouldn't lots of brain activity be required to have a highly functioning consciousness? Clearly, physicalism has a problem. And we're just getting started.

Science magazine has even admitted that the origin of consciousness remains a mystery, listing it *second* on its top twenty-five questions remaining in science.[11] To paraphrase, the question asks how consciousness comes from a brain.

Why does this question present such a big challenge? The brain is made of pieces of physical matter, whereas consciousness is abstract and can't be touched. Consciousness isn't physical, whereas the brain is. The big question is: How, then, could something nonphysical like consciousness magically pop out of something physical like a brain? No one knows. Perhaps *Science* magazine hasn't answered this question because the question itself erroneously assumes that consciousness comes from the brain, when in reality—I would argue—it does not.

The alternative to physicalism we'll explore says that consciousness is more fundamental than the body, the brain, or even physical matter. Furthermore, it serves as the basis of all reality and exists beyond space and time. Since it is beyond time, it exists without anything "causing" it to be. Consciousness simply *is*.

In fact, this notion of the "primacy" of consciousness would answer *Science* magazine's number-one question: "What is the universe made of?"[12] The answer here would be: consciousness. Max Planck, a Nobel Prize–winning physicist and pioneer of quantum mechanics, summed up the idea well in 1931: "I regard consciousness as fundamental. I regard matter as derivative from consciousness. We cannot get behind consciousness."[13] The figure that follows illustrates this very idea.

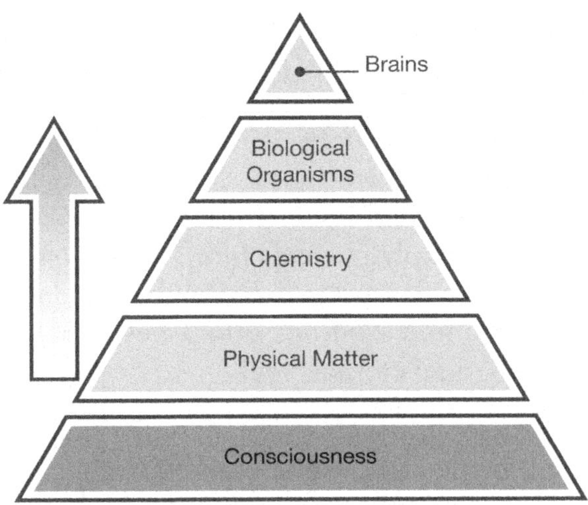

An alternative to physicalism: consciousness is primary. (Note: This is merely a visual approximation. If consciousness is truly the basis of reality, then everything in the pyramid is simply a modulation of consciousness itself.)

Kastrup has created a metaphor that can be used to think about consciousness in this way. He says that all reality is one universal consciousness represented by an infinite stream of water. Within the stream, there are whirlpools. A whirlpool is made of water, but it has the appearance of being an individual unit within the whole stream. Analogously, each of us is a whirlpool within the stream: we feel as if we're separate, but in fact, we're fundamentally interconnected. While in the form of a whirlpool, we experience life as an individual, and our brain blocks out the broader stream. **We'll refer to this universal stream of consciousness as the "One Mind" (derived from Nobel Prize–winning physicist Erwin Schrödinger's statement: "In truth, there is only one mind."**[14]) [emphasis added]

As Kastrup says, it's as if this One Mind has *dissociative identity disorder*—diversity and individuality appear within an underlying unity.[15]

What are the implications of all this? Imagine if a whirlpool allows water into it from another whirlpool in the stream. By analogy, some of one person's consciousness would be entering another person's consciousness. That's essentially mind-to-mind communication—"telepathy"—a psychic phenomenon. In effect, the mind is thus *nonlocal* (a term coined by author Larry Dossey, MD). Furthermore, if a whirlpool completely delocalizes, the water flows back into the broader stream. It doesn't leave the stream but instead simply changes form. Analogously, when the physical body dies, the associated consciousness does not die. It continues to exist and transitions into a new form. This idea is akin to the notion of an eternal "soul."

So, this model of consciousness would predict that psychic abilities are real, and that consciousness continues when the body dies. Put another way: **we're all psychic and we don't die**. The "paranormal" is actually "normal" once we alter the context.

And more than that, we're interconnected as part of the same underlying consciousness—the One Mind. This is another way of asserting the reality of "God." In this context, God is not a personal, anthropomorphic being separate from us, but instead is the infinite stream of consciousness itself. It is both within us ("immanent") *and* beyond us ("transcendent"). Furthermore, under this framework, our identity is not our body, but rather it is our consciousness: our consciousness is experiencing the physical world *through* the body.

Scientific Evidence for the "Paranormal"

The question then arises: "Is there any evidence for these 'paranormal' phenomena?" If there is, then we're getting closer to validating the primacy of consciousness and its inherently spiritual implications. And, indeed, the evidence is abundant (see the endnotes for exemplary scientific papers). **For example, the following "psychic" phenomena have produced Six Sigma statistical results under controlled conditions, meaning the odds against chance are more than a billion to one. So the phenomena are likely to be real rather than "chance" occurrences:**[16]

- Remote viewing (akin to clairvoyance; seeing or sensing at a distance, using the mind alone)

- Telepathy (mind-to-mind communication)
- Precognition (knowing or sensing the future before it happens)
- Psychokinesis (mind impacting matter)

Dean Radin, the chief scientist at the Institute of Noetic Sciences, compiled the "Six Sigma" studies for the above phenomena in his book *Real Magic* (2018), which was endorsed by two Nobel Prize–winning scientists. He summarizes the experiments:[17]

> Each of these experiments used protocols that avoided all known design flaws. An extensive due diligence of possible design faults has developed after years of intense scrutiny and criticism of these studies, leading to bulletproof designs. Each class of experiments has been repeated by a dozen to more than a hundred times by independent investigators at different labs around the world, with each class cumulatively involving hundreds to thousands of participants. The vast majority of the studies involved ordinary people, most of whom were not claiming any special [psychic] abilities.

Although many of the effects found in formal scientific studies are small—meaning the psychic abilities are sometimes subtle rather than dramatic—the statistical evidence is undeniably significant. **Dr. Jessica Utts, the 2016 president of the American Statistical Association, puts it well: "Using the standards applied to any other area of science, it is concluded that psychic functioning has been well established."**[18] [emphasis added] Also, *American Psychologist*, the official peer-reviewed scholarly journal of the mainstream American Psychological Association, published Dr. Etzel Cardeña's compilation and analysis of decades of psychic research. This 2018 paper showed strong statistical effects for multiple psychic phenomena—and it was able to withstand the editorial scrutiny of such a prominent academic outlet.[19]

Similar results have been validated at Princeton University in a lab run for nearly thirty years, up until 2007. And the CIA ran a psychic spying program in which the US government invested roughly $25 million over two decades to use psychic abilities, such as remote viewing, for national security during the Cold War and beyond. There are even *declassified CIA documents* that explicitly state: "Remote viewing is a real phenomenon[;]...Implications are revolutionary."[20]

Additionally, credible scientific research has been conducted in the following areas, which suggests that consciousness survives bodily death:

- *Near-death experiences:* People report a highly functioning consciousness with a highly dysfunctional brain, as previously discussed (and more to come soon).[21]
- *Mediumship (communicating with the deceased):* Early peer-reviewed studies conducted by the Windbridge Research Center—which employ five levels of blinding—suggest (statistically speaking) that mediums are at least sometimes able to obtain information about dead people that science can't explain.[22] Similarly, there have been many reports of more spontaneous after-death communications.[23]
- *Past lives:* More than 2,500 cases of young children who report memories of a previous life have been studied at the University of Virginia's Division of Perceptual Studies since the 1960s. The strongest cases include historical validation of the children's claims. And in some cases, the children have birthmarks or physical defects that align with the "previous life," sometimes confirmed by medical records.[24] The University of Virginia's Ian Stevenson, MD, concluded: "We should accept reincarnation as the most suitable interpretation for the cases only if we find other interpretations unsatisfactory. This is my situation....I therefore believe that reincarnation is the best explanation for most of the cases."[25]

When all of this evidence is put together, it's difficult to shoot down every single example. **If even *one* is real—which appears to be the case—physicalism has a big problem, whereas the One Mind is a much more sensible framework.**

Quantum Physics, Philosophy, and Spiritually Transformative Experiences

But the problem for physicalism extends beyond evidence of the so-called paranormal. For instance, quantum mechanics—a branch of physics that's gained traction since the early 1900s—needs to be considered. The phenomenon of "quantum entanglement" demonstrates that two particles physically separate from each other appear to be connected in ways we can't see with our eyes: When one particle is altered, the other one (no matter how far away it is) is *instantaneously* altered in a correlated manner. Change one, and the other changes at the exact instant. Albert Einstein famously called this phenomenon "spooky action at a distance," and he tried to disprove it. However, in attempting to disprove it, he only further demonstrated its reality. This finding is compatible with the notion of a hidden interconnectivity within the universe.[26]

The concept of *entangled minds*—a term used by Dean Radin in the title of his 2006 book—expresses the potential connection between quantum physics and consciousness. Moreover, in 1994, the editors of the *Journal of Consciousness Studies* echoed this sentiment: "There is increasing acknowledgement within the scientific community that there are some striking parallels between the properties of consciousness and those of quantum systems."[27]

Beyond quantum physics, there are also philosophical arguments that challenge physicalism. Some philosophers suggest that the One Mind framework—often likened to what's known as *metaphysical idealism*—is superior to physicalism because it offers a more "parsimonious" explanation of reality under Occam's Razor ("the simplest solution is usually the best"). The argument is complex, and I will only briefly summarize it here.

Consciousness is required in order to experience the world. Therefore, without consciousness we cannot prove that anything exists or existed externally. So to start with consciousness as the basis of reality is a *simpler* philosophical argument than the physicalist idea that consciousness emerged from biological organisms within an independent, preexisting world. The One Mind thus explains reality at least as well as physicalism, but requires fewer assumptions because it doesn't need to postulate anything about a hypothetical, unverifiable world prior to and outside of consciousness. More elaborate explanations are provided by Bernardo Kastrup in his book *The Idea of the World* (2019) and elsewhere.[28]

Finally, there are many instances of direct experiences of the One Mind—such as NDEs, psychedelic trips, meditation experiences, and spontaneous "awakenings." Although the specific nature of these experiences can vary within and across categories,[29] those who've had such "spiritually transformative experiences" often describe a distinctive feeling of love, oneness, and interconnectivity.

For example, a librarian describes a transformative experience she had while meditating during a retreat. Her account resembles what many others have reported: "There was a sudden seeing of complete, white, brilliant stillness everywhere. There was no 'me' thinking—there was nothing but white illumination and it was complete love. It was spacious, unbounded, undifferentiated, endless, and pure love. I became aware that everything is of love and there is nothing other than that."[30]

Similarly, Federico Faggin—**a world-renowned physicist, engineer, and entrepreneur who designed the world's first microprocessor at Intel in 1971**—had a spontaneous experience in 1990 after getting a drink of water in the middle of the night:

> I felt a powerful rush of energy-love emerge from my chest, the likes of which I had never felt before and couldn't even imagine possible.
>
> This feeling was clearly love, but a love so intense and so incredibly fulfilling that it surpassed any possible idea I had about what love is. Even more unbelievable was

the fact that *I was the source* of this love. I perceived it as a broad beam of shimmering white light, alive and beatific, gushing from my heart with incredible strength.

Then suddenly that light exploded and filled the room and then expanded to embrace the entire universe with the same white brilliance. I knew then, without a shadow of a doubt, that this was the "substance" of which all that exists is made. This was what created the universe out of itself. Then, with immense surprise, I knew that I was that light!

The entire experience lasted perhaps less than one minute, and it changed me forever.

My relationship with the world had always been as a separate observer perceiving the world as outside of me and separate from me. What made this experience astonishing was its "impossible" perspective, because I was both the experiencer and the experience.

For the first time in my life, I was simultaneously the world and the observer of the world. I was the world observing itself! And I was concurrently *knowing* that the world is made of a substance that feels like love. And that I am that substance!

In other words, the essence of reality is a substance that knows itself by self-reflection, and its self-knowing feels like an irrepressible and dynamic love....

I knew with certainty and for the first time that all is "made of" love. That experience also revealed the existence of another level of reality never before experienced: the spiritual level, in which I felt one with the world.

This was *direct knowing*, stronger than the certainty that human logic provides—a knowing *from the inside* rather than from the outside, one that involved for the first time the concurrent *resonance* of all my conscious

> aspects: the physical, emotional, mental, and spiritual.... [emphasis in original]
>
> [M]y identity is that unique point of view with which One—All that is, the totality of what exists—observes and knows itself. I am a point of view of One.[31]

These representative cases introduce a notion often discussed in such experiences: **love—more specifically *unconditional* love—is the nature of consciousness itself.** So "love" in that regard shouldn't be viewed as an emotion. Instead, it's the feeling of our true essence. Giving, receiving, and embodying love thus connects us with our source.

Additionally, there is an element of *universality* to what people describe in spiritually transformative experiences. But the specifics are difficult to articulate. Although the experiencers try to use words to explain what they felt, they often say that language is inadequate to capture it. **For those who haven't had these experiences, such abstract descriptions can be difficult to grasp, and therefore they sound like fantasy.** It's like trying to explain the taste of chocolate cake to someone who's never tasted a dessert. (Note: For reference, Rick Archer's podcast *Buddha at the Gas Pump* features hundreds of conversations with individuals who have had such spiritually transformative experiences and those who research related phenomena.)

As challenging as it might be for some of us to comprehend these experiences, they cannot be ignored. In fact, this idea of a unified, underlying field of consciousness lies at the core of mystical, spiritual beliefs all over the world, such as those in Hinduism, Buddhism, Gnosticism (mystical Christianity), Kabbalah (mystical Judaism), and Sufism (mystical Islam).

The accumulated evidence—from consciousness science, quantum physics, philosophy, and spiritually transformative experiences—suggests that perhaps the basis of many religions is rooted in reality. The mainstream scientific community just hasn't caught up.

Suppressed Science

You might be asking, as I've had to ask myself many times, "If there is so much evidence for all of this—something so central to life—how come it's not widely accepted yet?" For one thing, cognitive dissonance makes it difficult to accept. We're naturally inclined to reject information suggesting that we've been viewing the world incorrectly. Paradigm shifts don't happen overnight, and in this case we're talking about the metaparadigm for thinking about reality.

But beyond that, there's also active suppression of consciousness science. Psychologist Imants Barušs and cognitive neuroscientist Julia Mossbridge explain:

> As a result of studying anomalous phenomena or challenging [physicalism], scientists may have been ridiculed for doing their work, been prohibited from supervising student theses, been unable to obtain funding from traditional funding sources, been unable to get papers published in mainstream journals, had their teachings censored, been barred from promotions, and been threatened with removal from tenured positions. Students have reported being afraid to be associated with research into anomalous phenomena for fear of jeopardizing their academic careers. Other students have reported explicit reprisals for questioning [physicalism], and so on.[32]

Rupert Sheldrake, PhD, a former Cambridge University biochemist, has dealt with much of this as a researcher of consciousness "anomalies" in both humans and animals.[33] The first sentence of his *Wikipedia* page reads: "Alfred Rupert Sheldrake (born 28 June 1942) is an English author and researcher in the field of parapsychology, who proposed the concept of morphic resonance, a conjecture which lacks mainstream acceptance and has been characterised as pseudoscience."[34] If you don't know much about Sheldrake and that's the first thing you read about him, you might be inclined to assume that his work is not worth exploring. His

Wikipedia page is currently marked with a lock symbol that indicates "semiprotected." That limits the ability to edit his page.

Is something nefarious happening here? For one, The Skeptics Society often takes aim at claims of the paranormal, so one might wonder how that organization fits in.[35] Additionally, *Wikipedia*'s founder, Larry Sanger, stated in a July 2021 interview: "There are companies...where paid writers and editors will go in and change articles."[36] Sheldrake has even mentioned the "Guerrilla Skepticism" group that he claims "seizes control" of *Wikipedia* entries: it uses negative language within entries it seeks to demean, while bolstering the biographies of atheists.[37]

Sheldrake claims that this organization "captured" his *Wikipedia* page shortly after he gave a TEDx talk in 2013 that was subsequently banned. What was the subject matter? Challenging physicalism. He wrote a blog post about it:

> There is a conflict at the heart of science between the spirit of free enquiry and the [physicalist] worldview. I gave a talk on this subject at a TEDx event in London... in which I discussed the ten dogmas of modern science. I showed that by turning the dogmas into questions they can be examined critically in the light of the findings of science itself....
>
> My talk was removed from the TEDx web site after furious protests from militant skeptics, who accused me of propagating pseudoscience. This sparked off a controversy that went viral on the internet....Most participants in online discussions were very disappointed that TED had been frightened into submission, and TED themselves retracted the accusations against me.[38]

Isn't it anti-scientific to obstruct alternative scientific views? Is the scientific establishment simply afraid to change its paradigm?

In fact, many scientists reject the idea of a new paradigm offhand. Some even claim that no evidence of "anomalies" exists, in spite of the many examples we've summarized in this chapter. Others, while not acknowledging the evidence, admit that it would be a big deal to validate the paranormal. What follows is a table featured in chapter 1 of my first book, *An End to Upside Down Thinking*, which illustrates the divide in science.

Claims that psychic phenomena are real (examples)	**The other side (examples)**
"Using the standards applied to any other area of science, it is concluded that psychic functioning has been well established. The statistical results of the studies examined are far beyond what is expected by chance. Arguments that these results could be due to methodological flaws in the experiments are soundly refuted. Effects of similar magnitude to those found in government-sponsored research...have been replicated at a number of laboratories across the world. Such consistency cannot be readily explained by claims of flaws or fraud....This is a robust effect that, were it not in such an unusual domain, would no longer be questioned by science as a real phenomenon."[39] — Jessica Utts, member of the CIA's review panel for experiments on remote viewing run at Stanford University; she was also the 2016 president of the American Statistical Association (1995)	"It's perfectly acceptable to test psychic and paranormal phenomena like ESP [extrasensory perception]...and in fact those tests have been done. But they always fail."[40] — Jerry Coyne, University of Chicago professor, Department of Ecology and Evolution Sciences (2014)

Claims that psychic phenomena are real (examples)	**The other side (examples)**
"With regard to [psychic] phenomena, here I will simply say...the thousands of field and laboratory studies carried out by competent scientists over the 130-plus years since the founding of the Society for Psychical Research cumulatively provide an overwhelming body of evidence—*for those who will take the trouble to study it with an open mind*—that these phenomena really do exist as facts of nature."[41] [emphasis in original] — Ed Kelly, Harvard PhD, and University of Virginia professor of psychiatry and neurobehavioral sciences (2015)	"Psychic powers...don't exist. We can say that with confidence, even without digging into any controversies about this or that academic study. The reason is simple: what we know about the laws of physics is sufficient to rule out the possibility of true psychic powers."[42] — Sean Carroll, California Institute of Technology professor of physics (2016)
"Yes, I think telepathy exists...and I think quantum physics will help us understand its basic properties."[43] — Brian Josephson, Nobel Prize-winning physicist (2001)	"[Physicist Sean Carroll] deftly shows how current physics is so solid that it rules out ESP forever."[44] — Steven Pinker, Harvard professor of psychology (2016)
"It appears quite clear...that irrespective what interpretation is given to specific research reports, the overall results of [psychic] experimentation are indicative of an anomalous process of information transfer, and they are not marginal and neither are they impossible to replicate. In the face of this, the critic who merely goes on asserting there is no evidence for [psychic phenomena] is using a tactic reminiscent of Mohammed Saeed al-Sahaf, Iraq's former information Minister, in blindly asserting there are no American troops in Baghdad."[45] — Adrian Parker, Goteborg University professor of psychology; and Göran Brusewitz of the Swedish Society for Psychical Research (2003)	"It's not controversial at all. There's no scientific evidence for extrasensory perception."[46] — Lawrence Krauss, Arizona State University physicist (2017)

Claims that psychic phenomena are real (examples)	The other side (examples)
"The empirical evidence for the non-local nature of consciousness emerging from the research at [Princeton Engineering Anomalies Research Lab (PEAR)] and elsewhere inescapably predicates questions about the non-physical...dimensions of human experience."[47] — Robert Jahn, former dean of engineering at Princeton University, and PEAR Laboratory manager Brenda Dunne (2011)	In response to a study on precognition: "If any of his claims were true, then all of the bases underlying contemporary science would be toppled, and we would have to rethink everything about the nature of the universe."[48] — Douglas Hofstadter, cognitive scientist at Indiana University (2011)
"I assume that the reader is familiar with the idea of extrasensory perception, and the meaning of the four items of it, viz., telepathy, clairvoyance, precognition and psychokinesis. These disturbing phenomena seem to deny all our usual scientific ideas. How we should like to discredit them! Unfortunately the statistical evidence, at least for telepathy, is overwhelming."[49] — Alan Turing, pioneering computer scientist who helped to crack German codes in World War II (1950)	If telepathy occurred, it would "turn the laws of physics upside down."[50] — Richard Dawkins, evolutionary biologist formerly of Oxford University
"I never liked to get into debates with skeptics, because if you didn't believe that remote viewing was real, you hadn't done your homework."[51] — Major General Edmund R. Thompson, Army Assistant Chief of Staff for Intelligence, 1977–1981, and Deputy Director for Management and Operations, DIA, 1982–1984	Proof of remote viewing "would overturn almost everything we know in science."[52] — Ray Hyman, psychologist and professor emeritus at the University of Oregon (2002)

Claims that psychic phenomena are real (examples)	**The other side (examples)**
"Unless there is a gigantic conspiracy involving some thirty University departments all over the world, and several hundred highly respected scientists in various fields, many of them originally hostile to the claims of psychical researchers, the only conclusion the unbiased observer can come to must be that there does exist a small number of people who obtain knowledge existing in other people's minds, or in the outer world, by means as yet unknown to science."[53] — Professor H.J. Eysenck, chairman of the Psychology Department, University of London (1957)	Regarding psychic phenomena: "Any confirmation, no matter how weak an effect, would force a radical change in our worldview."[54] [emphasis in original] — Bruce Rosenblum and Fred Kuttner, physicists at UC Santa Cruz (2011)

Another Example of Mind Control?

Having now spent several years examining this space of "alternative consciousness research," it's become more and more difficult for me to explain the suppression and degradation of legitimate science by saying that "it's just cognitive dissonance" or "it's just people protecting their egos." Those issues are certainly part of the problem, but I think we need to be open to an additional possibility—although I cannot prove it.

We know that the State (alongside potential conspirators) utilizes mind control in many insidious ways. **But the greatest coup of all would be to convince the masses that their lives lack spiritual significance and that physical death means "lights out."** The fear of death is arguably the greatest fear, underlying practically all other fears. If that fear were to be alleviated *en masse* with the understanding that we are infinite and powerful beings whose lives are intrinsically meaningful, the State would lose leverage over its people. It would be less able to control the population with fear-mongering propaganda. And it would become less of a deity-like being that can magically solve society's problems for us.

Therefore, the State would be incentivized to try to "despiritualize" the masses, or at the very least, keep such ideas to a minimum and distort spiritual truth. Deriding the aforementioned science in the mainstream media and our education system—via the intellectual class—would be one way to achieve this. (And along these lines, we have to be open to the possibility that false ideas have been implanted into some religions to intentionally lead people astray.)

It's worth noting that ancient scripture points to the possibility of mind control. I must admit that I tend to be skeptical of ancient spiritual writings since there's so much we can't validate, and we don't know whether writings have been intentionally manipulated. However, the following example deserves mention here because it describes exactly what has happened in our world and can be linked to the general concept of mind control.

In 1945, the *Nag Hammadi* scriptures were found in Upper Egypt. Peasants who were searching for manure stumbled upon a large jar filled with buried books originally written in Greek (and translated into Coptic). According to scholar James Robinson, historical research suggests that the scriptures were likely buried around the fourth century CE. He asserted that this correlates with an edict made in 367 CE by Athanasius, the orthodox patriarch of Alexandria, which sought to eliminate certain writings and preserve others. What's now called the "New Testament" contains what was kept. Robinson noted: "It has been suggested that the Nag Hammadi codices were among the books that had to be excluded but were buried for safekeeping in a sealed jar by those who valued them."[55]

The first translation of the scriptures was published in 1977 and is often referenced by those adhering to Gnostic Christianity. The teachings contradict traditional Christian teachings in many ways and are therefore highly controversial.

The scriptures include origin stories that do have parallels to classic biblical ideas. They also emphasize the presence of a dark force that rules and influences our world, keeping us in ignorance of our innate spiritual connection.

One of the treatises, known as *The Nature of the Rulers*, narrates an origin story involving the Garden of Eden, in which Adam and Eve were forced out. The scripture says: **"The rulers threw humanity into great confusion and a life of toil, so that their people might be preoccupied with things of the world and not have time to be occupied with the holy Spirit."**[56] [emphasis added] (The term *holy Spirit* could be likened to the One Mind or some aspect thereof.)

Doesn't that sound like the plight of humanity?

When our attention is diverted away from our spiritual nature, we ignore our innate power and the deeper meaning embedded within the universe.

Metaphysical Evil?

Furthermore, the *Nag Hammadi* scriptures, as well as many other spiritual texts, introduce the idea of metaphysical evil: forms of intelligence that are perhaps multidimensional and yet exert a negative influence on human society. "Multidimensional" influences might even be inclusive of so-called extraterrestrial influences.

Once we acknowledge that consciousness can exist beyond the brain...ideas such as "dark spirits" and "demons"—and also "light spirits" and "angels"—become plausible. Alan Turing, the famous computer scientist mentioned previously, aptly acknowledged that once one accepts the "overwhelming" evidence for psychic phenomena such as telepathy, "it does not seem a very big step to believe in ghosts and bogies."[57]

Indeed, there are many such firsthand reports. For instance, John Mack, MD (1929–2004)—**a Pulitzer Prize winner and former head of the department of psychology at Harvard**—studied allegations of encounters with nonhuman intelligences from a psychiatric lens. He said: "There is no evidence that anything other than what [they] are telling us has happened to them.... [A]s far as I can tell, [they] are telling the truth, and this has been the impression of other...researchers."[58] His years of research led him to conclude: "The cosmos that is revealed by this opening of consciousness, far from being an empty place of dead matter and energy, appears to be filled with beings, creatures, spirits, intelligences, gods—the names vary according to the apparent worldview of the observer or function and behavior of the entity at hand—that have through the millennia been intimately involved with human existence."[59]

Along those lines, Dr. Ardy Clarke, professor emeritus at Montana State University, has also studied alleged interactions between humans and other intelligences. She initially collected almost one thousand stories spanning twenty years of research and found that individuals in many cultures—including the Mayans, Native Americans, and Pacific Islanders, for example—reported contact experiences with "Star People" and "Sky Gods."[60]

So—as far out as it might sound—we can't ignore the possibility that both "good" and "evil" on this planet are being influenced by unseen aspects of reality. That adds a whole new dimension to thinking about geopolitical power structures. Additionally, one might even wonder if psychopathic personalities merely represent the embodiment and mirroring of metaphysical evil that exists beyond what our eyes can ordinarily perceive.

Native American belief systems provide a relevant framework in this regard. They believe in the existence of a malevolent "psychic virus" (known as *wetiko* in Cree). Paul Levy explored this topic in his book *Dispelling Wetiko: Breaking the Curse of Evil* (2013) and referred to wetiko as a collective psychosis that functions as a "field phenomenon."[61] Furthermore, secretive "occult" practices have existed throughout history, and in extreme cases they include heinous rituals that attempt to invoke dark spirits and potentially bring power to the worshipers. Traumatized victims of such ritualistic abuse have been well documented by therapists and other researchers, as summarized, for example, in the book *Ritual Abuse in the Twenty-First Century: Psychological, Forensic, Social, and Political Considerations* (2008).

The point here is this: humanity's freedom—or, in the alternative, its enslavement—might have much greater cosmic, interdimensional, and even galactic significance than we realize. This possibility is rarely acknowledged or contemplated in traditional political theories. The One Mind framework—which posits that consciousness isn't produced by the brain—makes these notions conceivable.

CHAPTER 7

MORALITY EMBEDDED IN REALITY

If we accept the "One Mind"—rather than physicalism—as a reasonable approximation for thinking about reality, we can start to draw inferences about the meaning of life. This exploration leads us to a view on morality, which will be relevant to the exercise of building a more comprehensive political theory. **Ultimately, we'll see that statism is incompatible with the One Mind perspective because it endorses the initiation of aggression upon others and their private property. In fact, the State's existence is *dependent upon* such aggression. That behavior runs counter to spiritual principles built into the fabric of reality, thereby rendering statism an irreconcilably problematic structure around which to organize society. Voluntaryism, on the other hand, is much more aligned with the One Mind worldview.**

We'll begin this discussion with a "deep dive" into learnings uncovered through near-death experiences.

Near-Death Experiences (NDEs): The Basics

As previously discussed, NDEs might be instances in which the "blindfold comes off." When the brain is knocked out of the picture, the broader reality—the broader "stream"—becomes exposed; what always existed beyond our everyday perception becomes visible. Once the person is resuscitated, the whirlpool level of perception returns. If those experiences are real, rather than hallucinations, they would give us insights into the nature of reality.

Descriptions of NDEs have been reported for thousands of years in well-known texts such as *The Tibetan Book of the Dead*, *The Egyptian Book of the Dead*, and Plato's *Dialogues*.[1] However, NDEs are being reported with increased frequency in the modern era now that resuscitation technology has improved. Previously, individuals with such bodily trauma simply might have died. Now we have *millions* of reports from people who have lived to tell us what happened.[2] We can't know for sure whether NDEs are glimpses into what happens when our body truly dies, but it's worth keeping that possibility in the back of our minds.

The book *Life After Life* (1975), by Raymond Moody, MD, PhD, brought great attention to NDEs in the modern era. More recently, the bestselling book *Proof of Heaven* (2012) by former Harvard neurosurgeon Eben Alexander, MD, shined a mainstream spotlight on NDEs while also sparking great controversy. In spite of cries from "skeptics" who tried to debunk the veracity of Alexander's remarkable experiences during a weeklong coma,[3] an independent review of his medical records was published by three physicians in the peer-reviewed *Journal of Nervous and Mental Disease* (2018)—and the physicians confirmed Alexander's "severe brain impairment."[4]

NDEs are indeed remarkable. And although many aspects are consistently reported, they're not identical. NDE accounts come from adults and children, and even from the blind, who sometimes miraculously report being able to see during their NDEs.[5]

The typical elements of NDEs are as follows: ineffability (an inability to use language to describe what happened); positive emotions (some NDEs are distressing, however); heightened senses; acknowledgment of being dead; out-of-body experiences (the person's consciousness literally perceives from a vantage point outside the body); encountering heavenly realms; experiencing a dark space or tunnel; encountering a brilliant light, beings of light, or other mystical beings and deceased relatives; a sense that space or time is different (many say they felt a sense of timelessness or that the NDE was outside of time[6]); a panoramic life review (which we'll discuss further); learning special knowledge; a "flash-forward" to the future; and perceiving a boundary and returning to the body.[7]

Radiation oncologist and NDE researcher Jeffrey Long, MD, found within his database of NDE reports that **72.6 percent of survivors felt that "God definitely exists" following their NDE, whereas before the NDE, only 39.0 percent felt that way.**[8] His sample included 420 near-death experiences. [emphasis added]

Similarly, it's worth elaborating on the notion of encountering nonhuman intelligence during NDEs. As one NDE survivor described his experience: "I woke up [in the NDE] in communion with this being of light. It's a white light, but it's kind of gold around the edge....The light is a being, but it just kind of surrounds me. It's like I'm being held like a baby's being held in some arms and being rocked back and forth....The feeling was, 'I'm at home. I'm where I belong. I'm back.'...The being is a being I've known before. I've known this energy or this person or this being since the beginning of time, the beginning of eternity."[9]

Sometimes skeptics will dismiss these findings and claim that because there are differences in NDE reports—including cross-cultural disparities—they must be hallucinations. Although there are indeed differences, there are also many similarities. Dr. Gregory Shushan has examined this concept extensively. In his book *Near-Death Experiences in Indigenous Religions* (published in 2018 by Oxford University Press), he notes that scholars will sometimes "minimize the similarities between NDEs across cultures on the grounds that they do not live up to some ill-defined standard of being similar *enough*."[10] [emphasis in original]

Furthermore, because the experiences are often difficult to put into words, there are challenges in making comparisons. Different cultures use different words to describe things, so it's possible that two people with different descriptions of NDE elements actually experienced the same thing. For instance, the University of Virginia's Dr. Bruce Greyson notes that more "primitive" cultures do not use the word *tunnel* in their experiences but instead might use the word *cave*. Additionally, he mentions a truck driver who had an NDE and described going into a "tailpipe" rather than a "tunnel."[11]

Ultimately, there's still so much we don't know about NDEs. It might simply be the case that for different individuals, consciousness shifts into new dimensions in different ways, for reasons currently not well understood by science.

Are NDEs Hallucinations Caused by a Dying Brain?

We can't know for sure whether every single NDE account, out of the millions reported, is *definitely* legitimate. But it seems possible that at least some of them are, and that's incredibly significant. We'll now look at some extreme cases that are difficult to explain using "conventional" hypotheses.

For instance, NDEs sometimes occur in individuals during cardiac arrest and while they're under general anesthesia—conditions under which our traditional physicalist science would say "such a vivid consciousness shouldn't be possible." NDEs during cardiac arrest are particularly important case studies because scientists know how damaging this event is to brain activity: blood stops flowing to the brain, and it shuts off. This is severe. We're talking about cases of clinical death.[12]

Skeptics might still argue that any NDEs under cardiac arrest could be hallucinations caused by tiny amounts of brain activity that our measuring devices don't pick up. So the brain isn't actually "dead." But if that were true, it would still imply the need for a radical change in mainstream neuroscience because it would have to explain how a tiny, unmeasurable amount of brain activity could possibly cause such elaborate experiences. The more likely answer is that the brain doesn't hallucinate the experiences.

One of the most well-known studies in this area was conducted by Dutch cardiologist Pim van Lommel, MD, and his colleagues, and was published in the highly respected medical journal *The Lancet* in 2001. The research team examined 344 cardiac arrest cases and found that NDEs were reported in 62 of them (18 percent). Mainstream physicalist science would predict that there should be zero such cases. So something is clearly going on. It's not clear why not everyone recalls an NDE, and perhaps some of them did have NDEs but simply aren't able to remember them. (Note: If the brain is not the producer of consciousness, then memories might not be housed in the brain. Instead, they might exist elsewhere. If that were the case, then memories would be *accessed* by the brain.)

But if we really want to prove, beyond a reasonable doubt, that at least some NDEs are not hallucinations, we need to look at cases of the type referenced in the previous chapter: verified memories *during* the time of little or no measurable brain functioning. These are known as "veridical out-of-body experiences." If the memory is *verified*, then, by definition, it is not a hallucination. Such cases suggest that there is a highly functioning consciousness *during* the time in which there is a highly dysfunctional brain. And that is mind-blowing.

Greyson describes one such case in his book *After: A Doctor Explores What Near-Death Experiences Reveal about Life and Beyond* (2021). He tells a story from a support group he had started for those who had NDEs in which a man named Al spoke about his emergency quadruple coronary bypass surgery. Al said, "When I came to, I was looking down on the operating room from above....I was lying on the table covered with light blue sheets and I was cut open so as to expose my chest cavity. In this cavity I was able to see my heart. **I was able to see my surgeon....I thought he was flapping his arms as if he was trying to fly.**" [emphasis added]

Al then showed Greyson what it looked like, and Greyson was perplexed. He comments in his book: "In my years in the medical field, I'd never seen or heard of a surgeon doing such a thing." He thought it sounded "like a strange dream caused by the general anesthesia."[13]

Al then described experiences typical of NDEs: he was "enveloped in warmth, joy, and peace, a feeling of being loved," and then he encountered his deceased mother.

Greyson asked Al if he ever confronted his surgeon about the strange motions he claims to have seen during the operation. Indeed, he did, recalling, "Well, he was embarrassed. He got angry, and asked, 'Who told you that?'" Al replied, "No one told me. I was watching you from up there," as he pointed to the ceiling. The surgeon became defensive and felt like he was being accused.

Curious to learn more, Greyson sought out the surgeon to ask what had happened. Al signed a release form, which allowed Greyson to conduct the interview. Greyson described the surgeon as "a straightlaced Japanese American cardiac surgeon with an excellent reputation [who] did not seem to be someone prone to joking around in the operating room."

The surgeon validated what Al had told Greyson. Greyson comments:

> Much to my surprise, he confirmed what Al said. He told me that during his surgical training in Japan, he'd developed a peculiar habit that he'd never seen an American surgeon use. After he had "scrubbed in" to the operating room and donned sterile gloves, he didn't want to risk touching anything in the room that might transfer a contaminant, however small, to his hands. So while he watched his assistants begin the operation, he planted his hands on his chest, flat against his sterile gown, to make sure he didn't accidentally touch

> anything. He then supervised his team, using his elbows instead of his fingers to point out various things.
>
> Before that conversation, I'd suspected that Al's vision of the surgeon flapping his elbows had been a dream. But when I discovered that it had really happened, I had to search for another explanation....
>
> I began to wonder whether Al might have seen his surgeon "flapping his arms" before he was completely anesthetized. So in order to pinpoint the time, I asked Al what else he had observed at the time his surgeon was flapping his arms.
>
> He said that he saw his chest held open by metal clamps, and two other surgeons working on his leg.... In fact, the surgeons were at that time stripping a vein out of his leg to be used to create a bypass graft for his heart. **That detail clearly established that Al had been completely unconscious when he'd witnessed the cardiac surgeon flapping his arms. He couldn't possibly have seen that bizarre behavior with his eyes, because his brain was fully anesthetized and his eyes were taped shut—something that is often done to keep patients' eyes from drying out if they're going to be anesthetized for a long time and unable to blink. He shouldn't have been able to see anything. And yet he did.**[14] [emphasis added]

This is a veridical out-of-body experience: Al was able to perceive *accurately* during a time in which no perception should have been possible...if the physicalist view that "the brain creates consciousness" were true.

Similarly, in a 2014 paper in the medical journal *Resuscitation*, a cardiac-arrest survivor accurately described an automated noise he heard in the room during his procedure, which said, "Shock the patient, shock the patient." This was later confirmed to be a noise made by the automated external defibrillator used during his procedure. Since medical records confirmed the timing of this noise, the researcher, Sam Parnia, MD, was able to conclude that the memory occurred "during a three-minute period when there was no heartbeat. This is paradoxical, since the brain typically ceases functioning within 20-30 seconds of the heart stopping and doesn't resume again until the heart has been restarted."[15]

Another striking case was reported in a paper in *EXPLORE: The Journal of Science and Healing* (2020) by University of Oregon neuroscientist Marjorie Woollacott, PhD, and Bettina Peyton, MD. Peyton had verified memories during an NDE that occurred during complications in surgery. She had gone into cardiac arrest and was under general anesthesia. During the NDE, she felt as though she "exploded through some great barrier," saying to herself, "*I am free—and I am alive! Bodiless, eternal, pure being—This is who I really am!* I have always been so, and always will be so." [emphasis in original] The consciousness she experienced was "extraordinary—it's a consciousness that is all-pervasive, all-knowing, all-powerful!" She was also able to see the hospital room "from a vantage point above the scene" among other remarkable features of the event. The authors conclude in the paper that Peyton had "a deep NDE and **six perceptions during cardiac arrest that were verified by hospital personnel**, and which have no physiological explanation."[16] Peyton, who was an "avowed" physicalist before the NDE, has been forever transformed. **In her words: "I have seen the truth. I am deathless."**[17] [emphasis added]

These are just a few examples, and as mentioned previously, the book *The Self Does Not Die* includes more than one hundred such cases. Physicalist science cannot account for them: there aren't physiological explanations for veridical cases. Verified memories that occur during the time of such extreme brain impairment cannot be explained away as "hallucinations" due to a lack of oxygen to the brain, increased carbon dioxide levels, or chemicals in the brain. (Note: Even when examined outside the context of veridical cases, these sorts of physiological explanations for NDEs have fallen short.[18])

The point is: NDEs need to be taken seriously. They can inform us about a realm of expanded consciousness that might offer clues as to what life is all about, and we need these insights to build a comprehensive political framework.

The Life Review

One of the common features of NDEs is known as the life review. Jeffrey Long found in his NDE database that 21.8 percent of experiencers responded yes to the question "Did you experience a review of past events in your life?"[19] Bruce Greyson's findings are similar: "a quarter" of all the NDEs in his research included a life review.[20] Gregory Shushan's examination of cross-cultural NDEs, particularly those reported in indigenous cultures, notes a different pattern: "[W]hile the prototypical panoramic life review was apparently unknown in all these regions, the theme of being confronted with one's earthly actions occasionally occurs, such as in descriptions of afterlife record-keepers who have accounts of the soul's deeds."[21] So even if the life review per se isn't well documented in some cultures, and even if it is not reported in every NDE, the principle behind it still seems to exist—and that's what we'll focus on.

What is the life review, exactly? During the life review, people relive their lives, reexperiencing events and observing how they acted toward others. The events can be experienced through the eyes of others, as if, in this alternate dimension of reality, consciousness is able to switch "lenses" from one whirlpool to another. As one life-review experiencer states: "I perceived not only what I had done or thought, but even in what way it had influenced others, **as if I saw things with all-seeing eyes**"[22] [emphasis added]. That sounds like the One Mind.

In Greyson's research, he found that the "vast majority [of experiencers] described this life review as **more vivid than ordinary memories**....More than half experienced past events through their own eyes, but also...from viewpoints of others, **feeling those other people's emotions as well as their own**."[23] [emphasis added]

Even the indirect effects of one's actions can be felt. For example, Dannion Brinkley, the author of *Saved by the Light* (1994), had a life review in each of his *four* NDEs. His NDEs occurred as a result of being struck by lightning, open-heart surgery (on two separate occasions), and brain surgery. During his life reviews, he relived the deaths of the men he'd killed in combat in Vietnam, while also experiencing the pain of the children who would never see their fathers again (although he did not feel such indirect effects quite as strongly).[24]

In his book *Resonant Mind: Life Review in the Near-Death Experience* (originally published in 1990), David Lorimer includes many additional life-review reports. What follows are examples to give further context into this extraordinarily important phenomenon:

- A prisoner experienced a life review that appeared like a film: "And the only pictures on it were the pictures of people I had injured. It seemed there would be no end to it. A vast number of these people I knew or had seen. Then there were hundreds I had never seen. These were people who had been indirectly injured by me. The minute history of my long criminal career was thus relived by me, plus all the small injuries I had inflicted unconsciously by my thoughtless words and looks and omissions. Apparently nothing was omitted in this nightmare of injuries, but the most terrifying thing about it was that every pang of suffering I had caused others was now felt by me as the scroll unwound itself."[25]

- Another man recalled: "It wasn't like I was looking at a movie projector because I could feel these things; there was feeling, and particularly since I was with this knowledge...I found out that not even your thoughts are lost...every thought was there."[26]

- A woman described a sense of interconnectedness extending to all forms of nature: "For me it was a total reliving of every thought I had ever thought, every word I had ever spoken, and every deed I had ever done; plus the effect of each thought, word, and deed on everyone and anyone who had ever come within my environment or sphere of influence whether I knew them or not (including unknown passers-by on the street); plus the effect of each thought, word, and deed on weather, plants, animals, soil, trees, water, and air."[27] She also experienced a "sea or soup of each other's energy residue and thought waves," and being "held responsible for our contributions and the quality of the 'ingredients' we add."[28]

- A man recalled: "Things that I had completely forgotten about I was made cognisant [*sic*] of and these were the things that were important," including "working on a tubercular survey of schoolchildren at the age of nineteen."[29]
- A woman's life review made her feel ashamed because she realized that she "loved entirely for the gratification of the little self, the ego....I had used all that was at my disposal for my personal small ego-self, and not for larger mankind."[30]
- A car-accident victim described himself as "both observer and protagonist....My whole soul was a Sensitive instrument, my conscience immediately weighed up my actions."[31]
- A woman relived an event during which she took away her sister's Easter basket: "I felt her feelings of disappointment and loss and rejection." She added that in the life review, "I was the very people that I hurt, and I was the very people I helped to feel good."[32]

Clearly, life reviews help individuals understand the pain and joy they brought to others, but in some instances the reverse is experienced. For example, as Greyson puts it: "I've also heard people who have been abused, reliving in their life review the abuse and feeling it *from the abuser's perspective*, which gives them tremendous understanding and compassion for the abuser. So it works both ways."[33] [emphasis added]

Near-death experiencers' lives often change drastically upon being resuscitated because the NDE opens them up to a new way of looking at life. They frequently become less materialistic in their aims, live more spiritual lives, lose their fear of death, and can even change professions or get divorced.[34] Greyson explains the significance of the behavioral changes from his psychiatric lens: if they stemmed from mere mental illness, the experiencers might be "more frightened, more afraid of the world, afraid of living as well as dying [and] more concerned with their own safety; whereas, NDEs make people more outwardly focused, more altruistic, more full of love and enjoying life. When you get right down to it,...mental illness makes people less alive, [and] makes them withdraw from life....NDEs make you more engaged in life."[35]

Brinkley, for instance, became a hospice volunteer after his life-changing near-death and life-review experiences. And because he experienced additional NDEs later in life, he was afforded the unique opportunity to see his own evolution. In stark contrast to being a "vicious" combatant in Vietnam, in his later life reviews he felt what it was like to be a dying man in a hospice bed, looking into his own comforting eyes (through the perspective of the dying man). He felt—directly—the way in which his loving actions positively impacted others.[36]

A general theme is found in life-review research: **"The little things are the big things."** Interactions that we might consider "insignificant" in everyday life can be ones that are felt with great potency during the life review. For example, one person who had a life review saw how an unpleasant interaction with a grocery-store clerk put the clerk in a bad mood and impacted how that person treated every other person in line afterward.[37]

The life review is a visceral demonstration of the Golden Rule: treat others as you wish to be treated. This principle is found in spiritual traditions all over the world.[38] (A nuance worth noting: For a masochist, who enjoys experiencing pain, this definition of the Golden Rule would wrongly imply that he's justified in hurting others.[39] That's a distortion. Another way of thinking about the Golden Rule is that it counsels us to treat others with kindness and compassion because that is in alignment with the nature of consciousness itself.)

Greyson comments on the implications of the life review. **He suggests that the Golden Rule is beyond "mere" morality. It's more fundamental than that—it's natural law:** "Experiencers often describe the Golden Rule not as a moral guideline we should strive to follow, but as a description of how the world works, a law of nature as inescapable as gravity. They often say they have experienced this natural law firsthand in their NDEs, as they feel in their life reviews the effects of their actions upon others. Though they don't feel punished or judged for their misdeeds, they do receive back as part of their life review everything they have ever given out, measure for measure."[40]

For the remainder of this book—within the context of political and economic theory—we'll be referring to the Golden Rule as the primary aspect of natural law. But I don't mean to imply that it encompasses everything. Perhaps there are other, more nuanced aspects of natural law that aren't fully expressed or understood through existing life-review research. However, the Golden Rule is a reasonable starting point that seems to embody important overarching principles.

Spiritual Evolution

If we combine our knowledge of the life review with reincarnation research (for example, at the University of Virginia), we can infer that, more broadly, there exists an engine for the evolution of consciousness. Our individuated consciousness garners learning opportunities by inhabiting a different body after physical death: Water from one whirlpool is "recycled" into another. When our physical body dies, we take nothing from this world with us in a material sense. Our money, our car, our house, and even our family stays here. But we *do* take with us the way in which our consciousness has evolved. Some research even suggests that there could be an element of "choosing" before birth the incarnations that will afford the desired learning experience.[41] For example, University of Virginia researchers found that many children who report past-life memories also describe "intermission" memories between lives.[42]

Some even contend that the goal of life is to evolve to a level in which we "escape" the cycle of reincarnation—birth, death, and rebirth—and the associated struggles that come with this world.

The notion of "karma" becomes entirely plausible in this context, even though it might be much more complex than we could ever understand. The challenges we face in this life could be a result of restoring balance for things we did in the past (within our current life or past lives that we don't remember). In other words, there are *consequences* for our actions. David Hawkins likened humans to "karmic wind-up toys" who are let loose in the world, magnetically attracting into their lives that which is necessary for their evolution.

Implicit in the reincarnation process is the forgetting of our true nature, an "amnesia": in the same way that we don't remember many aspects of our current lives, such as being an infant, we're blocked from memories of our existence beyond this body. I acknowledge how difficult it might be to process this earth-shattering notion.

Why would life be structured this way? Perhaps, if we remembered everything, we wouldn't have the same learning experiences. So we temporarily forget who we are and identify ourselves with this individual bodily vessel. In essence, consciousness veils itself from itself.[43]

The struggles we go through in life, and even what we might call "evil," serve to stimulate evolution. We learn from difficulty. So in the end, challenging circumstances can actually help us. From one lens, suffering is painful and "bad," but from another lens, it's "good" because it forces us to evolve.

The evolutionary process seems to involve an impulse to "wake up from the dream," to remember that our ultimate identity is infinite consciousness, and to embody principles of unconditional love and oneness. An individual's "awakening" process is one of spiritual growth, moving toward elevated and blissful states of consciousness sometimes referred to as "enlightenment." The purpose of our lives as individuals, and collectively, might even be to achieve these levels of consciousness and unify with our source while existing in a body.

Eben Alexander's revelations from his profound near-death experience during a weeklong coma summarize these themes well. (Recall from the beginning of the chapter that his medical records were examined by independent researchers in 2018, and they validated the "severe brain impairment" during his coma.) He was a classically trained physicalist neurosurgeon from Harvard prior to his NDE, which makes his statements all the more impactful. In his words: **"Reincarnation was shown to me very strongly, in major form, in the midst of my [NDE] journey...as this beautiful tapestry that showed life reviews and all of our experiences together, but all in this process of growth towards oneness with the divine."** Additionally, he learned that we exist together **"down here"** in a **"dumbed-down"** state, **"not knowing all that our higher souls know....We do that intentionally. That's how we learn and teach these lessons of love and compassion and forgiveness in this world."**[44] [emphasis added]

CHAPTER 8
METAPHYSICS MEETS POLITICAL AND ECONOMIC THEORY

The view of reality summarized in the previous two chapters should not be regarded as precise. Rather, the analysis is an attempt to make reasonable inferences based on the convergence of evidence in many areas. It is a framework. However, even such a sketch—one of a universal consciousness evolving through individual "whirlpools" toward a state of unconditional love and unity—gives greater context with which to consider political and economic matters.

But first we need to elaborate on the framework further. Each of us individually possesses a degree of intelligence. And, since we're all part of the full stream of consciousness, it logically follows that the stream itself has intelligence. Furthermore, if the stream of consciousness is the "substance" underlying *everything* in this incredibly complex universe—from the tiniest subatomic levels to the grandest cosmic scales—how much intelligence must there be in the full stream? We could be taking about *infinite intelligence.*

If each of us is a vessel of that infinite intelligence, harnessing pieces of it, we don't need to take a big leap to infer that each of us is embodying something specific and meaningful. What we're embodying might be for some broader cosmic objective that we can't possibly comprehend. That objective could be related to what we've already discussed—achieving a collective state of unconditional love and unity—and it also might be more nuanced than that. For example, some people who have near-death experiences report being told (by nonphysical intelligences) that they needed to come back into their body to complete their "purpose."[1]

I sometimes envision it like an enormous puzzle. Each of us is a one-of-a-kind piece with a specific role. The unique attributes of our "private property"—such as our skills and material resources (including money)—offer us the potential to contribute to the world. But as individual whirlpools, we don't fully "own" our body and material property. Rather, we're more like stewards or custodians on behalf of our greater collective identity: the One Mind, the full stream of consciousness. So there's a deep responsibility for each of us to utilize and protect our gifts wisely in this life. When we do so to the fullest as individuals, we can then—together—build a cosmically designed, multidimensional piece of art.

This framework suggests that our lives are indeed meaningful, and thus the way in which we live matters. The way in which we live is intimately connected to the state of our society. The state of our society is dictated in large part by political systems. Politics is therefore an essential area of study from a metaphysical lens.

Those living in states of enslavement will have more restricted lives than those living in freedom. Yes, there are lessons to be learned from enslavement that can help us grow. But being enslaved naturally imposes inhibitions on our potential to fully embody and express our "puzzle piece." At the very least, expressing our full potential might be more difficult to achieve under states of enslavement.

Therefore, I propose, it follows that the promotion of liberty should be society's top priority: the function of society, and any of its governing systems, should be to enable liberty. The

State—an institution that legally initiates aggression upon its citizens and their private property—forges a pathway to enslavement. It is thus a metaphysical threat. Voluntaryism, on the other hand—and the liberty it naturally allows through the principle of nonaggression toward private property—is conceptually much more suitable for spiritual evolution. In fact, it might be the *most* suitable political stance for spiritual evolution: by providing individuals with the freedom to experience a range of "ups" and "downs," a truly liberated society offers each soul a diverse spectrum of opportunities to *learn and grow.*

Elevating Humanity's "Level" of Consciousness

A related inference we can make is that the state of the "collective" consciousness is not stagnant. That is, as people become more and more aligned with spiritual principles, the overall "sea level" rises.

The science of psychokinesis—mind impacting matter—suggests that this is possible. The classic study, including 2.5 *million* trials run at Princeton University[2] and elsewhere, often involves a "random-number generator" machine that usually generates "1's" and "0's" in a random fashion. Over time it approaches 50 percent "1's" and 50 percent "0's." But when a person puts his or her mental attention to the machine, "willing" it with the "intention" to produce more "1's" than "0's," there is a small but statistically significant deviation.[3] (As a reminder, psychokinesis is one of the research categories that has achieved "Six Sigma" statistical results: the odds against chance are more than a billion to one. Therefore, the psychic effect is very likely to be real rather than merely being an artifact of "coincidence.")

This has been shown to function on a collective level, as well. The Global Consciousness Project, which is run by former Princeton researchers, set up random-number generators all over the world. During major world events in which many people on the planet focus their attention in a similar direction (such as the 9/11 attacks), the machines have behaved statistically *non*randomly. Most people don't even know that the machines exist, and there's still an effect.[4] The implication is that our collective mindset literally changes the physical world. Physical reality is "malleable."

Additionally, there are twenty peer-reviewed studies and more than fifty demonstrations that suggest that when relatively small groups perform certain types of meditation, the "coherence in collective consciousness can result in improvements in the quality of life in society, increased governmental success and international cooperation without the use of armed force."[5] **In short, the research suggests that when people meditate together, the physical world becomes more peaceful.** This is known as the "Maharishi Effect"—named after Maharishi Mahesh Yogi, who taught a form of meditation often used in these studies, known as Transcendental Meditation.

In Barry Spivack and Patricia Anne Saunders's book, *An Antidote to Violence* (2020), the authors summarize the evidence for this phenomenon. They state:

> Examples include a rigorous study measuring a significant reduction of fatalities during the Lebanese civil war and known as the International Peace Project in the Middle East (IPPME); a case study detailing the impact of the Maharishi Effect on Mozambique's harsh civil war; and a summary of a two-month prospective experiment to reduce violent crime in Washington, DC. All three had a significant success rate.
>
> Evidence suggests the International Peace Project in the Middle East reduced war intensity and war deaths in Lebanon. President Chissano of Mozambique, who introduced Transcendental Meditation practice to a section of the military, credits the Maharishi Effect with a surge of political peace and balance in his country. Research from the Washington experiment indicates that the demonstration, carried out in the hot summer of 1993, was responsible not only for a reduction in the crime rate but also for greater media positivity towards the president and increased congressional bipartisanship.[6]

Although additional research is certainly warranted to show that meditation is repeatedly causing these effects, the implications here are massive—and the results are plausible in light of the existing psychokinesis science within the One Mind framework. Perhaps religious groups around the world attempt to achieve effects along these lines when they engage in various forms of group prayer.

David Edwards, a professor of government at the University of Texas at Austin, said of this work: "The claim can plausibly be made that the potential impact of this [Maharishi Effect] research exceeds that of any other ongoing social or psychological research program. The research has survived a broader array of statistical tests than most research in the field of conflict resolution. I think this work, and the theory that informs it, deserve the most serious consideration by academics and policy makers alike."[7]

Furthermore, Raymond Russ, PhD, a professor of psychology at the University of Maine, and former editor of the *Journal of Mind and Behavior*, commented: "The hypothesis definitely raised some eyebrows among our reviewers. But the statistical work is sound. The numbers are there. When you can statistically control for as many variables as these studies do, it makes the results much more convincing. **The evidence indicates that we now have a new technology to generate peace in the world.**"[8] [emphasis added]

Implicit in the phenomenon of "mind impacting matter" is the notion that reality isn't as solid as our senses would lead us to believe. The domain of physics supports this. For example, we know that atoms—units of matter—are 99.99999999 percent composed of *empty space*. This is completely counterintuitive. Matter only seems solid, but advancements in science suggest otherwise. We also know from physics that seemingly solid particles can behave like waves of probability (in other words, again, they aren't exactly solid). In fact, quantum physics suggests that consciousness might even be able to steer matter into being more particle-like than wave-like (as studied, for example, in the "double-slit laser experiment").[9] As Johns Hopkins physicist Richard Conn Henry concisely phrases it: "The Universe is mental."[10]

Or, as Nobel Prize–winning physicist Werner Heisenberg said, "Quantum theory does not allow a completely objective description of nature."[11]

Here's another way to think about it: If all reality is made of consciousness, then when we shift our state of consciousness, physical reality shifts as well. The bottom line is that we don't know what would happen if a "critical mass" of people began shifting their consciousness in a unified, positive direction. And we don't know what the tipping point might be.

Most political (and economic) theorists tend to assume a stagnant "human nature." I would argue that our nature is driven by our state of consciousness, and therefore our nature can change. Actually, it's not so much that our nature "changes," but instead that we become closer to aligning with what we really are. If consciousness is like the sun, even when blocked by clouds, it's always there—no matter how many clouds are getting in the way. What I'm talking about is removing clouds such that our overall condition is closer to the state of the One Mind (the sun).

This implies that on a societal level, what might have been impossible for one civilization to achieve could become possible over time. With collective shifts in consciousness, our potential as a civilization changes as a result.

Therefore, while a voluntarist society might seem unimaginable in today's world, I'm theorizing here that it—or something resembling it—could become more conceivable on larger and larger scales as the collective consciousness shifts toward a more evolved state. And as we become more aware of our truly spiritual nature, we'll instinctively value liberty, since it enables us to become greater stewards of our unique skills and resources. Statism will become less tolerable. In fact, statism is incompatible with spirituality: by its nature it initiates aggression upon individuals and their property without their explicit consent. It violates the Golden Rule. If we call the State's actions what they truly are without using euphemisms—taxation as coercive theft, conscription as slavery, and so on—how could its

aggression possibly be permissible while holding a spiritual worldview? I would argue, then, that voluntaryism and spirituality go hand in hand: moving toward voluntaryism and away from statism is indicative of spiritual evolution.

However, it's important to acknowledge that there are potential pitfalls, even if we do achieve an elevated state of consciousness as a society and move toward voluntaryism. This is evident in so-called enlightened spiritual teachers who objectively achieve extremely elevated states of consciousness individually but make big mistakes. Some of these "fallen gurus" succumb to glamorous seductions. In particular, the fall from grace usually comes from temptations related to money, sex, and/or power.[12] My point is that even if we reach an elevated state collectively, we have to remain vigilant. There's no guarantee that we'll remain there; the potential for the emergence of evil always exists.

For all of the reasons discussed in this book, eliminating the State would make any such transgressions less impactful because they would not be occurring within a centralized, monopolistic power structure. I'm certainly not suggesting that society would magically become perfectly peaceful. Rather, I contend, maintaining something close to a voluntarist society would do a relatively better job than statism of preventing widespread, centralized evil—in addition to its being an ideal political structure for enabling liberty and spiritual evolution.

Spiritual Economic Theory

Similarly, this spiritual perspective can influence views on the field of economics. As the Austrian School suggests, markets are driven by subjective consumer preferences. More fundamentally, economics begins with "human action" (which served as the title of Ludwig von Mises's seminal book, published in 1940). As Murray Rothbard summarized in his perhaps equally seminal book *Man, Economy, and State* (1962), "*Human action is defined simply as purposeful behavior*....The purpose of a man's act is his *end*; the desire to achieve this end is the man's *motive* for instituting the action."[13] [emphasis in original]

But we might wonder: *From where do purposeful behavior, desires, and motives arise? Are they mere products of our biological machinery? Do they arise from factors in our everyday environment, such as family, friends, the media, our education, and so on? Or is there more to the story?*

The One Mind framework suggests that the intelligence of the broader consciousness plays a role in all of this. Our behavior is being informed by this intelligence. Our bodies are enlivened and guided by it. This perhaps happens most when there are fewer clouds blocking the rays of consciousness that are always shining (when we live in alignment with spiritual principles, for example). And when we do so, we embody what our puzzle piece is here to do more fully.

This framework can be applied to the Austrian School's concept of a truly free-market economy. The famous capitalist Adam Smith (1723–1790) referred to an "invisible hand" that seemingly guides free markets and results in positive outcomes for society. In truly free markets, there are voluntary exchanges between individuals who want goods and services (consumers), and those who offer goods and services to meet consumers' needs (producers). The free market allows these exchanges to occur without intervention by the State. Advocates of the free market, such as Rothbard, often marveled at what emerges from what we might otherwise suspect would be a chaotic system. Rothbard called it a "beautiful and orderly structure"[14] that is "awe-inspiring."[15]

When considered from a metaphysical lens, this whole process could be attributed to the intelligence of the field of consciousness working its way *through* each individual. The "invisible hand" might more accurately be described as the "divine hand." Allowing this process to unfold naturally—thereby allowing the intelligence to flow into individuals as expressed by their preferences—might in fact be the most fundamental source of the "human action" that Austrian economists have so eloquently described.

We can also examine the production side of the economy from a spiritual perspective. The Austrian School emphasizes the importance of "division of labor," whereby individuals and firms specialize in certain aspects of production to make products most effectively. For example, someone with natural artistic talent might be best suited to work in a design role at a company, whereas a skillful writer might be assigned to a role that requires linguistic proficiency. From a spiritual lens, we could say that the division of labor allows each unique puzzle piece to embody its talents to the fullest—which enables businesses to satisfy consumers' needs, thereby benefiting society as a whole. As Rothbard said, "The enormous variety in human beings,"[16] can thus result in a "superiority in productivity."[17] The fully free market incentivizes producers to place each worker—each unique "puzzle piece"—in the optimal position.

But this whole process—which relies on consumers' subjective preferences and producers' efficient production—can become interrupted if a third party such as the State intervenes without consent. The State's actions and regulations can disrupt the natural consumption and production that's being guided by the One Mind. Therefore, when the State impacts the economy based on what *it* feels is best—rather than abiding by the will of all parties in the market—the "divine" intelligence of the system can become distorted, less pure, and less efficient. From this lens, the State's economic interventions could be viewed as immense acts of arrogance: What makes a group of individuals believe they can unilaterally impose their will—with their extremely limited knowledge—upon an entire population? **Is it a good idea to allow a group of politicians and bureaucrats to effectively "play God" with citizens' livelihoods?**

Thought of another way, the State's intervention creates one-way transactions: the State imposes its will on the entire system without the corresponding *consent from each participant* necessary for there to be voluntary exchanges. An involuntary exchange could thus be considered an indicator that an action is improper from a spiritual lens, whereas when two parties mutually consent, it's as if the spiritual intelligence is successfully implementing itself in the physical world through the vessels of biological entities.

This, of course, is a conceptual framework only. Trying to explain the countless interactions within a marketplace likely requires much more nuance and complexity, including the overlap with biological and environmental factors that play a role too. However, the overarching idea here is consistent with the notion of the One Mind. And at a high level, it might explain why truly free markets are so essential from a metaphysical standpoint. Perhaps they're an efficient means by which the One Mind works its way through society and encourages our collective evolution. Maybe that's why free markets seem to work with miraculous grace: they enable a "grand design"[18] comprised of countless "pixels" represented in the free market's voluntary exchanges—for some cosmic purpose that might be beyond human comprehension.

Individualism and Collectivism

One final matter needs to be explored with regard to the intersection of metaphysics and political systems: an understanding of individualism (a focus on one's individual needs) and collectivism (a focus on the needs of one's group). The aim here is to better contextualize the individual's role within a societal or political group, and furthermore to see how that fits within a voluntarist, free-market society.

We often hear about the notion of a "common good" that arises in the context of collectivism. Some people are willing to make personal sacrifices under the assumption that they're helping the collective. They might even feel that the common good should be preferred over the individual's needs. There certainly exists a spectrum of opinions on this, and each situation is different.

For example, if a political leader told a group of people to jump off a cliff because it will help the collective, should they do it? Or perhaps less dramatically, what if a political leader said that all citizens must take a medical intervention—case in point, a vaccine—in order to help the collective, even if some individuals have safety concerns? What if the government required its citizens to carry a "digital health passport" allegedly designed to enable collective safety, even if it restricts freedom and allows invasive surveillance?

Where is the threshold at which the individual's needs and values should be prioritized?

From a spiritual lens, *both* the individual and the collective are important. It's not a matter of "either/or." Rather, it's more appropriate to view this topic from a "both/and" lens.

The evolution of an individual's consciousness—being the best version of the puzzle piece you can be—is of utmost importance in one's life. Therefore, to ignore the individual's needs is profoundly anti-spiritual and obviously nonsensical.

Each of us is a whirlpool within the stream. You can't say that you care about the stream without also worrying about the whirlpool—since it's *part* of the stream. That means you have to look out for yourself and set boundaries where appropriate.

However, to ignore the collective is irresponsible too. As we learn from countless spiritually transformative experiences (such as life reviews), how we treat others *matters* in a big way. Altruism is, of course, essential: we are all interconnected. But a balance is needed in all of this. **Sometimes the pendulum swings too far in the direction of collectivism within spiritual and political circles such that the individual's needs are ignored or even derided as "selfish." That is a distortion.**

A comparison could be made to the advice given on airplanes in which we're told to put on our own oxygen mask before helping others. If we aren't in a stable position first, we're less able to be of assistance to third parties. So while it's certainly praiseworthy to want to "save the world," that will happen most effectively if we're at our strongest individually.

David Hawkins put it well: **"Our contribution to the world is the perfection of our own self."**[19] [emphasis added] We prioritize our own, individual evolution, and as a consequence, we positively impact the world. When we are in our best shape individually, we can be stronger warriors in service of the collective. Furthermore, when we elevate our individual consciousness, there could conceivably be a metaphysical "boost" within the collective field of consciousness.

The optimal blend might thus be regarded as "individualistic collectivism."

From the lens of political theory, the greatest danger to society is likely pure collectivism. In fact, scholars such as Nobel laureate F. A. Hayek[20] and author G. Edward Griffin[21] note that totalitarianism—*both* communism and fascism—stem from pure collectivism as an ideology. In these societies, the individual is blended in as part of the State—the collective.

As Hayek put it: "The principle that the end justifies the means… in collectivist ethics becomes necessarily the supreme rule. There is literally nothing which the consistent collectivist must not be prepared to do if it serves 'the good of the whole,' because that is to him the only criterion of what ought to be done. Once you admit that the individual is merely a means to serve the ends of the higher entity called society or the nation, most of those features of totalitarianism which horrify us follow of necessity."[22]

The related notion of "equality" has become similarly dangerous. We are not equal. We are distinct individuals who have countless differences. We are different puzzle pieces. At the same time, the essence of who we are (the One Mind) *is* in fact the same. We are both not equal and equal, simultaneously. It's a paradox, just like so many topics in the spiritual domain.

While residing in physical bodies, we express uniqueness. So to try to *force* equality upon the masses artificially is problematic, so long as the value of the individual is not maintained. In fact, it would be a hindrance to spiritual expression if any entity (such as the State) were to try to unilaterally force people to be the same puzzle piece. That is impossible and counter to spiritual reality. We're all on distinct evolutionary journeys, and we therefore *need* to have distinct learning experiences: our soul's growth requires opportunities for us to make mistakes, thrive, struggle, triumph, or whatever else is in store for us as we evolve. The precise formula differs by person. Thus, the individual's uniqueness needs the freedom to be expressed, which necessarily entails nonuniformity.

Along similar lines, it's worth examining the statist structure of "democracy" in which the individual is sometimes lost. Although this form of governance is often lauded as a positive development in human civilization, it has its dangers too. A "tyranny of the majority" is possible in which the individual's needs are diminished or altogether disregarded. Murray Rothbard said it well:

> With the rise of democracy, the identification of the State with society has been redoubled, until it is common to hear sentiments expressed which violate virtually every tenet of reason and commonsense such as, "we are the government." The useful collective term "we" has enabled an ideological camouflage to be thrown over the reality of political life. If "we are the government," then anything a government does to an individual is not only just and untyrannical but also "voluntary" on the part of the individual concerned. If the government has incurred a huge public debt which must be paid by taxing one group for the benefit of another, this reality of burden is obscured by saying that "we owe it to ourselves"; if the government conscripts a man, or throws him into jail for dissident opinion, then he is "doing it to himself" and, therefore, nothing untoward has occurred. Under this reasoning, any Jews murdered by the Nazi government were not murdered; instead, they must have "committed suicide," since they were the government (which was democratically chosen), and, therefore, anything the government did to them was voluntary on their part. One would not think it necessary to belabor this point, and yet the overwhelming bulk of the people hold this fallacy to a greater or lesser degree.
>
> We must, therefore, emphasize that "we" are not the government; the government is not "us." The government does not in any accurate sense "represent" the majority of the people. But, even if it did, even if 70 percent of the people decided to murder the remaining

> 30 percent, this would still be murder and would not be voluntary suicide on the part of the slaughtered minority. No organicist metaphor, no irrelevant bromide that "we are all part of one another," must be permitted to obscure this basic fact. It allows the State to program people into thinking they don't matter, in favor of some abstract "collective." The collective is made of individuals. That can't be ignored.[23]

Nondual Voluntaryism

With all of this context in mind, I assert that there exists a framework that serves to optimize both metaphysical and physical liberty—benefiting both the individual and the collective—which I'll call here **nondual voluntaryism**. The term *nondual* in spiritual parlance refers to "not two"—the idea that there is one reality that is a universal consciousness. This is simply another way of referencing the One Mind.[24] (Note: Using simpler, more general terminology, we could say nondual voluntaryism is a specific version of what one might call *spiritual libertarianism*.)

The nondual, spiritual aspect of this philosophy implies an overall way of looking at life: individuals make their decisions based on considerations around spiritual evolution, karma, and the Golden Rule—while also factoring in the impact on one's self *and* the collective. In other words, a compass for determining "right and wrong" is derived from spiritual principles rather than arbitrary standards mandated by compulsory government law. The nondual mindset will naturally encourage charitable, service-oriented behavior and will discourage overly materialistic aims; it will breed Good Samaritans.

The voluntarist aspect of this philosophy refers to a preference for a Stateless society based upon the principles of nonaggression, private-property rights, and fully free markets (as discussed in chapter 4). The State's functions would still exist (such as police, dispute resolution, and so on), but they would be managed by privately owned service providers, and citizens would voluntarily subscribe by contract to the services they want (as discussed in chapter 5).

However, the term *voluntaryism* alone doesn't specify a metaphysical underpinning, which is why I feel it's necessary to use the "nondual" qualifier. For example, one might be an atheistic physicalist while holding voluntarist beliefs, and that implies a very different outlook on the meaning of life and politics.

As I see it, we can view various categories of metaphysical-political theory within two distinct axes: one's level of spiritual focus and one's belief in the State's ideal involvement in society (see the illustration below). Additionally, as a reminder, I have included a side-by-side comparison of physicalism versus the One Mind (nonduality).

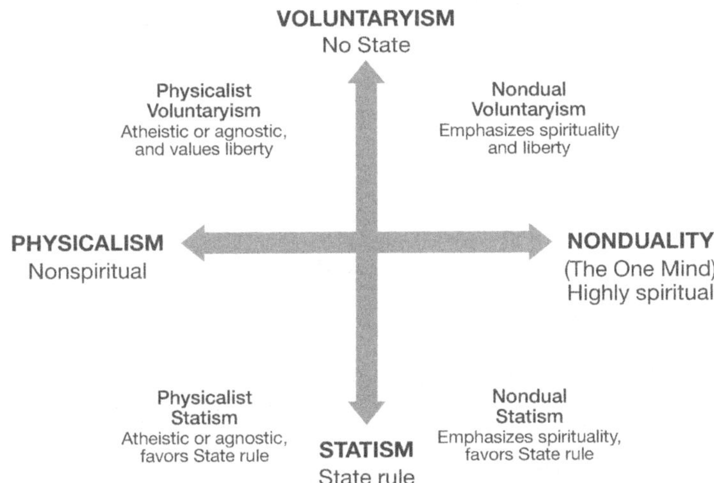

A spectrum of political theories on the axes of (a) level of spiritual focus and (b) level of the State's involvement in society. I contend that nondual voluntaryism represents the "ideal" metaphysical-political philosophy for organizing society.

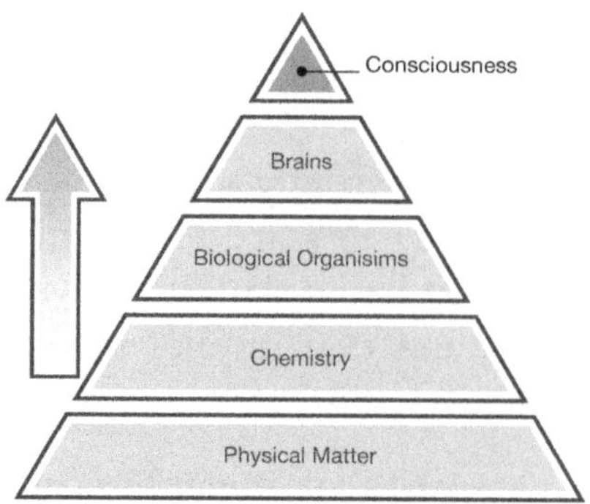

Physicalism: The interactions of units of matter (via chemistry) create biological organisms like human beings, which develop brains, out of which consciousness arises. This worldview supports atheism.

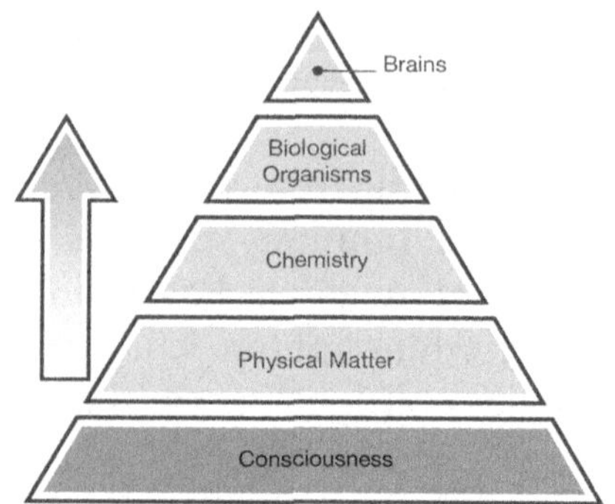

Nonduality (the "One Mind" view of reality): Consciousness is primary; everything we perceive in the apparently material world is simply a modulation of consciousness itself. This perspective supports a spiritual worldview found at the core of many religious traditions.

Applications

One might wonder how nondual voluntaryism can be applied to thinking about real-world matters, so we'll examine that here briefly.

The voluntarist aspect describes individuals' *rights* (based on the nonaggression principle). But it doesn't comment on whether those rights should be *exercised*.[25] The nondual, spiritual aspect fills in the voluntarist's gap by providing a moral compass to allow individuals to make their own decisions.

Let's consider drugs as an example. Nothing, from the voluntarist lens, would prohibit the ingestion of any substances, per se, because it's not an act of aggression upon anyone else's private property. That said, within various private properties, there would inevitably be rules and regulations. So perhaps in a voluntarist society there could exist communities in which all members—who joined the community voluntarily—agreed that certain substances are prohibited on their property. Therefore, any visitors would be obliged to adhere to those restrictions, or else face penalties as specified in the community's bylaws. If people don't like it, they can go somewhere else that doesn't have those rules.

From the nondual lens, an individual's decision to ingest any substances (on private property that allows such activities) would need to take into consideration potential spiritual, karmic implications. For example, one might ask: "Sure, I have the *freedom* to take this drug, but should I *exercise* that freedom and ingest it? Will it positively or negatively alter my body's spiritual connection? How will it impact my health? Will it make me a better or worse person around other people, and how will that affect their lives? If I treat people better or worse as a result of taking certain substances, will that impact my potential life review when I die? Will that negatively or positively impact my karma and overall spiritual evolution?" That's the line of thinking that a nondual adherent would take. Both the individual and the collective are considered.

This general exercise could be performed for any matter in society. **In summary: Under nondual voluntaryism, individuals would have the freedom to engage in activities that aren't initiating aggression upon anyone's private property, and they'd make their decisions about whether to exercise that freedom based upon spiritual principles.**

Yes, this philosophy encourages immense individual freedom and personal responsibility. Yes, that can sound scary in today's world. But the essential ingredient, which is lacking in many other political philosophies, is the spiritual perspective. **As a result of this worldview, certain harmful behaviors that exist in today's society will simply become irrational.** Living with a spiritual attitude will *incentivize* people to act with compassion and integrity: it will benefit their soul, which far outlasts this temporary stop in a body. And there will be a greater sense of responsibility to care for our world—including humans, animals, and the environment—rather than assuming "Mommy and Daddy government" will handle everything for us, with its mythical, supernatural wisdom and "master plans." **The nondual mindset would thus give voluntaryism the best chance of succeeding.**

I recognize that this might sound unrealistic given the state of the world today. However, I'm examining these matters with a forward-looking lens: I'm thinking about our future as a society—no matter how long it takes—in which consciousness is evolving and human nature itself is shifting. In such a world, the individual's responsibility will become critical and unavoidable. That is simply part of the spiritual, evolutionary process, as difficult as that might be to accept today. To reiterate the sentiment expressed in chapter 1, this is a "North Star" to guide our aspirations as a society. We have to start somewhere. So the mere act of examining the world with a nondual voluntarist mindset—and constantly questioning the State's sanctioned aggression against private property—is beneficial.

SECTION IV

WHAT IS THE PATH TO TRUE LIBERTY?

CHAPTER 9

A SHIFT IN CONSCIOUSNESS

The way to end upside down liberty—and break free from all manner of enslavement, whether subtle or explicit, whether metaphysical or physical—is easy to say, but challenging to implement. We need to (a) spiritualize our lives and (b) get government out of our lives.

Let's start with the spiritual aspect. Ken Wilber, a spiritual philosopher, provides a useful framework for thinking about this. He refers to multiple "lines of development" that one encounters during spiritual evolution. **In particular, he refers to the process of waking up, cleaning up, and growing up.**[1] These lines of development, each of which we'll examine shortly, are relatively independent from one another. For example, someone could be highly advanced and enlightened through the lens of "waking up" while lacking critical elements associated with "growing up." Furthermore, each and every one of us is going through these processes, whether we realize it or not (and whether we like it or not). Our evolutionary journey is built into the nature of reality itself.

"Waking up" involves breaking through our amnesia and remembering who and what we are. It is the realization that we're whirlpools within a stream, that our identity is both the whirlpool and the stream simultaneously, both the individual and the collective. Although it feels like I'm "Mark Gober," in reality I'm also the full stream of consciousness—the One Mind—which is temporarily experiencing the world through the body of Mark Gober. Consciousness is enlivening and activating the body, and not the other way around. The recognition and embodiment of this simple yet profound idea can be achieved by approaching life in a new way.

We might even engage in specific practices that help us reorient our consciousness, which can shift our fundamental values and priorities. For example, simply living in accordance with the Golden Rule can be immensely impactful. Additionally, more targeted "spiritual practices" can be incorporated into daily living and thinking. What follows are four general categories of practice commonly found in various traditions:

1. A focus on knowledge and wisdom: Trying to understand—at an intellectual level—the nature of reality, who we are, and why we're here. Methods can include reading books, listening to podcasts, attending lectures, or even finding a mentor or teacher.
2. A focus on selfless service: Finding ways to help people for the sake of helping rather than personal gain. Methods can vary depending on our life circumstances, but any such focus on service includes being mindful of our thoughts, words, and actions.
3. A focus on devotion: Holding a generally loving attitude toward all expressions of life, with the understanding that everything is derived from our single, common underpinning (the One Mind). We're all interconnected, even if we can't see the connections with our eyes. Methods can include holding a generally grateful attitude for all we've been gifted in life, prayer, chanting, dancing, appreciating nature, and seeing the "Divine" in everything.
4. A focus on "energetic" aspects: Caring for our bodily vessel and making it the best possible vehicle to embody

> its uniqueness. Methods can include meditation, breathing exercises, prolonged silence, sensory deprivation, yoga poses, qigong exercises, moving energy in the body (sometimes called "kundalini"), deep enjoyment of sensory experiences, and emphasizing physical health and nutrition.[2]

Having studied many awakening journeys in my research,[3] a behavioral pattern seems to emerge when one embarks on this path, which, over time, can include a diminished fear of death and the relinquishment of attachments to desires and fears. This is true psychological freedom. I'm not suggesting that one stops caring about life (that would be "detachment").[4] Rather, I'm talking about "nonattachment," which refers to a reduced *craving* of outcomes we think we want, and the recognition that outcomes are driven by a field of immense cosmic intelligence. In the nonattached state, the ups and downs of life are not quite as traumatic, and they cause less suffering. We begin to realize that even something seemingly "negative" can be viewed as a learning experience that helps us grow. Or it might have a broader, spiritual significance that's beyond human comprehension.

This overall way of living develops into enlightenment—an elevated, liberated joy leading into a blissful state of consciousness. Enlightenment can be viewed as a never-ending process rather than a final, stagnant state: there is *always* room to grow, evolve, and more fully express our innate gifts. And furthermore, since our true nature is ultimately the One Mind itself, part of us is already enlightened. Our quest, then, is really to remove blocks to enlightenment rather than to "achieve" something. As David Hawkins often joked, "The way to become enlightened is to stop being unenlightened."[5]

Hawkins summed up this inner journey in his seminal book *Letting Go: The Pathway of Surrender* (2012):

> There is one thing the world does not want us to find out and that is the truth about ourselves. Why? Because then we will become free. We can no longer

> be controlled, manipulated, exploited, drained, enslaved, imprisoned, vilified, or disempowered....
>
> What is the real truth about this voyage? The real truth is that, as we go within and discard one illusion after another, one falsehood after another, one negative program after another, it gets lighter and lighter. The awareness of the presence of love becomes stronger and stronger....Life becomes progressively more effortless.
>
> Every great teacher since the beginning of time has said to look *within* and find the truth, for the truth of what we really are will set us free.[6] [emphasis in original]

The notion of "cleaning up" is slightly different. It refers to the acknowledgment, processing, and healing of our individual traumas (or even achievements that have aggrandized our ego). It involves shining a light on whatever darkness lies dormant within us and allowing those emotions to be released and expressed so that they don't fester any longer. It requires deep introspection and a willingness to engage with unnerving parts of our psyches.

One aspect of the process involves recontextualizing the way in which we see ourselves and those who have hurt us. An easy healing technique in this regard is the Hawaiian practice of Ho'oponopono. You simply say the following four phrases to yourself: "I love you. I'm sorry. Please forgive me. Thank you."[7] Those words can be liberating—when directed both at ourselves and others (even supposed "enemies").

Cleaning up might also be occurring at the level of human civilization. Countless atrocities have been committed throughout our history, and part of our evolutionary process as a species could be to collectively acknowledge all that's happened, grieve, and clear the negativity that we might be suppressing societally.

On the whole, cleaning up can be an uncomfortable process, but it's essential. The avoidance of the process is known as **spiritual bypass** and can inhibit spiritual growth.

"Growing up," as I conceive it, refers to maturation. It means taking responsibility—and being fully accountable—for one's actions. Similarly, it moves us away from considering ourselves as victims. Growing up also involves seeing the world as it is rather than clinging to an idealized vision of what we hope it would be; it involves accepting the inevitability of upsetting aspects of life. It also entails an acknowledgment of the existence of evil rather than sticking our heads in the sand. When we do so, we become less susceptible to Trojan horses. We become more discerning, and acknowledge that sometimes people are not what they seem. In extreme cases, they might even be psychopaths. Even if we can't relate to their ways of thinking and lack of empathy, we can't hide from the fact that some people in this world are devoid of morality. If we ignore that, we risk becoming prey.

As we evolve on a metaphysical level—by waking up, cleaning up, and growing up—we naturally become free. Liberty is simply our "way of being" in the world.[8]

I often reference the nondual, spiritual philosopher Rupert Spira, who says that the world's problems are mere symptoms of an underlying disease. The disease is the physicalist view that consciousness comes from the brain—that we are finite beings who die when our body dies, and that we're fundamentally separate from one another.

I agree that this ignorance is the most fundamental problem in our world. And I would add to it the following: This "disease" is aided and abetted by the pervasive belief in the legitimacy of the State's authority. Governments throughout history have been responsible for immense death, destruction, enslavement, and brainwashing—and they're enabled by the widespread belief that this traditional governing structure is not only acceptable but necessary. We need to break the spell and recognize that it's not a requirement to have monopolistic, compulsory rulers who perpetrate aggression upon their subjects. Rather, our explicit consent is essential. Our engagements need to be voluntary.

From this lens, the two "most dangerous superstitions"[9] to humanity are physicalism and statism.

And that leads us into a discussion on getting government out of our lives.

Upon honest investigation, statism can be seen for what it is: a coercive and invasive system in which a ruling class makes itself exempt from morality—it is able to initiate aggression upon private property with impunity, and all the while it is often considered righteous for doing so. The State isn't formally policed by a global government: While it claims to control alleged "anarchy" at one level, it simultaneously exists within its own "international anarchy" of States. So, it doesn't even solve the anarchy "problem" it claims makes its existence necessary in the first place. And history has shown that this doesn't end well: States are unable to remain truly "limited" in their power. They eventually grow into intrusive entities.

When examined objectively, the State's features can be seen to align with those of an organized criminal enterprise. We've simply been brainwashed into accepting and praising it. It's difficult to accept that we've been deceived.

As we awaken to what's really happening, this becomes less tolerable. We begin to understand that endorsing statism is to contradict one's sense of morality. For instance, how can we feel good about forcing people, against their will, to hand over their honestly earned money—their private property—via taxation? Is it really okay to support a system that can coerce people, by law, into doing things that they consider immoral? Doesn't all of this go against the Golden Rule: treating others as we'd like to be treated?

Furthermore, we begin to notice that people in positions of authority often allow their egos to spiral out of control. Sometimes they lie, and they can become entangled in conspiracies. They might even create or weaponize emergencies to justify taking away citizens' freedoms (under the guise of "providing safety"). We start to acknowledge that some people are charlatans or psychopaths, others can transform into monsters when placed in positions of power, and others might be under the control of third parties via blackmail, bribery, and threats. And such individuals have the potential to do tremendous damage to society when placed into positions of power within a centralized government structure.

We start to recognize and nullify the impact of mind control, divide-and-conquer tactics, and censorship employed by all forms of media. That can even motivate us to seek out diverse, alternative media sources. We might then begin to resist the innate psychological instinct to obey and trust authority, simply because an authority figure "said so." Independent, critical thinking—rather than blind acceptance of an "expert's" narrative—starts to become more automatic.

We begin to understand that truly free markets—and the associated economic freedom they enable—are essential: they result in businesses with the accountability that government organizations lack. We start to realize that government isn't an all-knowing, supernatural entity. For instance, it couldn't possibly know how to optimally manage an economy consisting of countless exchanges and subjective consumer preferences. We begin to view the government as an extraneous, deleterious actor in the economy that distorts the natural intelligence of the system and obstructs economic freedom. We start to recognize that the government isn't uniquely qualified to do anything: private service providers operating within a free market can do better.

When all of this sinks in, we viscerally feel that the very foundation on which we used to view the world is shaken to its core through this new lens of liberty. Ludwig von Mises said it well: **"Government is essentially the negation of liberty....Liberty is always freedom from the government."**[10] [emphasis added]

And as Ron Paul stated during his farewell address to Congress in 2012:

> For thousands of years the acceptance of government force, to rule over the people, at the sacrifice of liberty, was considered moral and the only available option for achieving peace and prosperity. **What could be more utopian than that myth**—considering the results,

> especially looking at the [S]tate-sponsored killing, by nearly every government during the twentieth century, estimated to be in the hundreds of millions. It's time to reconsider this grant of authority to the [S]tate. No good has ever come from granting monopoly power to the [S]tate to use aggression against the people to arbitrarily mold human behavior. Such power, when left unchecked, becomes the seed of an ugly tyranny. **This method of governance has been adequately tested, and the results are in: reality dictates we try liberty.**[11] [emphasis added]

The practical path toward liberty and away from enslavement—toward voluntaryism and away from statism—is twofold, in my opinion. It involves the "building of the new" and the "dissolution of the old."

One could envision that small voluntarist communities might start to emerge and test the basic principles of a free society in practice. Those learnings would be valuable, and in theory these communities could coexist within a world that's dominated by statism. As more people awaken to the problems inherent in statism, and become increasingly disgruntled with our current political system, we might see an increased interest in such communities.

With regard to the existing States of the world, it will be up to the citizens to become less accepting of encroachments upon liberties. Once the populace—including law-enforcement personnel—begins to acknowledge that freedom is not something given to us by government and instead realizes that *it's our essential nature and natural right*, States might need to slow down their enactment of tyranny.

Some might even argue that freedom-focused individuals should enter the political sphere and dissolve the system from within. This seems like an uphill battle. In theory, such politicians, if elected, would vote against government interventions and regulations, and even advocate for the abolition of government agencies. Over time, as the thinking goes, they could meaningfully shrink the government's power from the inside. Others might refute this strategy on its face because, by working within the system of the State, we reinforce the legitimacy of the system.[12]

Regardless of the strategy taken, those who've shifted away from a purely statist worldview will begin to evaluate politicians very differently. All that starts to matter is one thing: **Does this person advocate liberty?** Period. It's not about whether the person seems "nice" on TV or makes politically correct statements. And it's not about whether the person promises to provide "safety." Instead, it's ultimately about whether the person advocates—*and acts on*—principles of nonaggression and respect for private property. Or, as Lew Rockwell summarizes the basic position, using different terminology: **"Anti-state, anti-war, pro-market."**[13] [emphasis added]

Decentralization of power is a critical aspect here—and that includes thinking about government structures on a global scale. During the COVID-19 era, we've seen firsthand the great influence of global powers, such as the World Health Organization, the United Nations, and the World Economic Forum. Although international collaboration is, of course, important, the downsides must be considered too. Centralized global power structures are potentially even more dangerous than any single State because they can influence the entire world's population. The handling of COVID-19 has demonstrated viscerally that the decisions and opinions of a relatively small number of leaders and "experts" can significantly impact the lives and livelihoods of the masses. From this lens, a "one-world government" would be the greatest threat to planetary liberty.

But to me, the most fundamental solution—which will translate into metaphysical and physical liberty—can be summed up with a single, all-encompassing phrase: **a shift in consciousness**. That is, the shift to a nondual voluntarist way of viewing the world—even if its literal implementation takes time, and even if that means playing by the rules within the State's system until then. So, most important of all is *education* about these matters and finding ways to help people open their minds and unwind their conditioned ways of thinking. Overcoming increasing levels of censorship and mind control is one of the greatest challenges in this regard.

A shift toward nondual voluntaryism—as a mindset—entails acknowledging that we're infinite, interconnected beings, and that third parties (such as the State) cannot own us, no matter what. We then start to exude the attitude expressed by Indian guru Sri Lahiri Mahasaya: **"Always remember that you belong to no one, and no one belongs to you."**[14] [emphasis added] We begin to recognize that people should be able to make their *own decisions* and shouldn't be coerced into doing what they don't want—so long as they're not initiating aggression against other people or their material private property. An individual's decision to exercise freedoms can be guided by a personal assessment of metaphysical concepts such as spiritual evolution and karma.

From a physicalist standpoint—which holds that consciousness exerts no influence on the physical world—such a "consciousness shift" among the masses wouldn't be sufficient to create great change. Who cares if people shift their mindset? All that happens is something inside their brains.

But from the nondual, spiritual perspective, a consciousness shift would be incredibly significant. If all reality is made of consciousness, then a shift in consciousness necessarily implies a shift in our physical reality: physical reality is malleable. The many studies on psychokinesis point to this idea. As discussed in chapter 8, The Global Consciousness Project suggests that when groups of people focus their consciousness in a similar direction (known as "coherence"), they unknowingly impact the behavior of random-number generators. Furthermore, the results of studies on the Maharishi Effect indicate the potential to bring about peace through group meditation—which is likewise a shift in consciousness. Shifting our internal state can stimulate shifts in the external world.

The mechanism and manifestation of this malleability still remains mysterious, however. We often tend to think in linear terms. For example, if you push a door, it will close at a rate proportional to the force you apply. If you just tap the door, it won't close very quickly; whereas if you push hard, the door will slam shut. A "linear" relationship can easily be seen between how hard you push the door and how quickly and forcefully it will close.

Other aspects of reality seem to be much more nonlinear, though. I'm often reminded of the "butterfly effect," which shows that tiny changes in initial conditions can ultimately cause massively different outcomes. This idea has been shown in meteorology, for example, where seemingly minuscule changes to initial conditions in weather models led to vastly different predictions. Mathematically speaking, this translates into the notion that a butterfly flapping its wings in China—thereby moving the air particles by just a tiny amount—could result in a hurricane in New York.[15]

This is precisely why a collective shift in mindset could have far-reaching impacts that we cannot conceive of with our limited human brains. Moreover, we shouldn't underestimate the possibility that a shift in each person's individual consciousness impacts the entire interconnected field of consciousness in meaningful ways. And who knows what that could mean from a quantum or even multidimensional lens? **Therefore, the simple—but profound—act of reconceptualizing liberty in our individual psyches could result in a powerful, global transformation.**

In fact, when we think about the composition of today's current power structures, the ruling class constitutes a tiny percentage of the total population. The masses outnumber the rulers significantly. Thus, if, at some point, a "critical mass" of the regular citizens and law enforcers were to recognize that no one has the right to coercively control our lives, the world's power structures might begin to exert less influence. The existing States' edicts would become less and less meaningful. New States would have a difficult time forming because citizens wouldn't accept the idea of involuntary political structures. And furthermore, some of the politicians themselves might begin to question the State and shift their policies and opinions accordingly. Their egos might actually compel them to do so: by advocating liberty, they could become immensely popular within a new global consciousness.

How exactly change might unfold is impossible to predict. We also can't know the time frame for change or whether it will occur gradually or suddenly. On the other hand, what each of us can do—today—is make a decision as to whether we want to start living with a *mindset* of liberty rather than fear. *We* have the power to make that choice.

When we look at the world around us, and observe the ways in which governments are controlling their citizens, it becomes evident that such a shift is *urgently* needed.

Murray Rothbard observed in his book *For a New Liberty* (1973): "Liberty has never been fully tried in the modern world."[16]

I ask: Why not now?

ACKNOWLEDGMENTS

I'm incredibly grateful for the opportunity to work with my publishers and friends, Bill and Gayle Gladstone, of Waterside Productions. Waterside has played an instrumental role in helping me refine my messages and bring them forth to broader audiences. Without Waterside, I would not be where I am today. It's also been a privilege to work with my talented editors Jill Kramer and Kenneth Kales. Joel Chamberlain has once again done a terrific job with design, and Ken Fraser's creativity has shined through once more with the cover art. Thanks, also, to Jennifer Uram for her assistance with contracts and to Sandi Schroeder for compiling the book's index.

I sincerely thank Dr. Walter Block and Rochel Leah Bernstein for providing such thoughtful and astute feedback. Additionally, I thank the Mises Institute for making so many books and lectures available to the public. I have been able to learn a tremendous amount through its resources. I'm blessed to have the unconditional support of so many friends and family members—particularly my parents and brothers. My podcast producers and friends from Blue Duck Media, Matt Ford and Gabe Goodwin, have also been immensely supportive throughout my journey over the last several years.

GLOSSARY

Anarcho-Capitalism: A political philosophy arguing for no compulsory government and a fully free-market economy. See "Voluntaryism."

Austrian Economics: A brand of free-market economics modeled after the work of Carl Menger (1840–1921); Eugen von Böhm-Bawerk (1851–1914); Ludwig von Mises (1881–1973); Henry Hazlitt (1894–1993); Nobel laureate F. A. Hayek (1899–1992); Murray Rothbard (1926–1995), and others; and continues today at the Mises Institute in Auburn, Alabama.

It argues against government intervention in the economy and emphasizes the subjectivity and unpredictability of consumer decision making. The complexity inherent in such a marketplace makes it impossible for even the most intelligent politicians to know what's best for the economy; therefore, anything the government does to the economy ends up distorting the natural intelligence of the system of free exchanges between consumers and producers. Austrian economists often emphasize the importance of entrepreneurship as well as savings and production. While elements of Austrian economics are compatible with voluntaryism, not all Austrian economists subscribe to voluntaryism, and vice versa.

Capitalism: In its pure form, capitalism allows the desire for profits and the aversion toward losses to govern the economy: producers are incentivized to service consumers' needs and minimize their dissatisfaction. In true capitalism, there's no government intervention in the economy whatsoever. Modern economies that are often called capitalistic are in fact only partially capitalistic because they include government intervention.

Cognitive Dissonance: Psychological stress experienced when confronted with information that contradicts one's worldview. This phenomenon makes it difficult for many people to shift their paradigms: they often reject information that's not aligned with their existing beliefs. So rather than shifting their beliefs, they improperly reject the evidence.

Communism: Akin to socialism, except the government takes an even more aggressive role as society's central planner (see "Socialism"). As reported by *The Black Book of Communism*, it has been responsible for nearly 100 million deaths.

Consciousness: The part of us that experiences life—our subjective awareness. Mainstream science tells us that consciousness comes from the brain (known as physicalism or scientific materialism). An alternative—promoted in this book—is that consciousness doesn't come from the brain but rather serves as the basis of all reality, existing beyond space and time. From this lens, the brain is more like a filtering mechanism or blindfold of consciousness, or an antenna-receiver-transmitter that taps into the "cloud" of consciousness. Consciousness could also be likened to the sun: it is always shining, but the "clouds" within our brain block the rays.

Crony-Capitalism: A term used to deride capitalism because the rich and powerful often collude with politicians to enhance their power at the expense of the masses. However, the term misunderstands what true capitalism is: under true capitalism, there's no State intervention in the economy whatsoever, so there would be no State with which to collude. The more accurate term is *cronyism*, which is rampant in economies featuring the State's intervention.

Cronyism: Collaboration between influential parties (corporations and individuals) and the State.

Exemption from Morality: A term used by political philosopher Larken Rose (among others) to convey the idea that the State ignores morality in its actions. For example, theft is illegal and immoral for normal citizens, but when the State does it through taxation, it's not only permitted but lauded as virtuous. Therefore, Rose notes that, unbeknownst to most citizens, the State is "exempt" from normal moral standards.[1]

Fascism: As defined by author Lew Rockwell: "Fascism is the system of government that cartelizes the private sector, centrally plans the economy to subsidize producers, exalts the police state as the source of order, denies fundamental rights and liberties to individuals, and makes the executive state the unlimited master of society."[2] Fascism is much more similar to communism and socialism than is typically acknowledged: like those other philosophies, fascist governments become domineering central planners with significant control over citizens' private property. Communism and socialism often profess egalitarianism as their alleged motive, whereas fascism tends to sound less altruistic and more nationalistic. The results for all of these forms of government have been catastrophic, however. Many millions have been murdered under these sorts of regimes. In fact, they all advocate a form of extreme collectivism in which the State matters more than the individual. That has proven to be a recipe for disaster—whether we call it "fascism," "communism," or "socialism."

The Global Consciousness Project: A group, led by former Princeton researchers, studying the behavior of random-number generators during events that arouse strong emotion. In many instances, such as the 9/11 attacks, they have behaved statistically nonrandomly. The results imply that when many people focus their consciousness in a certain direction, physical reality shifts (even if the results are sometimes extremely subtle, but statistically significant). The implication is that "collective intention" can have an impact on the world.

The Golden Rule: A principle found in spiritual traditions all over the world, which counsels people to treat others as they wish to be treated. In life reviews reported during near-death experiences, individuals sense the Golden Rule firsthand because they literally feel the pleasure or pain they inflicted upon others during their lives. This phenomenon suggests that the Golden Rule is built into reality itself, perhaps as an overarching "natural law."

Karma: The general idea that there's a "balancing" force in the universe, and that there are consequences to our actions—actions in this life and also in possible past lives that we don't remember. Simplistically stated, it's as if inflicting pain upon someone can boomerang back such that the person who inflicted pain later *feels* that pain through other life events. The same would apply to pleasure. However, karma is perhaps much more complex than described here. The life-review phenomenon in near-death experiences makes the notion of karma plausible because the pleasure and pain inflicted during one's life are directly experienced.

Keynesian Economic Policy: A policy that advocates government intervention in the economy—for example, through government spending. Austrian free-market economists tend to reject such interventionist activities as being more harmful than helpful.

Libertarianism: A political philosophy that advocates individual rights and limited government. Voluntaryism—which posits the absence of a traditional State—is a form of libertarianism, but not all libertarians would go as far as voluntarists. That is, some libertarians still believe in the existence of the State; they just want it to be limited in size. It's also worth noting that America was founded upon principles of limited government.

Life Review: Reported in many near-death experiences and involves reliving one's life. By some estimates, life reviews occur in roughly 20–25 percent of near-death experiences. Events are sometimes experienced through the eyes of those impacted by the events. Life reviews suggest that the Golden Rule is embedded within reality itself.

Lines of Development: A philosophy articulated by Ken Wilber in which spiritual evolution occurs in multiple, distinct ways that are effectively independent from one another. He summarizes the idea by talking about "waking up, cleaning up, and growing up." Being highly "awakened" doesn't necessarily imply that one has achieved the same level of mastery in the "growing-up" category, for example. These various lines of development are *all* essential as we evolve.

The Maharishi Effect: Meditation performed by relatively small groups of people can result in more peace and less violence within society. Barry Spivack and Patricia Anne Saunders's book, *An Antidote to Violence* (2020), summarizes the effect and current state of the associated science: there are twenty peer-reviewed studies and more than fifty demonstrations illustrating the impact of group meditation: "Coherence in collective consciousness can result in improvements in the quality of life in society, increased governmental success and international cooperation without the use of armed force."[3] The implication is that group meditation can alter the physical world in a positive way.

Mediumship: An ability to communicate with the deceased. The implication is that our consciousness does not die when the physical body dies, and that consciousness can be accessed by those still in bodies.

Mind Control: Techniques that enable brainwashing, often unbeknownst to the victims. Mind-control programs were active in the US following World War II, when it recruited Nazi scientists (Operation Paperclip). Mind control also seems to work through propaganda in the mainstream media, Hollywood, social media and technology platforms, and education systems.

Monetary Economic Policy: A policy that advocates government intervention in the economy—for example, through altering the money supply (via central banks such as the Federal Reserve). Austrian free-market economists tend to condemn such interventionist activities as being more harmful than helpful.

Near-Death Experiences (NDEs): Instances in which a person's brain, according to mainstream science, shouldn't be able to produce complex consciousness and yet it does. This can occur in individuals under general anesthesia or even when they're in cardiac arrest, among other physiologically traumatic events. Millions of cases have been reported. Experiencers often talk about being immersed in unconditional love, seeing mystical beings or deceased relatives, having an out-of-body experience, and having a life review, for instance. They are typically forever changed upon being resuscitated and become more spiritual and less materialistic.

Nonaggression Principle: A central tenet of voluntaryism that prohibits the initiation of aggression against anyone's private property, including theft, coercion, physical violence, fraud, extortion, and so on. When the nonaggression principle is violated, aggression and self-defense are permissible.

Nonduality: The notion that there's only one reality, and that reality is a universal consciousness of which each of us is a part. (See "One Mind.")

Nondual Voluntaryism: A metaphysical-political philosophy introduced in this book that blends voluntaryism with the spiritual notion of nonduality (the One Mind). Voluntaryism gives direction politically: it advocates a free society based upon nonaggression against private property. Whether or not an individual exercises those rights is examined from a nondual, spiritual lens—for example, the Golden Rule, karma, and spiritual evolution. Consider drugs as an example. Under voluntaryism, nothing would prevent someone from ingesting substances because that act doesn't initiate aggression against someone else's private property (unless, of course, a private-property owner had a rule that banned drugs). Under nonduality, whether or not one decides to exercise the right to ingest drugs depends on an assessment of how it would impact one's spiritual development. Individuals would thus have many rights, but while holding a spiritual worldview, the enactment of many of those rights would be irrational (that is, people would be less likely to engage in harmful behaviors). This book asserts that nondual voluntaryism is the optimal metaphysical-political philosophy when viewed in the context of the true nature of reality, as revealed by consciousness studies. Although our current society largely exists under the opposite philosophy (physicalist statism), nondual voluntaryism can be viewed as a North Star to guide our long-term aspirations as a society. A more general term for nondual voluntaryism would be *spiritual libertarianism*.

The One Mind: In contrast to physicalism, which suggests that consciousness stems from the brain, the One Mind view of reality asserts that consciousness is the basis of reality. The term is derived from Nobel Prize–winning physicist Erwin Schrödinger's statement "In truth, there is only one mind."[4] Additionally, Larry Dossey, MD, wrote a book called *One Mind* (2013) that makes a similar argument. The evidence for the One Mind, as opposed to physicalism, comes from four primary areas: consciousness "anomalies" (psychic phenomena and survival of bodily death), quantum physics, philosophy, and spiritually transformative experiences. The general idea is that we're all interconnected as part of this One Mind but appear to be separate (like whirlpools within an infinite stream, as stated by Bernardo Kastrup, PhD). The One Mind offers a spiritual view of reality that's in line with the notion of "nonduality."

Physicalism: The belief that reality ultimately stems from physical material (known as matter). More specifically, it posits that consciousness comes from the brain. This belief system is the popular metaparadigm for thinking about the nature of reality: it's the paradigm that underlies all other paradigms within modern science. Physicalism is also equated with the term *scientific materialism*. I argue in my books that physicalism is incorrect, and that consciousness does not come from the brain. Rather, consciousness is "fundamental," serving as the basis of reality. (See "One Mind" and "Nonduality.")

Precognition: Knowing or sensing the future before it happens, which suggests that consciousness exists beyond time.

Private-Property Rights: Ownership of one's body and material goods (such as land, money, homes, clothing, and anything else people own). Those advocating such rights are skeptical of the State's attempt to control or own individuals' private property, as often occurs in socialistic, communist, and fascistic forms of government.

Psychokinesis: Mind-matter interactions: the notion that consciousness can impact the physical world, even if the effect is sometimes small. If consciousness is the basis of reality, then it would make sense that a shift in consciousness could instigate a shift in the material world. Implied in this phenomenon is the notion that physical reality is malleable.

Psychopaths: People who lack empathy and are prone to wickedness. Sometimes they're charming and are thus able to fool unsuspecting individuals. Most people cannot relate to the mindset of psychopaths, and as a result, they often find it hard to believe that such individuals could be so evil.

Quantum Physics: A branch of physics that emerged in the early 1900s and often deals with the tiny scales of reality. One of the major findings is "quantum entanglement," which is suggestive of a hidden interconnectedness in the universe. Other experiments point to the wavelike aspect of matter (meaning matter is sometimes not solid), and perhaps consciousness is involved.

Reincarnation: The notion that our consciousness can exist in multiple bodies throughout time. The strongest evidence for this phenomenon comes from the University of Virginia's more than 2,500 cases of children who have past-life memories. In the strongest cases, historical or medical records validate what the children claim. Additionally, sometimes these children have distinctive birthmarks or physical defects that align with events from their alleged previous lives. Implicit in the notion of reincarnation is the fact that we all have *amnesia*—that is, we've forgotten our past lives (and more broadly, our true nature as the One Mind).

Remote Viewing: Seeing or otherwise perceiving something with the mind alone (and not with one's physical eyes). This form of "nonlocal consciousness" has been validated at Princeton University and in the US government's declassified psychic spying programs, for instance.

Socialism: A societal structure in which the government controls the means of production and the distribution of goods. In such an economy, the government plays the role of a central planner to redistribute wealth and prevent income inequality. However, embedded within this philosophy is a lack of respect for private property. So while it might sound "altruistic" because it preaches egalitarianism, it is a system that's inherently coercive to those who are forced to participate without their consent.

Spiritual Evolution: The notion that our individuated consciousness (some might call it our soul) evolves from lifetime to lifetime, working toward a state of unity and unconditional love with our source and true nature: the One Mind. Spiritual evolution might also occur at the level of society, almost like a sea level that rises as we each evolve individually.

The State: A term used to describe modern government. As Murray Rothbard defined it: "The State is that organization in society which attempts to maintain a monopoly of the use of force and violence in a given territorial area; in particular, it is the only organization in society that obtains its revenue not by voluntary contribution or payment for services rendered but by coercion. While other individuals or institutions obtain their income by production of goods and services and by the peaceful and voluntary sale of these goods and services to others, the State obtains its revenue by the use of compulsion; that is, by the use and the threat of the jailhouse and the bayonet."[5]

Statism: The belief that traditional government (the State) should run society. It includes the political Left and the Right because they both believe in the legitimacy of the State. They simply disagree over what the State's role should be. Those who believe in statism are known as "statists."

Telepathy: Mind-to-mind communication, which suggests that consciousness isn't stuck in our brains. Telepathy, along with remote viewing, psychokinesis, and precognition, is one of the categories for which there are Six Sigma statistical results: the odds against chance are more than a billion to one. In other words, they are likely real effects rather than chance coincidences.

Veridical Out-of-Body Experiences: Reports during near-death experiences in which a person's consciousness has complex perceptions that are later verified as accurate. Upon being resuscitated, third parties (such as operating-room doctors) confirm the claims that the experiencer says happened. For instance, this can involve a person's consciousness seeing an operating room from a vantage point above the body and accurately reporting what happened from that lens. These cases suggest that near-death experiences aren't hallucinations: if they were, the experiencers wouldn't be able to accurately recall events. *The Self Does Not Die* (2016) by Rivas et al. includes more than one hundred such well-documented cases.

Voluntaryism: A branch of libertarian political philosophy that endorses the principle of nonaggression against private property. Rothbard simply described such a society: "One where there is no legal possibility for coercive aggression against the person or property of any individual."[6] Because the State is an inherent aggressor against private property, voluntarists argue there should be no State, and any interactions between citizens and organizations should be voluntary. The functions currently under the State's purview would be managed by privately owned companies competing within a free market. Effectively, the State would turn into a set of nonmandatory service providers. Furthermore, the economy would be without the State's interventions because the State wouldn't exist. Contracts would be particularly important in a voluntarist society. Voluntaryism is sometimes called "anarcho-capitalism."

ENDNOTES

Preface

1 Anderson, *The Panopticon Is Already Here*, https://www.theatlantic.com/magazine/archive/2020/09/china-ai-surveillance/614197/.
2 "Epstein and Bill Gates with Whitney Webb" on RFK Jr / The Defender Podcast, https://anchor.fm/rfkjr/episodes/Epstein-and-Bill-Gates-with-Whitney-Webb-e11d5g1, May 22, 2021.
3 Modarressy-Tehrani and Murray, "'It just feels surreal': Military posted at checkpoints as Australian state extends COVID-19 lockdown," https://www.nbcnews.com/news/world/it-just-feels-surreal-military-posted-checkpoints-australian-state-extends-n1237068.
4 BBC News, "Covid in Sydney: Military deployed to help enforce lockdown," https://www.bbc.com/news/world-australia-58021718.
5 Thompson, *Rescue dogs shot dead by NSW council due to COVID-19 restrictions*, https://www.smh.com.au/national/nsw/rescue-dogs-shot-dead-by-nsw-council-due-to-covid-19-restrictions-20210821-p58ksh.html.
6 Annastacia Palaszczuk, Twitter post, August 25, 2021. https://twitter.com/AnnastaciaMP/status/1430739214035873795.
7 Justin Trudeau, Twitter post, March 29, 2021, https://twitter.com/justintrudeau/status/1376662503720112132?s=21.
8 Transcript of Farewell Address, http://www.campaignforliberty.org/national-blog/transcript-of-farewell-address/.
9 Video on Twitter post, July 12, 2021, https://twitter.com/dutchanddonts/status/1414833132822478849?s=20. Similar statements made here: https://www.youtube.com/watch?v=ENEUktOrQV8&t=2s.

10 "Robert F. Kennedy Jr on COVID: 'People in authority will abuse every power we relinquish to them!'" https://www.youtube.com/watch?v=EBSfsJBYqRo, December 21, 2020.
11 "'Above my pay grade': New Jersey governor claims Bill of Rights did not factor into his coronavirus executive orders," https://www.washingtonexaminer.com/news/above-my-pay-grade-new-jersey-governor-claims-bill-of-rights-did-not-factor-into-his-coronavirus-executive-orders, April 15, 2020.
12 Woods, *Nullification*, 2 (Kindle).
13 "COVID-19: Justice Alito overstepped judicial boundaries," https://www.msn.com/en-us/news/politics/covid-19-justice-alito-overstepped-judicial-boundaries/ar-BB1baUY5, November 19, 2020.
14 Transcript of Farewell Address, http://www.campaignforliberty.org/national-blog/transcript-of-farewell-address/.
15 Fauci: "Masks Forever!," https://youtu.be/mTTAWFjIPmg, May 2021.
16 Sagan, *The Demon-Haunted World*, 241.
17 Raschke, *Painted Black*, ix.
18 Twitter post, July 14, 2021, https://twitter.com/michaelmalice/status/1415393899598819331?s=21.

Chapter 1

1 Blackall, "People in England urged to be patient amid reports hugging may soon be allowed," https://www.theguardian.com/world/2021/may/01/england-urged-to-be-patient-amid-reports-hugging-may-soon-be-allowed.
2 Meeks, "With a worsening pandemic, California bans singing in places of worship," https://www.cnn.com/2020/07/03/us/california-places-of-worship-pandemiic-trnd/index.html.
3 Leshan, "DC has banned dancing at indoor and outdoor wedding receptions," https://www.wusa9.com/article/news/local/dc/dc-bans-dancing-at-wedding-receptions/65-bf89fd3f-9011-4d43-b356-9a836c832904.
4 Higham, "June 21: When will Boris Johnson announce if there is a delay to 'Freedom Day'?" https://www.express.co.uk/news/uk/1448541/June-21-boris-johnson-announcement-delay-freedom-day-evg.
5 Brady, "I believe the real purpose of masks is social control – it's time to turn down the fear dial, writes GRAHAM BRADY, Chairman of the Tory 1922 Committee," https://www.dailymail.co.uk/debate/article-9798365/GRAHAM-BRADY-believe-real-purpose-masks-social-control-time-stop-fear.html.
6 Reyes, "Novak Djokovic beats Rafael Nadal in French Open semifinals with fans allowed to defy curfew," https://www.usatoday.com/story/sports/tennis/french/2021/06/11/nadal-djokovic-french-open-match-allowed-end-fans-defy-curfew/7660733002/, June 11, 2021.
7 Hains, "CNN's Dr. Leana Wen: Make It Clear To People That The Vaccine Is Their 'Ticket Back To Pre-Pandemic Life' And Freedom," https://www.

realclearpolitics.com/video/2021/04/02/cnns_dr_leana_wen_make_it_clear_to_people_that_the_vaccine_is_their_ticket_back_to_pre-pandemic_life_and_freedom.html#!, April 2, 2021.

8 New South Wales Government, "New freedoms for vaccinated first step on state roadmap out of COVID." https://www.health.nsw.gov.au/news/Pages/20210826_01.aspx.

9 Hobbes, *Leviathan*, 76.

10 Adapted from Hans-Hermann Hoppe, for example, "Property and the Social Order | Hans-Hermann Hoppe," August 19, 2011, https://www.youtube.com/watch?v=AQmMe2IeGPU.

11 See Rose's book titled *The Most Dangerous Superstition*. In his book, Rose more generally refers to the belief in "authority" as the most dangerous superstition. That includes "all belief in 'government'" (p. 2). Many of the concepts in this chapter stem from the ideas discussed in Rose's book.

12 Rose, *The Most Dangerous Superstition*, 165.

13 Rothbard, *For a New Liberty*, 274.

14 Rothbard, *The Ethics of Liberty*, 161–162.

15 Woods, *Nullification*, 115 (Kindle).

16 Rose, *The Most Dangerous Superstition*, 16.

17 Ibid., 22.

18 "Society Without State: Private Law Society | Hans-Hermann Hoppe," https://youtu.be/TlWGA9H5An4, May 17, 2012.

19 Spike Cohen, Twitter post, June 30, 2021, https://twitter.com/RealSpikeCohen/status/1410267899625934848.

20 These arguments about morality are often explained in further detail by Larken Rose.

21 Rose, *The Most Dangerous Superstition*, 36.

22 Ibid.

23 Ibid., 34.

24 Ibid., 25.

25 Ibid., Part III (a) through (e).

26 These concepts are regularly discussed by Larken Rose.

27 Rose, *The Most Dangerous Superstition*, 28.

28 Ibid., 165.

29 Ibid., 37–40 (on "Altering Morality").

30 Ibid.

31 Rothbard, "Myth and Truth About Libertarianism," https://mises.org/library/myth-and-truth-about-libertarianism. The article notes: "This essay is based on a paper presented at the April 1979 national meeting of the Philadelphia Society in Chicago. The theme of the meeting was 'Conservatism and Libertarianism.'"

32 A comparison often made by Rothbard, for example, in *For a New Liberty*, 222.

33 Rothbard, *For a New Liberty*, 110.

34 Satter, *U.S. court: Mass surveillance program exposed by Snowden was illegal*, https://www.reuters.com/article/us-usa-nsa-spying-idUSKBN25T3CK.

35 History.com editors, *Patriot Act*, https://www.history.com/topics/21st-century/patriot-act.
36 As cited in Rossini, Chris, *The Decades-Long Obsession With "Safety At All Costs" Has Reached Its Culmination*, http://www.ronpaullibertyreport.com/archives/the-decades-long-obsession-with-safety-at-all-costs-has-reached-its-culmination.
37 Rose, *The Most Dangerous Superstition*, 32.
38 Ibid., 19.
39 Luigi Marco Bassani asserts in his book *Chaining Down Leviathan* (2021) that the modern, more oppressive version of the State is somewhat new. He points to the European model of the State, which has become the status quo. See chapter 1 of his book, for example.
40 Rothbard, *Anatomy of the State*, 11–12.
41 Ibid.
42 "Transcript of Farewell Address," http://www.campaignforliberty.org/national-blog/transcript-of-farewell-address/.
43 "Ep. 1875 Michael Malice on How to Make Radical Ideas Approachable," https://www.youtube.com/watch?v=k0jdavqhZe4&t=2182s, April 13, 2021.
44 Rothbard, *For a New Liberty*, 286–290.
45 "Michael Malice – What Is The Hardest Question For Anarchism To Answer?", https://www.youtube.com/watch?v=nzvgqlAkZcE, June 2, 2021.
46 See Kahneman and Tversky, "Prospect Theory: An Analysis of Decision under Risk," www.jstor.org/stable/1914185, 1979. The notion of "loss aversion" is relevant as well. The general principle here is losses feel worse than gains feel good, which impacts decision making and risk preferences accordingly. Individuals become more risk seeking when faced with the potential of a guaranteed loss, whereas they tend to be more risk averse when faced with the potential of a guaranteed gain.
47 Paul, *Liberty Defined*, 324.
48 This general theme often arises in modern libertarian thinking. For example, Ron Paul and Dave Smith have offered an overall sentiment along these lines.
49 "Thomas B. Reed: Quotes," https://www.britannica.com/biography/Thomas-B-Reed/quotes.
50 The quote is often attributed to Albert Einstein, but it's unclear whether he actually said it. Because of that uncertainty, the quote is used in the text without attribution.

Chapter 2

1 Rose, *The Most Dangerous Superstition*, 27.
2 Ibid., 31.
3 Ibid., 126.
4 Bates, "EXCLUSIVE: Jeffrey Epstein had surveillance cameras hidden throughout his properties worldwide in a 'blackmail scheme' to extort his

powerful friends, victims tell new Netflix doc about the pedophile," https://www.dailymail.co.uk/news/article-8361607/Jeffrey-Epsteins-surveillance-cameras-blackmail-scheme-extort-powerful-friends.html.

5 Rothbard, *Anatomy of the State*, 38. Here, Rothbard mentions this notion in the context of Professor J. Allen Smith's observation.

6 Zimbardo, *The Lucifer Effect*, 53, 62, 65-66, 74, 170, 172, and 202.

7 Ibid,. 161

8 Ibid., 2.

9 Ibid., 211–212.

10 Ibid., xii.

11 As cited in Moreell, *Power Corrupts*, https://www.acton.org/pub/religion-liberty/volume-2-number-6/power-corrupts.

12 Zimbardo, *The Lucifer Effect*, 218.

13 Milgram, *Obedience to Authority*, 4-6 (Kindle version).

14 Rose, *The Most Dangerous Superstition*, 175.

15 A related term, *sociopath*, is sometimes used interchangeably with *psychopath*. In other instances, the terms have slightly different connotations. Robert Hare, PhD, states: "In many cases the choice of term reflects the user's views on the *origins and determinants* of the clinical syndrome or disorder....Thus, some clinicians and researchers—as well as most sociologists and criminologists—who believe that the syndrome is forged entirely by social forces and early experiences prefer the term *socio*path, whereas those...who feel that psychological, biological, and genetic factors also contribute to the development of the syndrome generally use the term *psycho*path. The same individual therefore could be diagnosed as a sociopath by one expert and as a psychopath by another." See Hare, *Without Conscience*, 23–34.

16 Ibid., 1–2.

17 Ibid., 6.

18 Ibid., 38.

19 Ibid., 195.

20 Ibid., 216.

21 Ibid., 45.

22 Ibid., 113.

23 *The Bad Seed* by William March, as cited in *Without Conscience* (opening quotation).

24 Rose, *The Most Dangerous Superstition*, 62.

Chapter 3

1 Biko, *Black Consciousness and the Quest for True Humanity*, 6.

2 Instagram post, February 8, 2021, by @awakenwithjp, https://www.instagram.com/p/CLCFEP6FsAr/?igshid=kibupbvksqxe.

3 Griffin, "How Facebook's 'independent fact checkers' cited letter secretly organized by Wuhan lab funder Peter Daszak to 'debunk' leak theory and punish news outlets that explored it," https://www.dailymail.co.uk/news/

article-9655057/Facebook-fact-checkers-cited-Lancet-letter-Wuhan-lab-funder-Peter-Daszak-debunk-lab-leak.html.

4 As cited in Powell, *The ESP Enigma*, 229.

5 *Dispatch: Countering Criticism of the Warren Report, January 4, 1967*, https://history-matters.com/archive/jfk/cia/russholmes/104-10406/104-10406-10110/html/104-10406-10110_0002a.htm.

6 National Archives, JFK Assassination Records, *Summary of Findings*, https://www.archives.gov/research/jfk/select-committee-report/summary.html.

7 Rothbard, *Anatomy of the State*, 26–27.

8 Cadelago and Korecki, *MAGA media looks to turn White House briefing room into a battlefield*, https://www.politico.com/news/2021/01/25/maga-media-white-house-briefing-462015.

9 Tsakiris, *Kevin Annett, Whistleblower of an Evil Church |433|*, https://skeptiko.com/kevin-annett-whistleblower-of-an-evil-church-433/.

10 Robison, *Proofs of a Conspiracy*, 6.

11 Ibid.

12 Ibid., 7.

13 Wilson, *The New Freedom*, 24, 26. The book notes: "*The New Freedom* first appeared serially in *World's Work* from January to July, 1913." Archived at: https://archive.org/details/WoodrowWilsonTheNewFreedom/page/n3/mode/2up?q=small+group+of+men.

14 Hylan, *Mayor Hylan of New York: An Autobiography*, 41. Archived at: https://archive.org/details/autobiographyofj00hyla/page/n1/mode/2up?q=octopus.

15 As cited at the Ron Paul Institute for Peace and Prosperity website: http://ronpaulinstitute.org/archives/featured-articles/2016/october/24/the-path-to-total-dictatorship-americas-shadow-government-and-its-silent-coup/.

16 As cited in the foreword by Richard Grove in Stone, *New World Order*, xv.

17 Glass, *Eisenhower warns of 'military-industrial complex,' Jan. 17, 1961*, https://www.politico.com/story/2019/01/17/eisenhower-warns-of-military-industrial-complex-jan-17-1961-1099265.

18 Quigley, *Tragedy and Hope*, 690–691.

19 C-SPAN, *User Clip: Daniel Inouye Iran Contra Closing Remarks*, https://www.c-span.org/video/?c4593554/user-clip-daniel-inouye-iran-contra-closing-remarks.

20 Huxley, *Brave New World*, xvi.

21 Rapp and Jenkins, *Chart: These 6 Companies Control Much of U.S. Media*, https://fortune.com/longform/media-company-ownership-consolidation/.

22 "User Clip: Pelosi explaining Smear Tactics," https://www.c-span.org/video/?c4754168/user-clip-pelosi-explaining-smear-tactics, June 22, 2017.

23 Project Veritas, "PART 1: CNN Director ADMITS Network Engaged in 'Propaganda' to Remove Trump from Presidency … 'Our Focus Was to Get Trump Out of Office' … 'I Came to CNN Because

I Wanted to Be a Part of That,'" https://www.projectveritas.com/news/part-1-cnn-director-admits-network-engaged-in-propaganda-to-remove-trump/, April 13, 2021; and Project Veritas, "PART 2: CNN Director Charlie Chester Reveals How Network Practices 'Manipulation' to 'Change the World': 'There's an Art to Manipulation… Inflection, Saying Things Twice … It's Always Like Leading Them in a Direction Before They Even Open Their Mouths,'" https://www.projectveritas.com/news/part-2-cnn-director-charlie-chester-reveals-how-network-practices/, April 14, 2021; "PART 3: CNN Director Charlie Chester Says Network Is 'Trying To Help' The Black Lives Matter Movement By Protecting The Group's Narrative On Race … 'I Haven't Seen Anything About Focusing On The Color Of People's Skin That Aren't White,'" https://www.projectveritas.com/news/part-3-cnn-director-charlie-chester-says-network-is-trying-to-help-the-black/, April 15, 2021.

24 Weiss, https://www.bariweiss.com/resignation-letter.

25 Haddad, *[Investigation:] Lies, Newsweek and Control of the Media Narrative – First-Hand Account*, https://www.tareqhaddad.com/investigation-lies-newsweek-and-control-of-the-media-narrative-first-hand-account/.

26 US Senate's "Final Report of the Select Committee to Study Government Operations with Respect to Intelligence Activities," April 1976. Internet archives link: https://archive.org/details/finalreportofsel01unit/page/454/mode/2up?q=cia+currently+maintains.

27 Alford and Graham, *An offer they couldn't refuse*, https://www.theguardian.com/film/2008/nov/14/thriller-ridley-scott.

28 Patterson, *The caring, sharing CIA*, https://www.theguardian.com/film/2001/oct/05/artsfeatures. PR Week, *Barry named CIA entertainment liaison*, https://www.prweek.com/article/1257404/barry-named-cia-entertainment-liaison.

29 Alford and Graham, *An offer they couldn't refuse*, https://www.theguardian.com/film/2008/nov/14/thriller-ridley-scott.

30 Ibid.

31 Ibid.

32 Riffee, *CIA Pitches Scripts to Hollywood*, https://www.wired.com/2011/09/cia-pitches-hollywood/.

33 Ibid.

34 Evje, *'TOP GUN' BOOSTING SERVICE SIGN-UPS*, https://www.latimes.com/archives/la-xpm-1986-07-05-ca-20403-story.html.

35 Lowry, *The '24' Effect: How 'Liberal Hollywood' Carried Water For Torture*, https://variety.com/2014/tv/news/the-24-effect-how-liberal-hollywood-carried-water-for-torture-1201378516/#!.

36 IN-Q-TEL, *GOOGLE ACQUIRES KEYHOLE CORPORATION*, October 27, 2004, https://www.iqt.org/news/google-acquires-keyhole-corporation/.

37 Edwards, *Social Media Is a Tool of the CIA. Seriously*, https://www.cbsnews.com/news/social-media-is-a-tool-of-the-cia-seriously/.

38 Haddad, *Twitter Executive Revealed to Be 'Psyops' Soldier Linked to*

Spreading Disinformation Across Social Media: 'A Threat to Our Democracy,' https://www.newsweek.com/twitter-executive-revealed-psyops-soldier-spreading-disinformation-across-social-media-1462406.

39 Project Veritas, *UNDERCOVER VIDEO: Twitter Engineers To "Ban a Way of Talking" Through "Shadow Banning," Algorithms to Censor Opposing Political Opinions*, https://www.projectveritas.com/news/undercover-video-twitter-engineers-to-ban-a-way-of-talking-through-shadow-banning-algorithms-to-censor-opposing-political-opinions/.

40 "BREAKING: Facebook Whistleblowers Expose LEAKED INTERNAL DOCS Detailing New Effort to Secretly Censor Vaccine Concerns on a Global Scale," https://www.projectveritas.com/news/breaking-facebook-whistleblowers-expose-leaked-internal-docs-detailing-new/, May 24, 2021.

41 Fleetwood, "Fauci Colluded With Mark Zuckerberg On Facebook COVID-19 'Information Hub,' Emails Show," https://thefederalist.com/2021/06/02/fauci-colluded-with-mark-zuckerberg-on-facebook-covid-19-information-hub-emails-show/.

42 Schwartz, "WH's Psaki: "We're Flagging Problematic Posts For Facebook That Spread Disinformation," https://www.realclearpolitics.com/video/2021/07/15/psaki_were_flagging_problematic_posts_for_facebook_that_spread_disinformation.html.

43 "Facebook's New Extremism Warning! (For Your Protection)," https://www.youtube.com/watch?v=XPEKNYJ9gm0&t=277s, July 10, 2021.

44 Richardson, *'Orwellian': Facebook faces backlash for 'harmful extremist content' alerts*, https://www.washingtontimes.com/news/2021/jul/4/backlash-hits-facebook-over-new-extremist-content-/, July 4, 2021.

45 Kraemer, *Facebook's warning users of 'harmful, extremist content,'* https://justthenews.com/accountability/media/facebooks-warning-users-harmful-extremist-content-provide-support-exposed, July 2, 2021.

46 Culliford, "Facebook and tech giants to target attacker manifestos, far-right militias in database," https://www.reuters.com/technology/exclusive-facebook-tech-giants-target-manifestos-militias-database-2021-07-26/.

47 PR Newswire, "PayPal Partners with ADL to Fight Extremism and Protect Marginalized Communities," https://markets.businessinsider.com/news/stocks/paypal-partners-with-adl-to-fight-extremism-and-protect-marginalized-communities-1030645308.

48 Nix, "Facebook Removed 18 Million Misleading Posts on Covid-19," https://www.msn.com/en-us/money/other/facebook-removed-18-million-misleading-posts-on-covid-19/ar-BB1gUzo9.

49 Clarke, "Covid-19: Who fact checks health and science on Facebook?" https://www.bmj.com/content/373/bmj.n1170.

50 Manscar, Twitter, *Facebook censor Post over Hunter Biden exposé*, https://nypost.com/2020/10/14/facebook-twitter-block-the-post-from-posting/.

51 Iyengar, *Robert F. Kennedy Jr. has been banned from Instagram*, https://www.cnn.com/2021/02/10/tech/robert-kennedy-jr-instagram-ban/index.html, February 11, 2021.

52 Lovelace, *James O'Keefe of Project Veritas banned from Twitter*, https://www.washingtontimes.com/news/2021/apr/15/james-okeefe-project-veritas-banned-twitter/.

53 Sonmez and Wang, *YouTube suspends Ron Johnson for a week after GOP senator touts questionable drugs to fight covid-19*, https://www.washingtonpost.com/politics/sen-johnson-youtube-coronavirus-medicine/2021/06/11/1055ce46-caf0-11eb-81b1-34796c7393af_story.html.

54 Guzman, "Famous feminist Naomi Wolf banned from Twitter," https://thehill.com/changing-america/well-being/557120-famous-feminist-naomi-wolf-banned-from-twitter.

55 Halon, "Ex-Clinton adviser Naomi Wolf warns US becoming 'totalitarian state before our eyes' under Biden," https://www.foxnews.com/media/naomi-wolf-tucker-clinton-adviser-biden-lockdowns.

56 McGregor, "YouTube Censors North Carolina County Government Meeting," July 14, 2021.

57 Keane, "BREAKING: Twitter Suspends Arizona Audit And Audit War Room Accounts, Wendy Rogers Predicts 'I Will Be Next,' https://nationalfile.com/breaking-twitter-suspends-arizona-audit-and-audit-war-room-accounts-wendy-rogers-predicts-i-will-be-next/. Accounts related to election audits in Pennsylvania, Wisconsin, Nevada, and Georgia were also suspended: https://www.zerohedge.com/political/twitter-suspends-2020-election-audit-accounts-multiple-states.

58 Lovelace, "Trump announces lawsuits against Twitter, Facebook and Google," https://www.washingtontimes.com/news/2021/jul/7/donald-trump-plans-lawsuit-against-facebook-twitte/.

59 Riley, "Why Did Amazon Cancel Justice Thomas?" *Wall Street Journal*, March 2, 2021 https://www.wsj.com/articles/why-did-amazon-cancel-justice-thomas-11614727562

60 Svab, *Amazon Quietly Bans Books Containing Undefined 'Hate Speech,'* https://www.theepochtimes.com/amazon-quietly-bans-books-containing-undefined-hate-speech_3716038.html, March 1, 2021.

61 *Holocaust Encyclopedia*, *BOOK BURNING*, https://encyclopedia.ushmm.org/content/en/article/book-burning.

62 "Wikipedia co-founder: I no longer trust the website I created," https://unherd.com/thepost/wikipedia-co-founder-i-no-longer-trust-the-website-i-created/.

63 Rothbard, *For a New Liberty*, 13.

64 Ibid., 14.

65 Ibid., 14–15.

66 Kinzer, *Poisoner in Chief*, 24.

67 Ibid., 12.

68 Australia had a similar program called Matchbox. See Traynor, *UK arranged transfer of Nazi scientists to Australia*, https://www.theguardian.com/uk/1999/aug/17/iantraynor.

69 Kinzer, *Poisoner in Chief*, 21.

70 Schumm, *What Was Operation Paperclip?*, https://www.history.com/news/what-was-operation-paperclip.

71 Kinzer, *Poisoner in Chief*, 43.

72 According to Kinzer, Bluebird officials "injected captured North Korean soldiers with drugs including sodium amytal, a depressant that can have hypnotic side effects, and with three potent stimulants: Benzedrine, which affects the central nervous system; Coramine, which acts on the lungs; and Picrotoxin, a convulsant that can cause seizures and respiratory paralysis. While they were in the weakened state of transition between the effects of depressants and stimulants, CIA experimenters subjected them to hypnosis, electroshock, and debilitating heat. Their goal, according to one report, was 'to induce violent cathartic reactions, alternately putting subjects to sleep, then waking them up until they were sufficiently confused to be coerced into reliving an experience from their past.' CIA officials in Washington ordered the officers who carried out these experiments to keep their true nature secret even from the American military units with which they were working, and to say only that they were conducting 'intensive polygraph work.'" Ibid., 44.

73 Ibid., 55–56.

74 Cornwell, *Obituary: Sidney Gottlieb*, https://www.independent.co.uk/arts-entertainment/obituary-sidney-gottlieb-1080920.html.

75 Kinzer, *Poisoner in Chief*, 2.

76 Ibid.

77 Cornwell, *Obituary: Sidney Gottlieb*, https://www.independent.co.uk/arts-entertainment/obituary-sidney-gottlieb-1080920.html.

78 As cited in Rutz et al. in Noblitt and Noblitt (Ed.), *Ritual Abuse in the Twenty-First Century*, 34.

79 As cited in Ibid., 32. Additionally, Hal Pepinsky, professor emeritus of criminal justice at Indiana University–Bloomington, commented on the uniformity of the stories told by survivors of mind-control abuse (and also cult abuse): "If these narratives are essentially fabricated, they must have been fabricated in many different ways at once. It would require a more elaborate 'conspiracy' to account for how similar narratives could be falsely implanted in so many survivors' minds in so many different ways (e.g., 'memories' that arise before therapy in some cases and after therapy in others, in childhood in some cases and only long afterward in adulthood in others) than to account for how so many cults and mind-control programmers could operate in secret, with impunity." See S.M.A.R.T Ritual Abuse Pages, *The Official Story vs. Reality: Survivors as Whistleblowers*, https://ritualabuse.us/smart-conference/2011-conference/the-official-story-vs-reality-survivors-as-whistleblowers/.

80 Bain, *The Control of Candy Jones*, 8. This quotation comes from the opening segment of the 1977 edition of the book, written by Bain and included prior to the foreword, titled "Candy Jones Vindicated: The CIA Releases Its '*Behavior Modification Files.*'"

81 Ibid., 21–22.

82 Ibid., 25.

83 Ibid., 48.

84 Ibid., 51–52.

85 Ibid., 96.
86 Ibid., 209–212.
87 Ibid., 159, 172, 245.
88 Ibid., 263–264.
89 Ibid., 192.
90 Ibid., 198.
91 Ibid., 254.
92 Ibid., 256.
93 Ibid., 146.
94 Ibid., 10.
95 Ibid., 6–7.
96 Stebner, *Bobby Kennedy assassin still claims he was 'victim of mind control and his gun didn't fire fatal shot' in new appeal after parole is denied*, https://www.dailymail.co.uk/news/article-2066883/Robert-F-Kennedy-assassin-Sirhan-Sirhan-claims-victim-mind-control.html.
97 A framework often referenced by author David Icke.
98 False Flags with Richard Dolan, *False Flags of the Nazi Party* (August 22, 2017).
99 United States Holocaust Memorial Museum, *Reichstag Fire Decree*, https://www.ushmm.org/learn/timeline-of-events/1933-1938/reichstag-fire-decree.
100 *Memorandum for the Secretary of Defense, Unclassified*, https://archive.org/details/OperationNorthwoods.
101 A comparison often made by Murray Rothbard.
102 Stanton, "The Ten Stages of Genocide," https://www.genocidewatch.com/tenstages.
103 Information about the Star of David in Nazi Germany is summarized by the United States Holocaust Memorial Museum's website, https://www.ushmm.org/learn/timeline-of-events/1939-1941/jewish-badge-decreed.
104 *Testimony for Tom Lantos Human Rights Commission Hearing November 10, 2009 Wujian, citizen of the People's Republic of China*, https://chrissmith.house.gov/uploadedfiles/2_wujian_testimony.pdf. Mosher, *How Peru forced poor women to get sterilized — and robbed one mother of her life*, https://nypost.com/2019/12/07/how-peru-forced-poor-women-to-get-sterilized-and-robbed-one-mother-of-her-life/.
105 Mabuse, *Namibian women were sterilized without consent, judge rules*, https://www.cnn.com/2012/07/30/world/africa/namibia-forced-sterilization/index.html.
106 Morse, Sterilization Camps in India, https://www.pop.org/sterilization-camps-in-india/.
107 Ross, *The C.I.A. Doctors*, 22–23.
108 Ibid., 23–25.
109 Ibid., 28.

Chapter 4

1 Douglass, *Narrative of the Life of Frederick Douglass*, 10.
2 Larken Rose has often made this point.

3 As cited in Rothbard, *For a New Liberty*, 5.
4 As cited in Ibid., 6–7.
5 Ibid., 8.
6 Ibid., 84.
7 Rothbard, *The Ethics of Liberty*, 176.
8 Rose, *The Most Dangerous Superstition*, 149.
9 Rothbard, *Anatomy of the State*, 16.
10 Rothbard, *Society Without a State*, https://www.lewrockwell.com/1970/01/murray-n-rothbard/how-anarchism-can-work/. Instead of using the term *voluntarist society*, he calls it an *anarchist society*. The terms are conceptually equivalent in the context of this discussion.
11 Technically, one's body counts as private property, as defined in this book; however, it's often mentioned separately from other private property to avoid confusion. For example, many political economists might use the term *person and property* to make clear that individuals own themselves in addition to external property—even though this phrasing is redundant, since "person" *is* property. In several instances throughout the book, this sort of redundant phrasing is included, just in case readers need a reminder that our bodies shouldn't be excluded from the nonaggression principle.
12 Intellectual property, such as patent protection, is more abstract, and therefore its boundaries are more difficult to define. Concequently, the nature and extent of intellectual-property rights would need to be determined within various factions of a voluntarist society.
13 Block, *Defending the Undefendable II*, xiii.
14 Ibid., xiii–xiv. An additional note: With regard to land, homesteading implies ownership exclusively over the area into which labor has been mixed. That means the resources underground and the air above one's homesteaded property are not necessarily private property until they, too, have been homesteaded. The ground below could be homesteaded by way of mining, and the air above by trafficking airliners using airspace, for example.
15 Rothbard, *For a New Liberty*, 37.
16 Block, *Defending the Undefendable II*, xiii.
17 Rothbard, *For a New Liberty*, 50.
18 "Ten Things You Should Know About Socialism | Thomas J. DiLorenzo," https://www.youtube.com/watch?v=vFrrovr7GVs, July 22, 2019.
19 Ibid.
20 Rothbard, *For a New Liberty*, 51.
21 Ibid., 50–51.
22 Ibid., 52.
23 Ibid., 15.
24 In Marx and Engels's *The Communist Manifesto*, the authors mention "Abolition of property in land" as a core tenet of a communist society (p. 30). Furthermore, they comment, "[T]he theory of Communism may be summed up in the single sentence: Abolition of private property" (p. 23). The sentence seems to refer specifically to private property of the "bourgeois" class.

25 Rothbard, *For a New Liberty*, 34.
26 Ibid.
27 Courtois et al., *The Black Book of Communism*, 4.
28 Ibid.
29 The National WWII Museum New Orleans, "How Did Hitler Happen?" https://www.nationalww2museum.org/war/articles/how-did-hitler-happen.
30 Rockwell, "What Is Fascism? It's the System We've Been Living under for Decades," https://mises.org/wire/what-fascism-its-system-weve-been-living-under-decades.
31 For example, economist George Reisman explains how fascism in Nazi Germany obstructed private-property rights in his article "Why Nazism Was Socialism and Why Socialism Is Totalitarian": "What [Ludwig von] Mises identified was that private ownership of the means of production existed *in name only* under the Nazis and that the actual substance of ownership of the means of production resided in the German government. For it was *the German government* and not the nominal private owners that exercised all of the *substantive powers of ownership*: it, not the nominal private owners, decided what was to be produced, in what quantity, by what methods, and to whom it was to be distributed, as well as what prices would be charged and what wages would be paid, and what dividends or other income the nominal private owners would be permitted to receive. The position of the alleged private owners, Mises showed, was reduced essentially to that of government pensioners. *De facto* government ownership of the means of production, as Mises termed it, was logically implied by such fundamental collectivist principles embraced by the Nazis as that the common good comes before the private good and the individual exists as a means to the ends of the State. If the individual is a means to the ends of the State, so too, of course, is his property. Just as he is owned by the State, his property is also owned by the State. But what specifically established *de facto* socialism in Nazi Germany was the introduction of price and wage controls in 1936. These were imposed in response to the inflation of the money supply carried out by the regime from the time of its coming to power in early 1933. The Nazi regime inflated the money supply as the means of financing the vast increase in government spending required by its programs of public works, subsidies, and rearmament. The price and wage controls were imposed in response to the rise in prices that began to result from the inflation." [emphasis in original] See https://mises.org/library/why-nazism-was-socialism-and-why-socialism-totalitarian.
32 Rockwell, "What Is Fascism? It's the System We've Been Living under for Decades," https://mises.org/wire/what-fascism-its-system-weve-been-living-under-decades.
33 "Ten Things You Should Know About Socialism | Thomas J. DiLorenzo," https://www.youtube.com/watch?v=vFrrovr7GVs, July 22, 2019.
34 For example, see Hayek, *The Road to Serfdom*, chapter 12.
35 Ibid., 4.

36 Foreword by Martin Malia to Courtois et al., *The Black Book of Communism*, xvii.

37 For example, see Ep. 1940 of the Tom Woods Show titled "Helping the Poor Without the State," which features a new app called DonorSee. In a voluntarist society, many new technologies such as this might emerge.

38 In their 2017 paper published in the peer-reviewed academic journal *Economics, Management, and Financial Markets*, they note: "The acute problem lies within repeat users of the welfare system or people who get used to living in social assistance programs and they have no desire to depart. After a while these chronic recipients begin to expect things rather than be grateful for aid when they cannot help themselves." See Fast et al., *Welfare Harms Its Ostensible Beneficiaries*, 55.

39 Benjamin Franklin made an observation along these lines in 1766: "I am for doing good to the poor, but I differ in opinion of the means. I think the best way of doing good to the poor is not making them easy in poverty, but leading or driving them out of it. In my youth I travelled much, and I observed in different countries that the more public provisions were made for the poor, the less they provided for themselves, and of course became poorer. And, on the contrary, the less was done for them, the more they did for themselves, and became richer." See Franklin, Benjamin (1987), "'On the Price of Corn, and Management of the Poor,' *London Chronicle*, November 1766," in J. A. Leo Lemay (ed.), *Writings*. New York: Library of America, 587–588 (as cited in Fast et al.).

40 A central bank, or something like it, could theoretically be offered within a service provider's suite of services, and members of communities could voluntarily subscribe if they so choose.

41 As Rothbard states in *The Case Against the Fed*, 8: "The public, in the mythology of the Fed and its supporters, is a great beast, continually subject to a lust for inflating the money supply and therefore for subjecting the economy to inflation and its dire consequences. Those dreaded all-too-frequent inconveniences called 'elections' subject politicians to these temptations, especially in political institutions such as the House of Representatives who come before the public every two years and are therefore particularly responsive to the public will. The Federal Reserve, on the other hand, guided by monetary experts independent of the public's lust for inflation, stands ready at all times to promote the long-run public interest by manning the battlements in an eternal fight against the Gorgon of inflation. The public, in short, is in desperate need of absolute control of money by the Federal Reserve to save it from itself and its short-term lusts and temptations. One monetary economist, who spent much of the 1920s and 1930s setting up Central Banks throughout the Third World, was commonly referred to as 'the money doctor.' In our current therapeutic age, perhaps [former Fed chair Alan Greenspan] and his confreres would like to be considered as monetary 'therapists,' kindly but stem taskmasters whom we invest with total power to save us from ourselves."

42 The list of prominent Austrian economists can be found in Paul, *Liberty Defined*, 17. For a summary of the basics of the Austrian School of economics, the following lecture by Joseph Salerno is a good starting point: "The Birth of the Austrian School | Joseph T. Salerno," https://www.youtube.com/watch?v=xdepDj8C4D0, July 16, 2019.
43 I thank Dr. Walter Block for making this distinction clear in a personal correspondence.
44 Paul, *Liberty Defined*, 17.
45 The Attractiveness of Austrian Economics | Thomas E. Woods, Jr., https://www.youtube.com/watch?v=DStLhWMRERM, July 21, 2013.
46 von Mises, *Human Action*, 332.
47 Ibid., 427.
48 Block and Barnett, *Transitivity and the Money Pump*, 239. https://cdn.mises.org/qjae15_2_5.pdf.
49 Dr. Walter Block often explains pricing in this manner. For example, "An Austrian Critique of Mainstream Economics | Walter Block," https://www.youtube.com/watch?v=ua_tJbdmNmo, August 2, 2016.
50 Paul, *Liberty Defined*, 17.
51 This argument is often made by Austrian economists and is summarized in the article "4 Reasons Why Socialism Fails," https://mises.org/wire/4-reasons-why-socialism-fails. Also, see Rothbard, *For a New Liberty*, 247–248. Jonathan Newman's quotation is from his Twitter post on July 5, 2021, https://twitter.com/NewmanJ_R/status/1412154304623005701.
52 For those interested in learning more about the basics of these principles, the Mises Institute's YouTube channel includes a helpful "Economics for Beginners" series, https://www.youtube.com/playlist?list=PLALopHfWkFlFdEr_xv1hpqo65zq4eLBcG.
53 Rothbard, *Man, Economy, and State with Power and Market*, 1024.
54 "Ten Things You Should Know About Socialism | Thomas J. DiLorenzo," July 22, 2019, https://www.youtube.com/watch?v=vFrrovr7GVs.
55 Hayek, "The Pretense of Knowledge," https://cdn.mises.org/A%20Free-Market%20Monetary%20System%20and%20The%20Pretense%2z0of%20Knowledge_4.pdf.
56 Rockwell, "Why Professors Hate the Market," https://mises.org/library/why-professors-hate-market.
57 Rothbard, *For a New Liberty*, 71–72.
58 Paul, *Liberty Defined*, 168.
59 Ibid., 169.
60 Ibid.
61 Rothbard, *America's Great Depression*, xxvii.
62 Ibid., 186.
63 For example, see Ibid., 28–29.
64 Ibid., 336–337.
65 "The Mises View: 'Income Inequality' | Joseph T. Salerno," https://www.youtube.com/watch?v=HBIkj6UdlQg, February 5, 2014.
66 Ibid.

67 For a short explanation, see "What Is Cronyism?" https://www.youtube.com/watch?v=4b5cyrVmafU&t=4s, February 4, 2021.

68 "Monopoly Is Everywhere, Say Mainstream Economists; Austrians Roll Eyes," https://www.youtube.com/watch?v=3g7vkb_f89s, July 29, 2015.

69 Rothbard, *Man, Economy, and State with Power and Market*, 669.

70 Rothbard, *For a New Liberty*, 222.

71 Paul, *End the Fed*, 10. Paul continues: "I thought I was immune to being shocked by what our government does, but the actions of the Fed in 2008-2009 went beyond the pale. Not only did the Fed create many trillions of dollars and pass them out, it refused to explain its actions. This shows the arrogance of the members of the Fed and the complete apathy of the Congress in assuming its responsibility to protect the people and follow the law."

72 Rothbard, *The Case Against the Fed*, 3.

73 For more nuance on this topic, and the general theory of money from an Austrian perspective, see Block, "Bitcoin, the Regression Theorem, and the Emergence of a New Medium of Exchange," https://mises.org/library/bitcoin-regression-theorem-and-emergence-new-medium-exchange.

74 Paul, *Liberty Defined*, 201–202.

75 These terms are often used by Ron Paul, for example.

76 "Rothbard's Case Against the Fed," https://www.youtube.com/watch?v=Pv4CwF-579s, February 5, 2021.

Chapter 5

1 "The Curse of Economic Nationalism | Thomas J. Dilorenzo," July 22, 2021, https://www.youtube.com/watch?v=GNW5cMJOsPw.

2 Rothbard, *For a New Liberty*, 242.

3 "Ep. 1875 Michael Malice on How to Make Radical Ideas Approachable," https://www.youtube.com/watch?v=k0jdavqhZe4&t=2182s, April 13, 2021.

4 "The Curse of Economic Nationalism | Thomas J. Dilorenzo," July 22, 2021, https://www.youtube.com/watch?v=GNW5cMJOsPw.

5 Rose, *The Most Dangerous Superstition*, 153.

6 "Society Without State: Private Law Society | Hans-Hermann Hoppe," https://youtu.be/TlWGA9H5An4, May 17, 2012.

7 Rothbard, *For a New Liberty*, 268–269.

8 Ibid., 270. Creative ideas on the topic are insurance are also discussed frequently by Hans-Hermann Hoppe. For example, see Hoppe, "The Idea of a Private Law Society," https://mises.org/library/idea-private-law-society.

9 Rothbard, *For a New Liberty*, 273.

10 Ibid.

11 In fact, during a Mises Institute discussion in 2015 about crime management in a libertarian society, reference was made to an existing private security company in Detroit that does this. At the time of the interview, the company served roughly one thousand households and five hundred

businesses. While their clients were primarily from the upper class, the company also served lower-income individuals because of the profits it made elsewhere. As an example, it partnered with local prosecutors to serve domestic-violence victims (taking their children to school, guarding them, and transporting them to and from court). Also, the company provided free self-defense training to families with children. See "Tate Fegley: Crime and Punishment in a Libertarian Society," https://www.youtube.com/watch?v=8Tonyri5Xys, July 9, 2015.

12 Rothbard, *For a New Liberty*, 71.

13 Ibid., 298. Rothbard cites Joseph Peden, 'Stateless Societies,' p. 3; and Kathleen Hughes, introduction to A. Jocelyn Otway-Ruthven, *A History of Medieval Ireland* (New York: Barnes and Noble, 1968).

14 Ibid.

15 The ideas around military possibilities in a voluntarist society are summarized here from the work of Rothbard, *For a New Liberty*, 297–299.

16 Ibid., 277, 283, 290. With regard to arbitration, Rothbard commented: "[T]he modern arbitration movement began in full force in England during the time of the American Civil War, with merchants increasingly using the 'private courts' provided by voluntary arbitrators, even though the decisions were not legally binding. By 1900, voluntary arbitration began to take hold in the United States. In fact, in medieval England, the entire structure of merchant law, which was handled clumsily and inefficiently by the government's courts, grew up in private merchants' courts" (p. 277). Regarding admiralty law, Rothbard noted: "[T]he State was not interested [in admiralty law], and its jurisdiction did not apply to the high seas; so the shippers themselves took on the task of not only applying, but working out the whole structure of admiralty law in their own private courts. Again, it was only later that government appropriated admiralty law into its own courts" (p. 283).

17 Hoppe, "The Idea of a Private Law Society," https://mises.org/library/idea-private-law-society.

18 Hansas, "The Myth of the Rule of Law" in *The Anarchist Handbook*, 346.

19 Ibid., 345–346.

20 Rothbard, *For a New Liberty*, 278.

21 Ibid.

22 Hansas, "The Myth of the Rule of Law" in *The Anarchist Handbook*, 347.

23 Many of the ideas in this section are mere summaries of Walter Block's analysis in *The Privatization of Roads & Highways*. The ideas also draw from the foreword by Brad Edmonds.

24 For a discussion on pollution, see Rothbard, *For a New Liberty*, 319–323.

25 Rothbard, *For a New Liberty*, 327.

26 See the book summary of Block and Nelson, *Water Capitalism: The Case for Privatizing Oceans, Rivers, Lakes, and Aquifers*.

27 Many of the ideas here are summaries adapted from Rothbard, *For a New Liberty*, 301–327 (chapter on "Conservation, Ecology, and Growth").

Chapter 6

1 Figure reconstructed from NASA introduction to electromagnetic spectrum, https://science.nasa.gov/ems/01_intro. This figure and the associated caption were also included in Gober, *An End to Upside Down Thinking*, chapter 3.

2 *Radical humility* is a term often used by Dr. David Hawkins.

3 This pyramid and others in the book have been adapted from the work of Dr. Dean Radin (for example, see his book *Real Magic*).

4 An analogy along these lines is presented by Dr. Gary Schwartz, for example, see "Is Consciousness More than the Brain?" at http://open-sciences.org/gary-schwartz and the accompanying YouTube video at https://www.youtube.com/watch?v=x-6hosFAObI.

5 I initially heard of this analogy through the work of Dr. David Hawkins.

6 *Where Is My Mind?* Podcast, Ep. 2: "Blindfolded."

7 Ibid. and Gober, *An End to Upside Down Thinking*, chapter 2. Also see, for example, Kelly and Presti, "A Psychobiological Perspective on 'Transmission Models'" in *Beyond Physicalism*, by Kelly et al. Additionally, as summarized by Kastrup in his chapter in *Consciousness Unbound* (2021), edited by Edward Kelly and Paul Marshall: "Even more intriguingly, it is well known that psychedelic substances induce powerful experiences of self-transcendence and overwhelmingly richer conscious inner life" (Griffiths, Richards, McCann, & Jesse, 2006; Strassman, 2001; Strassman, Wojtowicz, Luna, & Frecska, 2008). It had been assumed that they did so by exciting parts of the brain. Yet recent neuroimaging studies have shown that psychedelics do largely the opposite (Carhart-Harris et al., 2012, 2016; Lewis et al., 2017; Palhano-Fontes et al., 2015). Moreover, "the magnitude of this decrease [in brain activity] predicted the intensity of the subjective effects" (Carhart-Harris et al., 2012, p. 2138). In other words, the less activated the brain becomes, the more intense the psychedelic experience." (p. 272, Kindle version). See Carhart-Harris, R. L., Erritzoe, D., Williams, T., Stone, J. M., Reed, L. J., Colasanti, A., . . . Nutt, D. J. (2012). Neural correlates of the psychedelic state as determined by fMRI studies with psilocybin. *Proceedings of the National Academy of Sciences*, 109, 2138–2143. Retrieved from https://doi.org/10.1073/pnas.1119598109.

8 Nahm et al. "Terminal Lucidity: A Review and a Case Collection," doi:10.1016/j.archger.2011.06.031.

9 Gober, *An End to Upside Down Thinking*, chapter 2. Also see *Where Is My Mind?* Podcast, Ep. 2: "Blindfolded."

10 Kastrup, *Transcending the Brain*, https://blogs.scientificamerican.com/guest-blog/transcending-the-brain/.

11 *Science* magazine's 125th-anniversary issue, http://www.sciencemag.org/site/feature/misc/webfeat/125th/. The question is phrased as follows: "What is the Biological Basis of Consciousness?"

12 Ibid.

13 Interview with Max Planck, *The Observer* (1931).

14 Schrödinger, *What Is Life? with Mind and Matter*, 139.
15 See Dr. Bernardo Kastrup's books *Why Materialism is Baloney* and *The Idea of the World*, for example.
16 For a discussion on "Six Sigma" statistical results, see Radin, *Real Magic*, 97. Also see Radin, *Supernormal*, *Entangled Minds*, and *The Conscious Universe*. Additional resources include: Tressoldi, *Extraordinary claims require extraordinary evidence: The case of non-local perception, a classical and Bayesian review of evidences*; Williams, *Revisiting the ganzfeld ESP debate: A basic review and assessment*; Mossbridge, Tressoldi, & Utts, *Predictive physiological anticipation preceding seemingly unpredictable stimuli: A meta-analysis*; Bem, Tressoldi, Raberyon, & Duggan, *Feeling the future: A meta-analysis of 90 experiments on the anomalous anticipation of random future events*; Bosch, Steinkamp, & Boller, *Examining psychokinesis: The interaction of human intention with random number generators—a meta-analysis*; Radin, Nelson, Dobyns, & Houtkooper, *Re-examining psychokinesis: Commentary on the Bösch, Steinkamp and Boller meta-analysis*; Nelson, Radin, Shoup, & Bancel, *Correlations of continuous random data with major world events*. Also see global-mind.org/results.html. Additionally, for a summary of Dr. Radin's studies, see https://www.deanradin.com/publications.
17 Radin, *Real Magic*, 97. This book was endorsed by Brian Josephson, Nobel Laureate in physics; and Kary Mullis, PhD, Nobel Laureate in chemistry.
18 Utts, *An Assessment of Evidence for Psychic Functioning*, https://www.ics.uci.edu/~jutts/air.pdf.
19 Cardeña, *The Experimental Evidence for Parapsychological Phenomena: A Review*.
20 See Gober, *An End to Upside Down Thinking*, chapter 4; and *Where Is My Mind?* Podcast, Ep. 4, "CIA Psychic Spying and Knowing the Future." Both the book and the podcast also discuss the Princeton University Engineering Anomalies Research Lab (Dr. Robert Jahn, Brenda Dunne, and Dr. Roger Nelson, for instance).
21 See Gober, *An End to Upside Down Thinking*, chapter 9; and *Where Is My Mind?* Podcast, Eps. 5 ("Near Death Experiences") and 6 ("The Life Review").
22 For example, see Beischel et al. "Anomalous Information Reception by Research Mediums Under Blinded Conditions II: Replication and Extension." Also See Gober, *An End to Upside Down Thinking*, chapter 10; and *Where Is My Mind?* Podcast, Ep. 7 ("Mediumship and Reincarnation").
23 For example, see Guggenheim and Guggenheim, *Hello from Heaven!* Also See Gober, *An End to Upside Down Thinking*, chapter 10; and *Where Is My Mind?* Podcast, Ep. 7 ("Mediumship and Reincarnation").
24 See Gober, *An End to Upside Down Thinking*, chapter 11; and *Where Is My Mind?* Podcast, Ep. 7 ("Mediumship and Reincarnation").
25 Stevenson, *Reincarnation and Biology: Volume I*, 1145.
26 Gober, *An End to Upside Down Thinking*, chapter 3.
27 As cited in Spivack and Saunders, *An Antidote to Violence*, 95.

28 See Gober, *An End to Upside Down Living*, chapter 2 (section titled "Philosophy"). Also see Kastrup, *The Idea of the World*.
29 For example, see Dr. Greyson's chapter "Near-Death Experiences" in *Consciousness Unbound* (2021), edited by Edward Kelly and Paul Marshall. Greyson notes: "NDEs have substantial commonalities with, but can be differentiated from, mystical experiences" (p. 22, Kindle version).
30 Greenwell, *When Spirit Leaps*, 9–10.
31 Faggin, "Consciousness Comes First," 284–285, Kindle version in *Consciousness Unbound,* edited by Edward Kelly and Paul Marshall.
32 Barušs and Mossbridge, *Transcendent Mind*, 25.
33 See Gober, *An End to Upside Down Thinking*, chapter 7, for evidence on psychic abilities in animals (which includes Dr. Sheldrake's work). Also see *Where Is My Mind?* Podcast, Ep. 3: "Telepathy."
34 "Rupert Sheldrake" *Wikipedia* page, accessed on March 1, 2021, https://en.wikipedia.org/wiki/Rupert_Sheldrake.
35 Skeptic, *Skepticism 101*, https://www.skeptic.com/academic-discipline/parapsychology/.
36 "Wikipedia co-founder: I no longer trust the website I created," https://unherd.com/thepost/wikipedia-co-founder-i-no-longer-trust-the-website-i-created/.
37 Sheldrake, *Wikipedia Under Threat*, http://dev.sheldrake.org/about-rupert-sheldrake/blog/wikipedia-under-threat.
38 Ibid.
39 Utts, *An Assessment of Evidence for Psychic Functioning*.
40 Coyne, *Science Is Being Bashed by Academics Who Should Know Better*, https://newrepublic.com/article/117244/jeffrey-kripals-anti-materialist-argument-promotes-esp.
41 Kelly, 'Introduction: Science and Spirituality at a Crossroads' in *Beyond Physicalism*, Kelly et al., xv.
42 Carroll, *The Big Picture*, 154.
43 McKie, *Royal Mail's Nobel guru in telepathy row*, https://www.theguardian.com/uk/2001/sep/30/robinmckie.theobserver.
44 Pinker, Praise for Carroll's *The Big Picture*.
45 Parker and Brusewitz, *A Compendium of the Evidence for Psi*.
46 Closer to Truth. "Lawrence Krauss—Does ESP Make Sense?" YouTube video, 8:30. Posted July 17, 2017. https://youtu.be/5NweHLQmbZE.
47 Jahn and Dunne, *Consciousness and the Source of Reality*, 32.
48 Hofstadter, A Cutoff for Craziness, https://www.nytimes.com/roomfordebate/2011/01/06/the-esp-study-when-science-goes-psychic/a-cutoff-for-craziness.
49 Turing, *Computing Machinery and Intelligence*.
50 Sheldrake, *Dogs That Know When Their Owners Are Coming Home*, 330.
51 Schnabel, *Remote Viewers*, 7.
52 Interview with Ray Hyman, *Austin American-Statesman*, July 14, 2002.
53 Eysenck, *Sense and Nonsense in Psychology*.
54 Rosenblum and Kuttner, *Quantum Enigma*, 255.
55 Robinson, Preface to *The Nag Hammadi Scriptures*, xi–xii.

56 *The Nature of the Rulers* from Ibid., 194.
57 As cited in Radin, *Entangled Minds*, 73.
58 Blumenthal, *The Believer*, 3.
59 Mack, *Passport to the Cosmos*, 288.
60 Tsakiris, *211. Montana State University's Ardy Sixkiller Clarke Compiles 1,000 Accounts of American Indian Contact With UFO Phenomena*, https://skeptiko.com/ardy-sixkiller-clarke-1000-accounts-of-american-indian-contact-with-ufo-phenomena/.
61 Levy, *Dispelling Wetiko*, 45.

Chapter 7

1 See Gober, *An End to Upside Down Thinking*, chapter 9.
2 As noted by the International Association of Near-Death Studies, "The Gallup Organization and near-death research studies have estimated that, as of 1982, some 13 million adults [*sic*] NDEs in the U.S. alone had had one or more NDEs. Add children's NDEs, all experiences world-wide, and all experiences since 1982, and the figure would be much larger. Near-death experiences are uncommon but not rare." https://iands.org/ndes/about-ndes/common-questions.html.
3 For example, see *Esquire's* 2013 article "The Prophet," https://www.esquire.com/entertainment/interviews/a23248/the-prophet/; *The Atlantic's* 2013 article "The 'Proof of Heaven' Author Has Now Been Thoroughly Debunked by Science," https://www.theatlantic.com/culture/archive/2013/07/proof-heaven-author-debunked/313681/; Sam Harris's 2012 article, "This Must Be Heaven," https://samharris.org/this-must-be-heaven/; and Michael Shermer's 2013 article, "Why a Near-Death Experience Isn't Proof of Heaven Did a neurosurgeon go to heaven?" https://www.scientificamerican.com/article/why-near-death-experience-isnt-proof-heaven/.
4 Alexander, "INDEPENDENT MEDICAL REVIEW VALIDATES FACTS," http://ebenalexander.com/independent-medical-review-validates-facts/. Also see Khanna et al., "Full Neurological Recovery From Escherichia coli Meningitis Associated With Near-Death Experience," https://med.virginia.edu/perceptual-studies/wp-content/uploads/sites/360/2018/09/Greyson_-Alexander-JNMD-2018.pdf.
5 As discussed in Gober, *An End to Upside Down Thinking*, chapter 9. Also see *Mindsight: Near-Death and Out-of-Body Experiences in the Blind* by Kenneth Ring and Sharon Cooper.
6 Greyson, *After*, 33.
7 As described in Gober, *An End to Upside Down Living*, chapter 2.
8 Long, *God and the Afterlife*, 40.
9 Mark Gober interview with Alan Hugenot, see https://markgober.com/podcast/.
10 Shushan, *Near-Death Experiences in Indigenous Religions*, 4.
11 See *Where Is My Mind?* Podcast, Ep. 5: "Near-Death Experiences." The

story referenced was mentioned by Dr. Bruce Greyson. Also see the full-length interview with Dr. Greyson at https://www.youtube.com/watch?v=-QYBhzi67NY.

12 See Gober, *An End to Upside Down Thinking*, chapter 9. Also mentioned by van Lommel et al. who noted, "NDE are reported in many circumstances: cardiac arrest in myocardial infarction (clinical death)." From "Near-death experience in survivors of cardiac arrest: a prospective study in the Netherlands" in *The Lancet* (2001), https://pimvanlommel.nl/wp-content/uploads/2017/11/Lancet-artikel-Pim-van-Lommel.pdf.

13 Greyson, *After*, 64–65.

14 Ibid., 67–68.

15 International Association for Near Death Studies, Inc, *AWARE study initial results are published*, https://iands.org/resources/media-resources/front-pagenews/1060-aware-study-initial-results-are-published.html.

16 Woolacott and Peyton, "Verified account of near-death experience in a physician who survived cardiac arrest," *Explore* (2020).

17 "Near-Death Experiences and Mystical Experiences (IANDS Video)," March 7, 2021, https://www.youtube.com/watch?v=3esgYXr9-LY.

18 For example, see Dr. Greyson's chapter "Near-Death Experiences" in *Consciousness Unbound* (2021), edited by Edward Kelly and Paul Marshall.

19 Long, *God and the Afterlife*, 20.

20 Greyson, *After*, 41.

21 Shushan, *Near-Death Experiences in Indigenous Religions*, 223.

22 Van Lommel, *Near-Death Experience, Consciousness, and the Brain*.

23 Greyson, *After*, 41–42.

24 See *Where Is My Mind?* Podcast, Ep. 6: The Life Review. Also see "Mark Gober interviews Dannion Brinkley: The Life Review (in Near-Death Experiences)" at https://www.youtube.com/watch?v=nAm_0LZteCQ.

25 Lorimer, *Resonant Mind*, 401–407 (Kindle).

26 Ibid., 384.

27 Ibid., 390.

28 Ibid., 390–395.

29 Ibid., 313.

30 Ibid., 336.

31 Ibid., 349.

32 Ibid., 372.

33 "Spiritual Notes from Dr. Greyson, Dr. Alexander, and Suzanne Giesemann." https://www.youtube.com/watch?v=0XdGDt9QCUY, April 7, 2021.

34 For more on near-death experiences, see Gober, *An End to Upside Down Thinking*, chapter 9.

35 "Spiritual Notes from Dr. Greyson, Dr. Alexander, and Suzanne Giesemann." https://www.youtube.com/watch?v=0XdGDt9QCUY, April 7, 2021.

36 See *Where Is My Mind?* Podcast, Ep. 6: "The Life Review." Also see "Mark Gober interviews Dannion Brinkley: The Life Review (in Near-Death Experiences)" at https://www.youtube.com/watch?v=nAm_0LZteCQ.

37 See *Where Is My Mind?* Podcast, Ep. 6: "The Life Review."
38 Gober, *An End to Upside Down Living*, 68.
39 As noted by Sean Stone. For example, see his interview with John Lamb Lash: https://www.youtube.com/watch?v=jukIPVRlnDs.
40 Greyson, *After*, 182.
41 Gober, *An End to Upside Down Living*, chapter 3.
42 Sharma and Tucker, *Cases of the Reincarnation Type with Memories from Intermission Between Lives.*
43 This sort of terminology often appears in nondual, spiritual circles. For example, see the work of Rupert Spira.
44 "Spiritual Notes from Dr. Greyson, Dr. Alexander, and Suzanne Giesemann." https://www.youtube.com/watch?v=0XdGDt9QCUY, April 7, 2021.

Chapter 8

1 For example, see *Where Is My Mind?* Podcast, Ep. 5: "Near-Death Experiences," and Ep. 8: "Revolution."
2 As summarized by researcher Helané Wahbeh: "The Princeton Engineering Anomalies Research (PEAR) Laboratory at Princeton University published a paper in 2007 reporting on 12 years of psychokinetic research with RNGs [Random-Number Generators]. The analysis included 12 years of data with 91 participants and 2.5 million trials and produced highly significant results (z = 3.8) demonstrating a psychokinetic effect. Another group at the Institut für Grenzgebiete der Psychologie und Psychohygiene in Freiburg in collaboration with the PEAR aimed to replicate these findings in another large study. Data was collected over three years and included 750,000 trials per condition (experimental/control) and 227 participants. This study did not replicate the same findings of a positive psychokinetic effect for their primary hypothesis (z= 0.6). There were two outlier participants in the PEAR database which resulted in incorrect power calculations for the replication study. Thus, some suggest that the failed replication was 'not the result of elusive micro-PK [psychokinesis] but simply as due to an underpowered study.' Despite the non-significant result of the primary hypothesis of the replication, six pre-planned secondary hypotheses were significant. *Furthermore, when the data of the original PEAR dataset are combined with the replication data, they produce a z score of 3.2 which is still a highly significant effect. Furthermore, regardless of the results of the primary hypothesis of the replication, the positive results of the original PEAR analysis are still valid.*" See Jahn RG, Dunne BJ, Nelson R, et al. "Correlations of random binary sequences with pre-stated operator intention: A review of a 12-year program." *Explore*. 2007; 3: 244–253.
3 See Gober, *An End to Upside Down Thinking*, chapter 8. Also see *Where Is My Mind?* podcast, Ep. 8: "Revolution." A primer on mind-matter interactions was published in 2021 in *Cardiology & Vascular Research* by

Wahbeh from the Institute of Noetic Sciences, titled "Collective Consciousness and Our Sense of Interconnectedness" and is available here: https://25u5243lh1hm2x5eq12ubot6-wpengine.netdna-ssl.com/wp-content/uploads/2021/06/collective-consciousness-and-our-sense-of-interconnectedness.pdf?fbclid=IwAR1OcE1wnhXN60uF13EKvgns2wA-g15eRcuOcty-x-_MBzclgt5fKgk6K1w. Also see Bosch, Steinkamp, & Boller, *Examining psychokinesis: The interaction of human intention with random number generators—a meta-analysis* and Radin, Nelson, Dobyns, & Houtkooper, *Re-examining psychokinesis: Commentary on the Bösch, Steinkamp and Boller meta-analysis*. As Radin et al. state about scientific results on psychokinesis: "We agree with Bösch et al. that the existing experimental database provides high-quality evidence suggestive of a genuine [psychokinetic] effect….In summary, we believe that the cumulative data are now sufficiently persuasive to advance beyond the timid conclusion of 'not proven' and that it is more fruitful to focus on understanding the nature of [psychokinesis] rather than to concentrate solely on the question of existence." Additionally, see Nelson, Radin, Shoup, & Bancel, *Correlations of continuous random data with major world events*; global-mind.org/results.html.

4 Ibid.

5 Spivack and Saunders, *An Antidote to Violence*, 16.

6 Ibid., 20–21.

7 As cited in Ibid., 93.

8 As cited in Ibid., 22.

9 See Gober, *An End to Upside Down Thinking*, chapter 3. In particular, Dean Radin and his colleagues have presented preliminary data suggesting that the mind might indeed have an impact on the physical world. For example, see "Psychophysical modulation of fringe visibility in a distant double-slit optical system," among other related studies, by Radin et al.

10 Conn Henry, *The Mental Universe*.

11 Heisenberg, *Physics and Philosophy: The Revolution in Modern Science*, 80–81.

12 See Gober, *An End to Upside Down Living*, chapter 6; and Caplan, *Eyes Wide Open: Cultivating Discernment on the Spiritual Path*.

13 Rothbard, *Man, Economy, and State with Power and Market*, 1.

14 Ibid., 569.

15 Ibid., 669.

16 Ibid., 96.

17 Ibid., 97.

18 Physicist Stephen Hawking used the term *grand design* in the title of his 2010 book.

19 Hawkins, "Transcending the Levels of Consciousness: A review of the work, 09/06," Audible, chapter 8.

20 For example, see Walter Williams's Introduction to Hayek, *The Road to Serfdom*, 11.

21 "G Edward Griffin on 'Collectivism,'" https://www.youtube.com/watch?v=-nH2Igq1gh8, April 8, 2021.
22 Hayek, *The Road to Serfdom*, 53.
23 Rothbard, *Anatomy of the State*, 9–11.
24 The term *nonduality* is derived from the Hindu philosophy of Advaita Vedanta.
25 For example, often referenced in Rothbard's book *The Ethics of Liberty*.

Chapter 9

1 *Buddha at the Gas Pump* episode with Ken Wilber, April 30, 2018, https://batgap.com/ken-wilber/.
2 These four categories are adapted from the yogic tradition, broadly defined (Jhana Yoga, Karma Yoga, Bhakti Yoga, and Raja Yoga). In the true yogic tradition, there are more specific meanings related to each path. I've intentionally compressed, combined, and simplified the ideas in an attempt to make them accessible here.
3 See Gober, *An End to Upside Down Living*. Also see *Buddha at the Gas Pump* podcast.
4 The distinction between "nonattachment" and "detachment" was often made by David Hawkins.
5 I'm paraphrasing a sentiment he often expressed, though he might have used slightly different wording on different occasions.
6 Hawkins, *Letting Go*, 103–104 (Kindle).
7 Taught by Dr. Ihaleakala Hew Len, for example: https://hooponopono miracle.com/iloveyou-imsorry-pleaseforgiveme-thankyou-mantra/.
8 Dr. Hawkins often used the phrase *way of being in the world*.
9 This phrase comes from Larken Rose, based on his book *The Most Dangerous Superstition*, in which he refers to the belief in the State's authority as the most dangerous superstition (also mentioned in chapter 1).
10 von Mises, *Liberty & Property*, 34–35, https://cdn.mises.org/Liberty%20and%20Property_3.pdf.
11 "Transcript of Farewell Address," http://www.campaignforliberty.org/national-blog/transcript-of-farewell-address/.
12 Larken Rose, in particular, makes this point often.
13 Rockwell, https://www.lewrockwell.com/.
14 Yogananda, *Autobiography of a Yogi*, 332.
15 See Gober, *An End to Upside Down Thinking*, chapter 3.
16 Rothbard, *For a New Liberty*, 403.

Glossary

1 Rose, *The Most Dangerous Superstition*, 34.
2 Rockwell, "What Is Fascism? It's the System We've Been Living under for Decades," https://mises.org/wire/what-fascism-its-system-weve-been-living-under-decades.

3 Spivack and Saunders, *An Antidote to Violence*, 16.
4 Schrödinger, *What Is Life? with Mind and Matter*, 139.
5 Rothbard, *Anatomy of the State*, 11–12.
6 Rothbard, *Society Without a State*, https://www.lewrockwell.com/1970/01/murray-n-rothbard/how-anarchism-can-work/. Instead of using the term *voluntarist society*, he calls it an *anarchist society*. The terms are conceptually equivalent in the context of this discussion.

BIBLIOGRAPHY

Alexander, Eben. "INDEPENDENT MEDICAL REVIEW VALIDATES FACTS." *Dr. Eben Alexander* website, n.d., http://ebenalexander.com/independent-medical-review-validates-facts/.

Alford, Matthew, and Robbie Graham. "An offer they couldn't refuse." *The Guardian*, November 13, 2008. https://www.theguardian.com/film/2008/nov/14/thriller-ridley-scott.

Anderson, Ross. "The Panopticon Is Already Here." *The Atlantic*, September 2020. https://www.theatlantic.com/magazine/archive/2020/09/china-ai-surveillance/614197/.

Archer, Rick. "452. Ken Wilber." *Buddha at the Gas Pump* website, April 30, 2018.

AwakenWithJP. "Facebook's New Extremism Warning! (For Your Protection)." YouTube video, July 10, 2021. https://www.youtube.com/watch?v=XPEKNYJ9gm0&t=277s.

Bain, Donald. *The Control of Candy Jones*. Chicago, Illinois: Playboy Press, 1976.

Barušs, Imants, and Julia Mossbridge. *Transcendent Mind: Rethinking the Science of Consciousness*. Washington, DC: American Psychological Association, 2017.

Bassani, Luigi Marco. *Chaining Down Leviathan: The American Dream of Self-Government 1776–1865*. McClellanville, SC: The Abbeville Institute Press, 2021.

Bates, Daniel. "EXCLUSIVE: Jeffrey Epstein had surveillance cameras hidden throughout his properties worldwide in a 'blackmail scheme' to extort his powerful friends, victims tell new Netflix doc about the pedophile." *Daily Mail*, May 17, 2020. https://www.dailymail.co.uk/news/article-8361607/Jeffrey-Epsteins-surveillance-cameras-blackmail-scheme-extort-powerful-friends.html.

BBC News. "Covid in Sydney: Military deployed to help enforce lockdown." *BBC News* website, July 30, 2021.

Beischel, Julie. *Investigating Mediums: A Windbridge Institute Collection*. Tuscon, AZ: Windbridge Institute, 2015.

Beischel, Julie. "Research into Mental Mediumship." In *Surviving Death: A Journalist Investigates Evidence for an Afterlife*, edited by Leslie Kean. New York: Crown Archetype, 2017.

Beischel, Julie, et al. "Anomalous Information Reception by Research Mediums Under Blinded Conditions II: Replication and Extension." *EXPLORE: The Journal of Science and Healing* 11, no. 2 (2015): 136–42.

Bem, Daryl et al. "Feeling the Future: A Meta-Analysis of 90 Experiments on the Anomalous Anticipation of Random Future Events." *F1000 Research* 4 (2015): 1188. doi: 10.12688/f1000research.7177.1, https://f1000research. com/articles/4-1188/v1.

Biko, Steve. "Black Consciousness and the Quest for True Humanity." *SASO Newsletter*, 1972. https://disa.ukzn.ac.za/sites/default/files/pdf_files/remar72.3.pdf.

Blackall, Molly. "People in England urged to be patient amid reports hugging may soon be allowed." *The Guardian*, May 1, 2021. https://www.theguardian.com/world/2021/may/01/england-urged-to-be-patient-amid-reports-hugging-may-soon-be-allowed.

Block, Walter. *Defending the Undefendable II*. Auburn, AL: Mises Institute, 2018.

Block, Walter. *The Privatization of Roads & Highways: Human and Economics Factors*. Auburn, AL: The Ludwig von Mises Institute, 2009.

Block, Walter, and Peter Nelson. *Water Capitalism: The Case for Privatizing Oceans, Rivers, Lakes, and Aquifers*. Lanham, Maryland: Lexington Books, 2016.

Block, Walter, and William Barnett II. "Transitivity and the Money Pump." *The Quarterly Journal of Austrian Economics*. 15(2), 237–251, 2012.

Blumenthal, Ralph. *The Believer: Alien Encounters, Hard Science, and the Passion of John Mack*. Albuquerque: University of New Mexico Press, 2021.

Bosch, Holger, Fiona Steinkamp, and Emil Boller. "Examining Psychokinesis: The Interaction of Human Intention with Random Number Generators; A Meta-Analysis." *Psychological Bulletin* 132, no. 4 (2006): 497–523.

Brady, Graham. "I believe the real purpose of masks is social control - it's time to turn down the fear dial, writes GRAHAM BRADY, Chairman of the Tory 1922 Committee." *The Daily Mail*, July 17, 2021. https://www.dailymail.co.uk/debate/article-9798365/GRAHAM-BRADY-believe-real-purpose-masks-social-control-time-stop-fear.html.

Britannica. "Thomas B. Reed: Quotes." https://www.britannica.com/biography/Thomas-B-Reed/quotes.

Cadelago, Christopher, and Natasha Korecki. "MAGA media looks to turn White House briefing room into a battlefield." *Politico*, January 25, 2021. https://www.politico.com/news/2021/01/25/maga-media-white-house-briefing-462015.

Caplan, Mariana. *Eyes Wide Open: Cultivating Discernment on the Spiritual Path*. Boulder: Sounds True, 2009.

Cardeña, Etzel. (2018). "The experimental evidence for parapsychological phenomena: A review." *American Psychologist*, 73(5), 663–677. https://doi.org/10.1037/amp0000236.

Carroll, Sean. *The Big Picture: On the Origins of Life, Meaning, and the Universe Itself*. New York: Dutton, 2017.

Chief, Woview. "Dispatch: Countering Criticism of the Warren Report." January 4, 1967, https://history-matters.com/archive/jfk/cia/russholmes/104-10406/104-10406-10110/html/104-10406-10110_0002a.htm.

Clarke, Laurie. "Covid-19: Who fact checks health and science on Facebook?" *BMJ*, 373 (1170): 2021. https://www.bmj.com/content/373/bmj.n1170.

Closer to Truth. "Lawrence Krauss: Does ESP Make Sense?" YouTube Video, July 17, 2017. https://youtu.be/5NweHLQmbZE.

Cohen, Spike. Twitter post, June 30, 2021. https://twitter.com/RealSpikeCohen/status/1410267899625934848.

Cornwell, Rupert. "Obituary: Sidney Gottlieb." *Independent*, October 23, 2011. https://www.independent.co.uk/arts-entertainment/obituary-sidney-gottlieb-1080920.html.

Courtois, Stephane et al. *The Black Book of Communism: Crimes, Terror, Repression*. Cambridge, MA: Harvard University Press, 1999.

Coyne, Jerry. "Science is Being Bashed by Academics Who Should Know Better." *New Republic*, April 3, 2014. https://newrepublic.com/article/117244/jeffrey-kripals-anti-materialist-argument-promotes-esp.

C-SPAN User Clip. "Daniel Inouye Iran Contra Closing Remarks." *C-SPAN*, n.d. https://www.c-span.org/video/?c4593554/user-clip-daniel-inouye-iran-contra-closing-remarks.

C-SPAN User Clip. "Pelosi explaining Smear Tactics." *C-SPAN*, June 22, 2017, https://www.c-span.org/video/?c4754168/user-clip-pelosi-explaining-smear-tactics.

Culliford, Elizabeth. "Facebook and tech giants to target attacker manifestos, far-right militias in database." *Reuters*, July 26, 2021. https://www.reuters.com/technology/exclusive-facebook-tech-giants-target-manifestos-militias-database-2021-07-26/.

Davidson, Laura. "Bitcoin, the Regression Theorem, and the Emergence of a New Medium of Exchange." *The Mises Institute*, September 28, 2018. https://mises.org/library/bitcoin-regression-theorem-and-emergence-new-medium-exchange.

Dittrich, Luke. "The Prophet." *Esquire*, July 2, 2013. https://www.esquire.com/entertainment/interviews/a23248/the-prophet/.

Dolan, Richard. *False Flags of the Nazi Party*, August 22, 2017. https://www.amazon.com/False-Flags-Season-1/dp/B0759YTZPW.

Douglass, Frederick. *Narrative of the Life of Frederick Douglass*. 1846.

Edwards, Jim. "Social Media Is a Tool of the CIA. Seriously." *CBS News*, July 11, 2011. https://www.cbsnews.com/news/social-media-is-a-tool-of-the-cia-seriously/.

Evje, Mark. "'TOP GUN' BOOSTING SERVICE SIGN-UPS." *Los Angeles Times*, July 5, 1986. https://www.latimes.com/archives/la-xpm-1986-07-05-ca-20403-story.html.

Eysenck, H. J. *Sense and Nonsense in Psychology*. Middlesex, UK: Penguin, 1957.

Faggin, Federico. "Consciousness Comes First." In *Consciousness Unbound: Liberating Mind from the Tyranny of Materialism*, edited by Edward Kelly and Paul Marshall. New Lanham, MD: Rowman & Littlefield, 2021.

Fast, Richard et al. "WELFARE HARMS ITS OSTENSIBLE BENEFICIARIES." *Economics, Management, and Financial Markets*. 12(3), 51–66, 2017.

Fleetwood, Shawn. "Fauci Colluded With Mark Zuckerberg On Facebook COVID-19 'Information Hub,' Emails Show." *The Federalist*, June 2, 2021. https://thefederalist.com/2021/06/02/fauci-colluded-with-mark-zuckerberg-on-facebook-covid-19-information-hub-emails-show/.

"Formal Results: Testing the GCP Hypothesis." *Global Consciousness Project* website, n.d. global-mind.org/results.html.

Glass, Andrew. "Eisenhower warns of 'military-industrial complex,' Jan. 17, 1961." *Politico*, January 17, 2019. https://www.politico.com/story/2019/01/17/eisenhower-warns-of-military-industrial-complex-jan-17-1961-1099265.

Gober, Mark. *An End to Upside Down Living: Reorienting Our Consciousness to Live Better and Save the Human Species*. Cardiff-by-the-Sea, CA: Waterside Press, 2020.

Gober, Mark. *An End to Upside Down Thinking: Dispelling the Myth That the Brain Produces Consciousness, and the Implications for Everyday Life*. Cardiff-by-the-Sea, CA: Waterside Press, 2018.

Gober, Mark and Blue Duck Media. *Where Is My Mind?* Podcast (Eps. 1 through 8). June–September 2019.

Gober, Mark. "Mark Gober interviews Dannion Brinkley: The Life Review (in Near-Death Experiences)." YouTube video, April 7, 2020. https://www.youtube.com/watch?v=nAm_0LZteCQ&t=3893s.

Gober, Mark. "Mark Gober interviews Dr. Bruce Greyson from the University of Virginia: Near-Death Experiences." YouTube video, December 5, 2019. https://www.youtube.com/watch?v=-QYBhzi67NY.

Greenwell, Bonnie. *When Spirit Leaps: Navigating the Process of Spiritual Awakening*. Oakland, CA: Non-Duality Press, 2018.

Greyson, Bruce. *After: A Doctor Explores What Near-Death Experiences Reveal about Life and Beyond*. New York: St. Martin's Essentials, 2021.

Greyson, Bruce. "Near-Death Experiences." In *Consciousness Unbound: Liberating Mind from the Tyranny of Materialism*, edited by Edward Kelly and Paul Marshall. New Lanham, MD: Rowman & Littlefield, 2021.

Griffin, Keith. "How Facebook's 'independent fact checkers' cited letter secretly organized by Wuhan lab funder Peter Daszak to 'debunk' leak theory and punish news outlets that explored it." *Daily Mail*, June 5, 2021. https://www.dailymail.co.uk/news/article-9655057/Facebook-fact-checkers-cited-Lancet-letter-Wuhan-lab-funder-Peter-Daszak-debunk-lab-leak.html.

Guggenheim, Bill, and Judy Guggenheim. *Hello from Heaven!* London: Watkins, 1995.

Guzman, Joseph. "Famous feminist Naomi Wolf banned from Twitter." *The Hill* website, June 7, 2021. https://thehill.com/changing-america/well-being/557120-famous-feminist-naomi-wolf-banned-from-twitter.

Haddad, Tareq. "[Investigation:] Lies, Newsweek and Control of the Media Narrative – First-Hand Account." *Tareq Haddad Writer and Journalist*, December 14, 2019. https://www.tareqhaddad.com/investigation-lies-newsweek-and-control-of-the-media-narrative-first-hand-account/.

Haddad, Tareq. "Twitter Executive Revealed to Be 'Psyops' Soldier Linked to Spreading Disinformation Across Social Media: 'A Threat to Our Democracy.'" *Newsweek*, October 1, 2019. https://www.newsweek.com/twitter-executive-revealed-psyops-soldier-spreading-disinformation-across-social-media-1462406.

Hains, Tim. "CNN's Dr. Leana Wen: Make It Clear To People That The Vaccine Is Their 'Ticket Back To Pre-Pandemic Life' And Freedom." *Real Clear Politics*, April 2, 2021. https://www.realclearpolitics.com/video/2021/04/02/cnns_dr_leana_wen_make

_it_clear_to_people_that_the_vaccine_is_their_ticket_back_to_pre-pandemic_life_and_freedom.html#!.

Halon, Yael. "Ex-Clinton adviser Naomi Wolf warns US becoming 'totalitarian state before our eyes' under Biden." *Fox News*, February 22, 2021. https://www.foxnews.com/media/naomi-wolf-tucker-clinton-adviser-biden-lockdowns.

Hansas, John. "The Myth of the Rule of Law," 1995. In *The Anarchist Handbook*, organized by Michael Malice. Michael Malice, 2021.

Hare, Robert. *Without Conscience: The Disturbing World of the Psychopaths Among Us*. New York, NY: The Guilford Press, 1999.

Harris, Sam. "THIS MUST BE HEAVEN." *Sam Harris* website, October 12, 2012. https://samharris.org/this-must-be-heaven/.

Hawkins, David. *Letting Go: The Pathway of Surrender*. Alexandria, Australia: Hay House, 2014.

Hawkins, David. *Transcending the Levels of Consciousness: A Review of the Work, 09/06*. Audible, chapter 8. Veritas: 2006.

Hayek, F. A. *The Road to Serfdom*. London and New York: Routledge Classics, 2001.

Hayek, F. A. "The Pretense of Knowledge." *The American Economic Review*, 79 (6), 3, 1989.

Heisenberg, Werner. *Physics and Philosophy: The Revolution in Modern Science*. New York: HarperPerennial, 1958.

Henry, Richard Conn. "The Mental Universe." *Nature* 436 (July 2005): 29.

Higham, Aliss. "June 21: When will Boris Johnson announce if there is a delay to 'Freedom Day'?" *Express*, June 12, 2021. https://www.express.co.uk/news/uk/1448541/June-21-boris-johnson-announcement-delay-freedom-day-evg.

History.com editors. "Patriot Act," *History.com*, August 21, 2018. https://www.history.com/topics/21st-century/patriot-act.

Hobbes, Thomas. *Leviathan*. USA: Pacific Publishing Studio, 2011.

Hofstadter, Douglas. "A Cutoff for Craziness." *New York Times*, January 7, 2011. https://www.nytimes.com/roomfordebate/2011/01/06/the-esp-study-when-science-goes-psychic/a-cutoff-for-craziness.

Holocaust Encyclopedia. "BOOK BURNING," n.d. https://encyclopedia.ushmm.org/content/en/article/book-burning.

Hoppe, Hans-Hermann. "The Idea of a Private Law Society." *The Mises Institute* website, July 28, 2006. https://mises.org/library/idea-private-law-society.

Huxley, Aldous. *A Brave New World*. New York and London: Harper & Brothers Publishers, 1946.

Hylan, John Francis. *Mayor Hylan of New York: An Autobiography*. New York: Broadway Press, 1922. https://archive.org/details/autobiographyofj00hyla/page/n1/mode/2up?q=octopus.

IANDS. "FREQUENTLY ASKED QUESTIONS ABOUT NDES." *IANDS* website, May 18, 2015. https://iands.org/ndes/about-ndes/common-questions.html.

IANDSvideos. "Near-Death Experiences and Mystical Experiences (IANDS Video)." YouTube video, March 7, 2021. https://www.youtube.com/watch?v=3esgYXr9-LY.

IANDSvideos. "Spiritual Notes from Dr. Greyson, Dr. Alexander, and Suzanne Giesemann." April 7, 2021. https://www.youtube.com/watch?v=0XdGDt9QCUY.

IN-Q-TEL. "GOOGLE ACQUIRES KEYHOLE CORPORATION." *IN-Q-TEL*, October 27, 2004. https://www.iqt.org/news/google-acquires-keyhole-corporation/.

International Association for Near Death Studies. "AWARE Study Initial Results Are Published!" IANDS webpage, July 18, 2017. https://www.iands.org/news/news/front-page-news/1060-aware-study-initial-results-are-published.html.

"Interview with Max Planck." *The Observer*, January 25, 1931.

"Interview with Ray Hyman." Austin American-Statesman, July 14, 2002. As cited in Stephan A. Schwartz, Opening to the Infinite: The Art and Science of Nonlocal Awareness (Buda, TX: Nemoseen Media, 2007).

Iyengar, Rishi. "Robert F. Kennedy Jr. has been banned from Instagram." CNN, February 11, 2021. https://www.cnn.com/2021/02/10/tech/robert-kennedy-jr-instagram-ban/index.html.

Jahn, Robert, and Brenda Dunne. *Consciousness and the Source of Reality: The PEAR Odyssey*. Princeton, NJ: ICRL, 2011.

Kahneman, D., & Tversky, A. (1979). Prospect Theory: An Analysis of Decision under Risk. *Econometrica*, 47(2), 263-291. doi:10.2307/1914185.

Kastrup, Bernardo. "Analytic Idealism and Psi: How a More Tenable Metaphysics Neutralizes a Physicalist Taboo." In *Consciousness Unbound: Liberating Mind from the Tyranny of Materialism*, edited by Edward Kelly and Paul Marshall. New Lanham, MD: Rowman & Littlefield, 2021.

Kastrup, Bernardo. *The Idea of the World: A Multi-Disciplinary Argument for the Mental Nature of Reality*. Hampshire, UK: Iff, 2019.

Kastrup, Bernardo. "Transcending the Brain: At Least Some Cases of Physical Damage Are Associated with Enriched Consciousness or Cognitive Skill." *Scientific American* blog, March 29, 2017. https://blogs.scientificamerican. com/guest-blog/transcending-the-brain/.

Kastrup, Bernardo. *Why Materialism Is Baloney: How True Skeptics Know There Is No Death and Fathom Answers to Life, the Universe and Everything*. Winchester, UK: Iff, 2014.

Keane, Gabriel. "BREAKING: Twitter Suspends Arizona Audit And Audit War Room Accounts, Wendy Rogers Predicts 'I Will Be Next.'" *National File* website, July 27, 2021. https://nationalfile.com/breaking-twitter-suspends-arizona-audit-and-audit-war-room-accounts-wendy-rogers-predicts-i-will-be-next/.

Kelly, Edward, Adam Crabtree, and Paul Marshall, eds. *Beyond Physicalism: Toward Reconciliation of Science and Spirituality*. Lanham, MD: Rowman & Littlefield, 2015.

Kelly, Edward. "Introduction: Science and Spirituality at a Crossroads." In *Beyond Physicalism: Toward Reconciliation of Science and Spirituality*, edited by Edward Kelly, Adam Crabtree, and Paul Marshall. Lanham, MD: Rowman & Littlefield, 2015.

Kelly, Edward, and David Presti. "A Psychobiological Perspective on 'Transmission Models.'" In *Beyond Physicalism: Toward Reconciliation of Science and Spirituality*, edited by Edward Lanham, Adam Crabtree, and Paul Marshall. Lanham, MD: Rowman & Littlefield, 2015.

Kennedy Jr., Robert F. "Epstein and Bill Gates with Whitney Webb." *The Defender Podcast*, May 22, 2021. https://anchor.fm/rfkjr/episodes/Epstein-and-Bill-Gates-with-Whitney-Webb-e11d5g1.

Khanna, Surbhi et al. "Full Neurological Recovery From *Escherichia coli* Meningitis Associated With Near-Death Experience." *The Journal of Nervous and Mental Disease*, 206 (9): 744–747, 2018. https://med.virginia.edu/perceptual-studies/wp-content/uploads/sites/360/2018/09/Greyson_-Alexander-JNMD-2018.pdf.

Kinzer, Stephen. *Poisoner in Chief: Sidney Gottlieb and the CIA Search for Mind Control.* New York, NY: Henry Holt and Company, 2019.

Kraemer, Brianna. "Facebook's warning users of 'harmful, extremist content.'" *Just the News*, July 2, 2021. https://justthenews.com/accountability/media/facebooks-warning-users-harmful-extremist-content-provide-support-exposed.

Leonardi, Anthony. "'Above my pay grade': New Jersey governor claims Bill of Rights did not factor into his coronavirus executive orders." *Washington Examiner*, April 15, 2020, https://www.washingtonexaminer.com/news/above-my-pay-grade-new-jersey-governor-claims-bill-of-rights-did-not-factor-into-his-coronavirus-executive-orders.

Leshan, Bruce. "DC has banned dancing at indoor and outdoor wedding receptions." *WUSA9*, April 29, 2021. https://www.wusa9.com/article/news/local/dc/dc-bans-dancing-at-wedding-receptions/65-bf89fd3f-9011-4d43-b356-9a836c832904.

Levy, Paul. *Dispelling Wetiko: Breaking the Curse of Evil.* Berkeley, CA: North Atlantic Books, 2013.

LibertyInOurTime. "Society Without State: Private Law Society | Hans-Hermann Hoppe." YouTube video, May 17, 2012. https://www.youtube.com/watch?v=TlWGA9H5An4.

Long, Jeffrey, with Paul Perry. *God and the Afterlife: The Groundbreaking New Evidence for God and Near-Death Experience.*" New York: HarperCollins, 2016.

Lorimer, David. *Resonant Mind: Life review in the near-death experience.* Hova Villas, UK: White Crow Books, 2017.

Lovelace, Ryan. "James O'Keefe of Project Veritas banned from Twitter." *The Washington Times*, April 15, 2021. https://www.washingtontimes.com/news/2021/apr/15/james-okeefe-project-veritas-banned-twitter/.

Lovelace, Ryan. "Trump announces lawsuits against Twitter, Facebook and Google." *The Washington Times*, July 7,

2021. https://www.washingtontimes.com/news/2021/jul/7/donald-trump-plans-lawsuit-against-facebook-twitte/.

Lowry, Brian. "The '24' Effect: How 'Liberal Hollywood' Carried Water For Torture." *Variety*, December 14, 2014. https://variety.com/2014/tv/news/the-24-effect-how-liberal-hollywood-carried-water-for-torture-1201378516/#!.

Mabuse, Nkepile. "Namibian women were sterilized without consent, judge rules." CNN, July 31, 2012. https://www.cnn.com/2012/07/30/world/africa/namibia-forced-sterilization/index.html.

Mack, John E. *Passport to the Cosmos: Human Transformation and Alien Encounters* (Commemorative Edition). Guildford, United Kingdom: White Crow Books, 2011 (original version 1999).

Malice, Michael. Twitter post, July 14, 2021. https://twitter.com/michaelmalice/status/1415393899598819331?s=21.

Manskar, Noah. "Twitter, Facebook censor Post over Hunter Biden exposé." *New York Post*, October 14, 2020. https://nypost.com/2020/10/14/facebook-twitter-block-the-post-from-posting/.

Marx, Karl, and Frederick Engels. *The Communist Manifesto*. New York: International Publishers, 1948.

McGregor, Matt. "YouTube Censors North Carolina County Government Meeting." *The Epoch Times*, July 14, 2021. https://www.theepochtimes.com/north-carolina-county-government-meeting-censored-by-youtube_3901107.html.

McKie, Robin. "Royal Mail's Nobel Guru In Telepathy Row." *The Observer*, September 29, 2001. https://www.theguardian.com/uk/2001/sep/30/robinmckie.theobserver.

Meeks, Alexandra. "With a worsening pandemic, California bans singing in places of worship." CNN, July 3, 2020. https://www.cnn.com/2020/07/03/us/california-places-of-worship-pandemiic-trnd/index.html.

"Memorandum for the Secretary of Defense, Unclassified." March 13, 1962. https://archive.org/details/OperationNorthwoods.

Milgram, Stanley. *Obedience to Authority: An Experimental View*. New York: HarperPerennial, 2017.

misesmedia. "The Attractiveness of Austrian Economics | Thomas E. Woods, Jr." YouTube video, July 21, 2013. https://www.youtube.com/watch?v=DStLhWMRERM.

misesmedia. "An Austrian Critique of Mainstream Economics | Walter Block." YouTube video, August 2, 2016. https://www.youtube.com/watch?v=ua_tJbdmNmo.

misesmedia. "The Birth of the Austrian School | Joseph T. Salerno." YouTube video, July 16, 2019. https://www.youtube.com/watch?v=xdepDj8C4D0.

misesmedia. "The Curse of Economic Nationalism | Thomas J. Dilorenzo." YouTube video, July 22, 2021. https://www.youtube.com/watch?v=GNW5cMJOsPw.

misesmedia. "The Mises View: "Income Inequality" | Joseph T. Salerno." YouTube video, February 6, 2014. https://www.youtube.com/watch?v=HBIkj6UdlQg.

misesmedia. "Property and the Social Order | Hans-Hermann Hoppe." YouTube video, August 19, 2011. https://www.youtube.com/watch?v=AQmMe2IeGPU.

misesmedia. "Rothbard's Case Against the Fed." YouTube video, February 5, 2021. https://www.youtube.com/watch?v=Pv4CwF-579s.

misesmedia. "Tate Fegley: Crime and Punishment in a Libertarian Society." YouTube video, July 9, 2015. https://www.youtube.com/watch?v=8Tonyri5Xys.

misesmedia. "Ten Things You Should Know About Socialism | Thomas J. DiLorenzo," YouTube video, July 22, 2019.

misesmedia. "What Is Cronyism?" YouTube video, February 4, 2021. https://www.youtube.com/watch?v=4b5cyrVmafU&t=4s.

Modarressy-Tehrani, Caroline and Grace Murray. "'It just feels surreal': Military posted at checkpoints as Australian state extends COVID-19 lockdown." *NBC News*, August 19, 2020. https://www.nbcnews.com/news/world/it-just-feels-surreal-military-posted-checkpoints-australian-state-extends-n1237068.

Moreell, Ben. "Power Corrupts." *Acton Institute*, July 20, 2010. https://www.acton.org/pub/religion-liberty/volume-2-number-6/power-corrupts.

Morse, Anne Roback. "Sterilization Camps in India." *Population Research Institute*, March 19, 2015. https://www.pop.org/sterilization-camps-in-india/.

Mossbridge J., P. Tressoldi, and J. Utts. "Predictive Physiological Anticipation Preceding Seemingly Unpredictable Stimuli: A Meta-Analysis." *Frontiers in Psychology* 3 (2012): 390. https://www.frontiersin.org/articles/10.3389/ fpsyg.2012.00390/full.

Mueller, Antony P. "4 Reasons Why Socialism Fails." *The Mises Institute*, September 10, 2018. https://mises.org/wire/4-reasons-why-socialism-fails.

Nahm, M. et al. "Terminal Lucidity: A Review and a Case Collection." Archives of Gerontology and Geriatrics 55, no. 1 (2011): 138–42. doi:10.1016/j.archger.2011.06.031

NASA. "Tour of the Electromagnetic Spectrum: Introduction to the Electromagnetic Spectrum." NASA website, n.d. https://science.nasa.gov/ems/01_intro.

National Archives. *JFK Assassination Records: Summary of Findings*, based on 1979 report. https://www.archives.gov/research/jfk/select-committee-report/summary.html

The National WWII Museum New Orleans. "How Did Hitler Happen." *The National WWII Museum New Orleans* website, n.d. https://www.nationalww2museum.org/war/articles/how-did-hitler-happen.

The Nature of the Rulers (author unknown). In *The Nag Hammadi Scriptures*, edited by Marvin Meyer. New York, NY: HarperOne, 2007.

Nelson, Roger et al. "Correlations of Continuous Random Data with Major World Events." *Foundations of Physics Letters*, 15 (2002): 537–50.

Newman, Jonathan. Twitter post, July 5, 2021. https://twitter.com/NewmanJ_R/status/1412154304623005701.

New South Wales Government. "New freedoms for vaccinated first step on state roadmap out of COVID." *New South Wales Government* website, August 26, 2021. https://www.health.nsw.gov.au/news/Pages/20210826_01.aspx.

Nix, Naomi. "Facebook Removed 18 Million Misleading Posts on Covid-19." *Bloomberg*, May 19, 2021. https://www.msn.com/en-us/money/other/facebook-removed-18-million-misleading-posts-on-covid-19/ar-BB1gUzo9.

Noblitt, Randy et al. *Ritual Abuse in the Twenty-First Century: Psychological, Forensic, Social, and Political Considerations*. Brandon, Oregon: Robert D. Reed Publishers, 2008.

Noordhoek, Stefan. Twitter post, July 12, 2021. https://twitter.com/dutchanddonts/status/1414833132822478849?s=20.

1A with Robin. "Robert F. Kennedy Jr on COVID: 'People in authority will abuse every power we relinquish to them!'" YouTube video, December 21, 2020 https://www.youtube.com/watch?v=EBSfsJBYqRo.

"125th Anniversary Issue." *Science* magazine website. http://www.sciencemag.org/site/feature/misc/webfeat/125th/.

O'Neill, Tom with Dan Piepenbring. *CHAOS: Charles Manson, the CIA, and the Secret History of the Sixties*. New York: Hachette Book Group, 2019. Parker, Adrian, and Göran Brusewitz. "A Compendium of the Evidence for Psi." *European Journal of Parapsychology* 18 (2003): 33–51.

Palaszczuk, Annastacia. Twitter post, August 25, 2021. https://twitter.com/AnnastaciaMP/status/1430739214035873795

Patterson, John. "The caring, sharing CIA." *The Guardian*, October 4, 2011. https://www.theguardian.com/film/2001/oct/05/artsfeatures.

Paul, Ron. *End the Fed*. New York, NY: Grand Central Publishing, 2009.

Paul, Ron. *Liberty Defined: 50 Essential Issues That Affect Our Freedom*. New York: Grand Central Publishing, 2011.

Prestigiacomo, Amanda. "'The End Of Conservative Books': Amazon Quietly Bans Books They Deem Offensive, 'Hate Speech.'" *Daily Wire*, February 27, 2021. https://www.dailywire.com/news/the-end-of-conservative-books-amazon-quietly-bans-books-they-deem-offensive-hate-speech.

PR Newswire. "PayPal Partners with ADL to Fight Extremism and Protect Marginalized Communities." *Markets Insider*, July 26, 2021. https://markets.businessinsider.com/news/stocks/paypal-partners-with-adl-to-fight-extremism-and-protect-marginalized-communities-1030645308.

Project Veritas. "BREAKING: Facebook Whistleblowers Expose LEAKED INTERNAL DOCS Detailing New Effort to

Secretly Censor Vaccine Concerns on a Global Scale." Project Veritas, May 24, 2021. https://www.projectveritas.com/news/breaking-facebook-whistleblowers-expose-leaked-internal-docs-detailing-new/.

Project Veritas. "PART 1: CNN Director ADMITS Network Engaged in 'Propaganda' to Remove Trump from Presidency ... 'Our Focus Was to Get Trump Out of Office' ... 'I Came to CNN Because I Wanted to Be a Part of That.'" Project Veritas, April 13, 2021. https://www.projectveritas.com/news/part-1-cnn-director-admits-network-engaged-in-propaganda-to-remove-trump/.

Project Veritas. "PART 2: CNN Director Charlie Chester Reveals How Network Practices 'Manipulation' to 'Change the World': 'There's an Art to Manipulation... Inflection, Saying Things Twice ... It's Always Like Leading Them in a Direction Before They Even Open Their Mouths.'" Project Veritas, April 14, 2021. https://www.projectveritas.com/news/part-2-cnn-director-charlie-chester-reveals-how-network-practices/.

Project Veritas. "PART 3: CNN Director Charlie Chester Says Network Is 'Trying To Help' The Black Lives Matter Movement By Protecting The Group's Narrative On Race ... 'I Haven't Seen Anything About Focusing On The Color Of People's Skin That Aren't White.'" Project Veritas, April 15, 2021. https://www.projectveritas.com/news/part-3-cnn-director-charlie-chester-says-network-is-trying-to-help-the-black/.

Project Veritas. "UNDERCOVER VIDEO: Twitter Engineers To 'Ban a Way of Talking' Through 'Shadow Banning,' Algorithms to Censor Opposing Political Opinions." Project Veritas, January 11, 2018. https://www.projectveritas.com/news/undercover-video-twitter-engineers-to-ban-a-way-of-talking-through-shadow-banning-algorithms-to-censor-opposing-political-opinions/.

Powell, Diane Hennacy. *The ESP Enigma*: The Scientific Case for Psychic Phenomena. New York: Walker, 2010.

Quigley, Carroll. *Tragedy and Hope: A History of the World in Our Time.* New York, NY: Macmillan, 1966. https://archive.org/details/tragedyhopehisto0000quig_d0s3/page/689/mode/2up?q=network.

Radin, Dean. *The Conscious Universe: The Scientific Truth of Psychic Phenomena.* New York: HarperEdge, 1997.

Radin, Dean. *Entangled Minds Extrasensory Experiences in a Quantum Reality*. New York: Paraview, 2006.

Radin, Dean. "Publications." *Dean Radin* website, n.d. https://www.deanradin.com/publications

Radin, Dean. *Real Magic: Ancient Wisdom, Modern Science, and a Guide to the Secret Power of the Universe*. New York: Harmony, 2018.

Radin, Dean et al. "Re-Examining Psychokinesis: Commentary on the Bösch, Steinkamp, and Boller Meta-Analysis." *Psychological Bulletin* 132 (2006): 529–32.

Radin, Dean. *Supernormal: Science, Yoga, and the Evidence for Extraordinary Psychic Abilities*. New York: Random House, 2013.

Radin, D. Michel, L., Delorme, A. (2016). "Psychophysical modulation of fringe visibility in a distant double-slit optical system." *Physics Essays*. 29 (1), 14-22.

Riley, Jason. "Why Did Amazon Cancel Justice Thomas?" Wall Street Journal, March 2, 2021. https://www.wsj.com/articles/why-did-amazon-cancel-justice-thomas-11614727562.

Rapp, Nicholas, and Aric Jenkins. "Chart: These 6 Companies Control Much of U.S. Media." *Fortune*, July 24, 2018. https://fortune.com/longform/media-company-ownership-consolidation/.

Raschke, Carl A. *Painted Black: From Drugs Killing to Heavy Metal—The Alarming True Story of How Satanism Is Terrorizing Our Communities*. San Francisco, CA: Harper & Row Publishers, 1990.

Reisman, George. "Why Nazism Was Socialism and Why Socialism Is Totalitarian." *The Mises Institute*. November 11, 2005. https://mises.org/library/why-nazism-was-socialism-and-why-social ism-totalitarian.

Reuters Staff. "Ex-Olympic gymnastics coach faces human trafficking, other charges." *Reuters*, February 25, 2021. https://www.reuters.com/article/us-sports-geddert-charges-idUSKBN2AP2OS.

Reyes, Lorenzo. "Novak Djokovic beats Rafael Nadal in French Open semifinals with fans allowed to defy curfew." *USA Today*, June 11, 2021. https://www.usatoday.com/story/sports/tennis/french/2021/06/11/nadal-djokovic-french-open-match-allowed-end-fans-defy-curfew/7660733002/.

Richardson, Valerie. "'Orwellian': Facebook faces backlash for 'harmful extremist content' alerts." *The Washington Times*, July 4, 2021.

https://www.washingtontimes.com/news/2021/jul/4/backlash-hits-facebook-over-new-extremist-content-/.

Riffee, Mark. "CIA Pitches Scripts to Hollywood." *Wired*, September 16, 2011. https://www.wired.com/2011/09/cia-pitches-hollywood/.

Ring, Kenneth, and Sharon Cooper. *Mindsight: Near-Death and Out-of-Body Experiences in the Blind*. New York: iUniverse, 2008.

Rivas, Titas, Anny Dirven, and Rudolf H. Smit. *The Self Does Not Die: Verified Paranormal Phenomena from Near-Death Experiences*. Durham: IANDS Publications, 2016.

Robinson, James. "Preface." In *The Nag Hammadi Scriptures*, edited by Marvin Meyer. New York, NY: HarperOne, 2007.

Robison, John. *Proofs of a Conspiracy: Against All The Religions and Governments Of Europe, Carried On In The Secret Meetings of Freemasons, Illuminati, and Reading Societies*. 1798 (original publication).

Rockwell Jr., Llewellyn H. *LewRockwell.com* website, https://www.lewrockwell.com/.

Rockwell Jr., Llewellyn H. "What Is Fascism? It's the System We've Been Living under for Decades." *The Mises Institute*: January 15, 2021. https://mises.org/wire/what-fascism-its-system-weve-been-living-under-decades.

Rockwell Jr., Llewellyn H. "Why Professors Hate the Market." *The Mises Institute*, June 5, 2000. https://mises.org/library/why-professors-hate-market.

RonPaulLibertyReport. "Fauci: 'Masks Forever!'" YouTube video, May 10, 2021. https://www.youtube.com/watch?v=mTTAWFjIPmg.

Rose, Larken. *The Most Dangerous Superstition*. Larken Rose, 2012.

Rosenblum, Bruce, and Fred Kuttner. *Quantum Enigma: Physics Encounters Consciousness*. Oxford: Oxford University Press, 2011.

Ross, Colin A. *The C.I.A. Doctors: Human Rights Violations By American Psychiatrists*. Richardson, Texas: Manitou Communications, Inc., 2006.

Rossini, Chris. "The Decades-Long Obsession With 'Safety At All Costs' Has Reached Its Culmination." *Ron Paul Liberty Report*, August 25, 2021. http://www.ronpaullibertyreport.com/archives/the-decades-long-obsession-with-safety-at-all-costs-has-reached-its-culmination.

Rothbard, Murray N. *America's Great Depression*. Auburn, AL: The Ludwig von Mises Institute, 2000.

Rothbard, Murray N. *Anatomy of the State*. Auburn, AL: The Ludwig von Mises Institute, 2009.

Rothbard, Murray N. *The Case Against the Fed*. Auburn, AL: The Ludwig von Mises Institute, 2007.

Rothbard, Murray N. *The Ethics of Liberty*. New York, NY: New York University Press, 2002.

Rothbard, Murray N. *For a New Liberty: The Libertarian Manifesto*. Auburn, AL: The Ludwig von Mises Institute, 2006.

Rothbard, Murray N. *Man, Economy, and State: A Treatise on Economic Principles* with *Power and Market: Government and the Economy*. Auburn, AL: The Ludwig von Mises Institute, 2009.

Rothbard, Murray N. "Myth and Truth About Libertarianism." *The Mises Institute* website, July 20, 2019. https://mises.org/library/myth-and-truth-about-libertarianism.

Rothbard, Murray N. *Society Without a State*. December 28, 1974. https://www.lewrockwell.com/1970/01/murray-n-rothbard/how-anarchism-can-work/.

Sagan, Carl. *The Demon-Haunted World: Science As a Candle in the Dark*. New York, NY: Random House, 1995.

Schnabel, Jim. *Remote Viewers: The Secret History of America's Psychic Spies*. New York: Dell, 1997.

Schrödinger, Erwin. *What Is Life? With Mind and Matter and Autobiographical Sketches*. London: Cambridge University Press, 1969.

Schumm, Laura. "What Was Operation Paperclip?" *History.com*, March 4, 2020. https://www.history.com/news/what-was-operation-paperclip.

Schwartz, Gary. "Is Consciousness More than the Brain?" *Gary Schwartz* webpage, video, n.d. http://opensciences.org/gary-schwartz and https://www.youtube.com/watch?v=x-6hosFAObI.

Schwartz, Ian. "WH's Psaki: "We're Flagging Problematic Posts For Facebook That Spread Disinformation." *Real Clear Politics*, July 15, 2021. https://www.realclearpolitics.com/video/2021/07/15/psaki_were_flagging_problematic_posts_for_facebook_that_spread_disinformation.html.

Sears, JP. Instagram post (@awakenwithjp). February 8, 2021, https://www.instagram.com/p/CLCFEP6FsAr/?igshid=kibupbvksqxe.

Select Committee to Study Government Operations with Respect to Intelligence Activities, *Final Report*. April 1976, https://archive.org/details/finalreportofsel01unit/page/n3/mode/2up (Internet Archive).

Sharma, Poonam, and Jim Tucker, MD. "Cases of the Reincarnation Type with Memories from the Intermission Between Lives." *Journal of Near-Death Studies* 23 (2) (2004), 101–118.

Sheldrake, Rupert. *Dogs That Know When Their Owners Are Coming Home*. New York, New York: Crown, 1999.

"Sheldrake, Rupert." *Wikipedia*, accessed March 1, 2021. https://en.wikipedia.org/wiki/Rupert_Sheldrake.

Shermer, Michael. "Why a Near-Death Experience Isn't Proof of Heaven – Did a neurosurgeon go to heaven?" *Scientific American*, April 1, 2013. https://www.scientificamerican.com/article/why-near-death-experience-isnt-proof-heaven/

Shushan, Gregory. *Near-Death Experiences in Indigenous Religions*. New York, NY: Oxford University Press, 2018.

Singleton, Norm. "Transcript of Farewell Address" (referring to Ron Paul's farewell address to Congress). *Campaign for Liberty*, November 12, 2012. http://www.campaignforliberty.org/national-blog/transcript-of-farewell-address/.

Skeptic. *Skepticism 101*, June 26, 2012. https://www.skeptic.com/academic-discipline/parapsychology/.

Sonmez, Felicia and Amy B Wang. "YouTube suspends Ron Johnson for a week after GOP senator touts questionable drugs to fight covid-19." *The Washington Post*, June 11, 2021. https://www.washingtonpost.com/politics/sen-johnson-youtube-coronavirus-medicine/2021/06/11/1055ce46-caf0-11eb-81b1-34796c7393af_story.html.

Spivack, Barry, and Patricia Anne Saunders. *An Antidote to Violence*. Winchester, UK: Changemakers Books, 2020.

Stanton, Gregory. "THE TEN STAGES OF GENOCIDE." *Genocide Watch* website, n.d. https://www.genocidewatch.com/tenstages.

Stebner, Beth. "Bobby Kennedy assassin still claims he was 'victim of mind control and his gun didn't fire fatal shot' in new appeal after parole is denied." *Daily Mail*, December 15, 2001. https://www.dailymail.co.uk/news/article-2066883/Robert-F-Kennedy-assassin-Sirhan-Sirhan-claims-victim-mind-control.html.

Stevenson, Ian. *Reincarnation and Biology: A Contribution to the Etiology of Birthmarks and Birth Defects*. Vol. 1, *Birthmarks*. Westport, CT: Praeger, 1997.

Stone, Sean. "G Edward Griffin on 'Collectivism.'" YouTube video, April 8, 2021. https://www.youtube.com/watch?v=-nH2Igq1gh8.

Stone, Sean. "John Lamb Lash on the Archon Empire." YouTube video, March 5, 2021. https://www.youtube.com/watch?v=jukIPVRlnDs.

Stone, Sean. *New World Order: A Strategy of Imperialism*. Chicago, IL: Independent Publishers Group, 2012.

Thompson, Angus. "Rescue dogs shot dead by NSW council due to COVID-19 restrictions." *The Sydney Morning Herald*, August 22, 2021. https://www.smh.com.au/national/nsw/rescue-dogs-shot-dead-by-nsw-council-due-to-covid-19-restrictions-20210821-p58ksh.html.

TomWoodsTV. "Ep. 1875 Michael Malice on How to Make Radical Ideas Approachable." YouTube video, April 13, 2021. https://www.youtube.com/watch?v=k0jdavqhZe4&t=2182s.

TomWoodsTV. "Ep. 1940 Helping the Poor Without the State." *Tom Woods.com website*, July 21, 2021. https://tomwoods.com/ep-1940-helping-the-poor-without-the-state/.

TomWoodsTV. "Monopoly Is Everywhere, Say Mainstream Economists; Austrians Roll Eyes." July 29, 2015. https://www.youtube.com/watch?v=3g7vkb_f89s.

Traynor, Ian. "UK arranged transfer of Nazi scientists to Australia." *The Guardian*, August 16, 1999. https://www.theguardian.com/uk/1999/aug/17/iantraynor.

Tressoldi, P. E. "Extraordinary Claims Require Extraordinary Evidence: The Case of Non-Local Perception, a Classical and Bayesian Review of Evidences." *Frontiers in Psychology* 2, no. 117 (2011).

Tsakiris, Alex. "Kevin Annett, Whistleblower of an Evil Church |433|." *Skeptiko* website, November 15, 2019. https://skeptiko.com/kevin-annett-whistleblower-of-an-evil-church-433/.

Tsakiris, Alex. "211. Montana State University's Ardy Sixkiller Clarke Compiles 1,000 Accounts of American Indian Contact With UFO Phenomena." *Skeptiko* website, May 28, 2015, https://skeptiko.com/ardy-sixkiller-clarke-1000-accounts-of-american-indian-contact-with-ufo-phenomena/.

Trudeau, Justin. Twitter post, March 29, 2021. https://twitter.com/justintrudeau/status/1376662503720112132?s=21.

Turing, Alan Mathison. "Computing Machinery and Intelligence." Mind: A Quarterly Review of Psychology and Philosophy LIX, no. 236 (1950): 433–60.

United States Holocaust Memorial Museum. "Jewish Badge," n.d. https://www.ushmm.org/learn/timeline-of-events/1939-1941/jewish-badge-decreed.

United States Holocaust Memorial Museum. "Reichstag Fire Decree," n.d. https://www.ushmm.org/learn/timeline-of-events/1933-1938/reichstag-fire-decree.

Utts, Jessica. "An Assessment of the Evidence for Psychic Functioning." *Journal of Parapsychology* 59, no. 4 (1995): 289–320.

van Lommel et al. "Near-death experience in survivors of cardiac arrest: a prospective study in the Netherlands." *The Lancet*, Vol. 358, 2001. https://pimvanlommel.nl/wp-content/uploads/2017/11/Lancet-artikel-Pim-van-Lommel.pdf.

van Lommel, Pim. "Near-Death Experience, Consciousness, and the Brain: A New Concept about the Continuity of Our Consciousness Based on Recent Scientific Research on Near-Death Experience in Survivors of Cardiac Arrest." *World Futures* 62 (2006): 134–51.

von Mises, Ludwig. *Human Action: A Treatise on Economics*. Auburn, AL: The Ludwig von Mises Institute, 1998.

von Mises, Ludwig. *Liberty & Property*. Auburn, AL: The Ludwig von Mises Institute, 2009. https://cdn.mises.org/Liberty%20and%20Property_3.pdf

Wahbeh, Helané. "Collective Consciousness and Our Sense of Interconnectedness." *Cardiology & Vascular Research*, 5(1), 2021.

"Wikipedia co-founder: I no longer trust the website I created." *Unherd* website, July 14, 2021. https://unherd.com/thepost/wikipedia-co-founder-i-no-longer-trust-the-website-i-created/.

"Wikipedia Under Threat." Rupert Sheldrake webpage, n.d. https://www.sheldrake.org/about-rupert-sheldrake/blog/wikipedia-under-threat.

Wehle, Kimberly. "COVID-19: Justice Alito overstepped judicial boundaries." *The Hill*, November 19, 2020. https://www.msn.com/en-us/news/politics/covid-19-justice-alito-overstepped-judicial-boundaries/ar-BB1baUY5.

Weiss, Bari. *Resignation Letter*. https://www.bariweiss.com/resignation-letter.

Whitehead, John W. "The Path to Total Dictatorship: America's Shadow Government and Its Silent Coup." *Ron Paul Institute for Peace and Prosperity*, October 24, 2016. http://ronpaulinstitute.org/archives/featured-articles/2016/october/24/the-path-to-total-dictatorship-americas-shadow-government-and-its-silent-coup/.

Williams, B. J. "Revisiting the Ganzfeld ESP Debate: A Basic Review and Assessment." *Journal of Scientific Exploration* 25, no. 4 (2011): 639–61.

Williamson, Chris. "Michael Malice – What Is The Hardest Question For Anarchism To Answer?" YouTube video, June 2, 2021. https://www.youtube.com/watch?v=nzvgqlAkZcE.

Wilson, Woodrow. *The New Freedom: A Call for the Emancipation of the Generous Energies of a People*. Edgewood Cliffs, New Jersey: Prentice-Hall Inc, 1961 (material cited from 1913 version contained in the 1961 publication). https://archive.org/details/Woodrow WilsonTheNewFreedom/page/n3/mode/2up?q=small+group+of+men.

Woods Jr., Thomas E. *Nullification: How to Resist Federal Tyranny in the 21st Century*. Washington, DC: Regnery Publishing, Inc, 2010.

Woolacott, Marjorie, and Bettina Peyton. "Verified account of near-death experience in a physician who survived cardiac arrest." *Explore*, 17(3): 213–219, 2021. https://www.sciencedirect.com/science/article/abs/pii/S1550830720301117?via%3Dihub.

Wujian. "Testimony for Tom Lantos Human Rights Commission Hearing, November 10, 2009, Wujian, citizen of the People's Republic of China." https://chrissmith.house.gov/uploadedfiles/2_wujian_testimony.pdf

Yogananda, Paramahansa. *Autobiography of a Yogi*. UK: Rider, 1955.

Zimbardo, Philip. *The Lucifer Effect: Understanding How Good People Turn Evil.* New York, NY: Random House, 2008.

Zuckerman, Esther. "The 'Proof of Heaven' Author Has Now Been Thoroughly Debunked by Science." *The Atlantic*, July 2, 2013. https://www.theatlantic.com/culture/archive/2013/07/proof-heaven-author-debunked/313681/.

INDEX

A

Abdication of responsibility, 30–31
Acton, Lord, 30
After: A Doctor Explores What Near-Death Experiences Reveal about Life and Beyond (Greyson), 151
Alexander, Eben, 148, 161
Alito, Samuel, xvii
Alternative consciousness research, 142
Alzheimer's disease, 127
Amazon
    business model of, 106
    censorship of content, 54
American intelligentsia, capacity for denial, xix
America's Great Depression (Rothbard), 97
Amnesia, xi, 160, 183, 204
Anarchism, 79
Anarcho-capitalism, 79, 197, 206
Anarchy, 188
    international, 9
    State and elimination of, 9
Anatomy of the State (Rothbard), 39–40
Annett, Kevin, 40
Anomalies, lack of evidence on existence of, 138
An Antidote to Violence (Spivack and Saunders), 166, 201
Archer, Rick, 136
Artificial intelligence, application of, xiii
Atoms, 124
AT&T/Time Warner, 45
Australia
    COVID-19 in, xvi, 5
    COVID-19 vaccine in, 5
Austrian School of economics, 88–95, 169–171, 197–198
Authority
    obedience to, 31–32
    of State as illegitimate, 8

B

Bailyn, Bernard, 77
Bain, Donald, 62, 63
Barnett, William, 90–91
Barušs, Imants, 137
Bias in the media, 48–49

Biden, Joe, in presidential election of 2020, 47
Big Bang theory, 124
Biko, Steve, 37
The Black Book of Communism (Courtois et al.), 84, 198
Block, Walter
on people's preferences, 90–91
on private property, 80, 81
on privatization, 115, 116
Blome, Kurt, 57–58
BMJ, 53
Böhm-Bawerk, Eugene von, 88, 197
Brady, Graham, 4
Brain, dying, as cause of hallucinations, 150–155
Brainwashing in mind control, 25, 37
Brave New World (Huxley), 44
Brinkley, Dannion, 155–156, 158
Britain. *See also* England
conquest of West Africa, 112
Buddha at the Gas Pump (Archer), 136
Buddhism, 136
Business, destruction of the environment, 115–118
Butterfly effect, 193

C

Camp King, 58
Canada, COVID-19 travel regulations in, xv
Capitalism, 198
laissez-faire, 88
Cardeña, Etzel, 131
Carroll, Sean, 140
The Case Against the Fed (Rothbard), 100
"Cato's Letters," 77
CBS, 45
CDC, 55
Censorship, 53–54
Central banks, monetary policy and, 100–103
Central Cancer Institute, 58
Centralized global power structures, 191
CHAOS: Charles Manson, the CIA, and the Secret History of the Sixties, 65
Chemistry, 124
Chile
life in, xiv–xv
as test lab, xv
China
depopulation tactics in, 70
pilot "social credit" schemes in, xiv
surveillance cameras in, xiii
Chissano, President of Mozambique, 166
Christianity, Gnostic, 143
CIA
assassination of Kennedy, John, and, 39
establishment of Entertainment Liaison Office, 50–51
psychic spying program of, 131–132
The CIA Doctors: Human Rights Violations by American Psychiatrists (Ross), 70–71
Civil liberties, erosion to, xii
Clarke, Ardy, 145
Classification as stage in genocidal situations, 68
Cleaning up, 186
Climate, 48
Clinton, Bill, 54
apology to Tuskegee subjects, 71
CNN
propaganda and, 46–48
weaponization of fear and, 48
Cognitive dissonance, xvii–xx, 15, 28, 46, 122, 137, 142, 198
Cohen, Jeremy (Spike), 13
Coherence, 166, 192
Collective evolution, 172
Collectivism, 172–176

Comcast, 45
Common good, 172
Commons, tragedy of the, 117
Communism, 81–84, 198
death toll at the hands of regimes in, 84
The Communist Manifesto (Marx and Engels), 83
Competition in encouraging innovation, 93
Consciousness, 198
as abstract, 128
elevating humanity's level of, 165–169
as enlivening, 184
nonlocal, 205
origin of, 128
science of, 136
as sense of experiencing life, 124
shift in, 183–194
unified field of, xi
Conscription as function for society, 17
Conspiracy theories, 38–40
public's negative view of, 38–39
Constitution, importance of enforcing, xvi–xvii
Consumer-producer dynamic, 89–90
The Control of Candy Jones (Bain), 62
Copper, exhaustion of, 117
Coronavirus Information Hub, 52
Corporate behavior, State regulation of, 115–118
COVID-19
in Australia, xvi
in France, 4–5
global trends in, 5–6
handling of, 191
as leak from Wuhan Institute of Virology, 38
in United Kingdom, 4
COVID-19 crisis, 3
as constitutional stress test, xvii
COVID-19 vaccine
in Australia, 5
convincing people to take, 5
plans to curb hesitancy, 52
Coyne, Jerry, 139
Crisis. weaponization of, xv–xvi
Critical mass, 193
Crony-capitalism, 98, 198–199
Cronyism, 97–98, 199
Cryptocurrencies, 102

D

Dangerous psychology, 27–35
Decentralization of power, 23, 191
Defending our nation, 68
Dehumanization, 30
as stage in genocidal situations, 69
Democracy
rise of, 175
statist structure of, 175
Denial, xix
as stage in genocidal situations, 69
Deny, Discredit, and Distract, 40
Depopulation, 25
mind control and, 68–71
Detachment, 185
Devotion, focus on, 184
Dialogues (Plato), 148
Digital health passport, carrying of, 172–173
DiLorenzo, Thomas, 81–82, 85, 105–106, 107
Direct knowing, 135
Discernment, xx
Discrimination as stage in genocidal situations, 69
Dispelling Wetiko: Breaking the Curse of Evil (Levy), 145
Disputes
management of, 113
resolution of, 112–114
Dissociative identity disorder, 129
Dissonance, cognitive, 198
Diversionary tactic, 45
Divine hand, 170

Division of labor, 171
Division, sowing of, 55
Djokovic, Novak, 5
DNA, 124
Domino effect, xx
Dossey, Larry, 130, 203
Double standard of morality, 95
Douglass, Frederick, memoir of, on escaping from slavery, 75–76
Dulles, Allen, 58
Dying brain, as cause of hallucinations, 150–155

E

Earth, 6
  resources of, 6
Ecologists, modern, 116
Economics
  Austrian School of, 88–95, 169–171, 197–198
  human action and, 169
  Keynesian, 95–97, 200
  relationship of metaphysics to politics and, 121–180
Economy, State intervention in the, 198–199
Education, 55–57
Edwards, David, 167
Egalitarianism, 199
The Egyptian Book of the Dead, 148
Einstein, Albert, 133
Eisenhower, Dwight, farewell speech of, 42–43
Elections, fairness of, 28–29
Electromagnetic spectrum, 123
Empty space, 167
End the Fed (Paul), 100
An End to Upside Down Living (Gober), 122
An End to Upside Down Thinking (Gober), 122, 139
Energetic aspects, focus on, 184–185
Engels, Frederick, 83
England. *See also* Britain
  challenges in conquering Ireland, 111–112
Enlightenment, 161
Enslavement
  on a metaphysical level, xi–xii
  on a physical level, xii
Entangled minds, 133
Environment, business destruction of, 115–118
Epstein, Jeffrey, 28
Equality, 174
Erosions to civil liberties, xii
Essence versus perception, xx
Eugenics, Nazis' endorsement of, 68
Evil
  accepting the reality of hidden, xix
  metaphysical, 144–146
Evolution, spiritual, 159–161, 169, 192, 202, 205
Exemption from morality, 14, 199
Extermination as stage in genocidal situations, 69
Externalities, negative, 116
Extraterrestrial influences, 144
Eysenck, H. J., 142

F

Facebook
  censoring articles, 38
  efforts to curb extremism, 53
  plans to curb vaccine hesitancy, 52
Faggin, Federico, 134–136
False-flag operations, 25, 65–68
Fascism, 85–86, 199
  defined, 85
Fauci, Anthony, 52
Federal Reserve, 100–101
Field phenomenon, 145
For a New Liberty (Rothbard), 194
Foreign Intelligence Surveillance Act, 18
France, COVID-19 in, 4–5
Franklin, Benjamin, 87
Freedom of speech, 82
Free markets, 115, 189
  advocates of, 170

systems of, 92–94

G

Genocidal situations, stages of, 68–69
Genocide Watch, 68
Germany
burning of the Reichstag in, 66
Hitler Youth program in Nazis, 55–56
life in Nazi, xii, 15–16, 30, 58, 68
Global Consciousness Project, 165–166, 192, 199–200
Gnostic Christianity, 143
Gnosticism, 136
Gober, Mark, 184
God, reality of, 130
Gold as a precious metal, 101
Golden Rule
defined, 200
as embedded in reality, 25
life review and, 201
living in accordance with, 184, 188
as primary aspect of natural law, 158–159
statism and, 168
voluntaryism and, 176, 202
Gold-standard test, 118
Good Samaritans, 176
existence of, 110
Google, acquisition of Keyhole, 51
Google Earth, 51
Gottlieb, Sidney, 58, 60–61
Government
gospel of, 15
intervention by, 102
as organized crime, 3–26
privatizing functions of, 105–118
Government-sponsored mind-control programs
Jones, Candy, case study as, 61–65
Nazi-influenced, 58
Operation Paperclip as, 57–58
of the United States, 58–61
universality of reports and, 61
Grant, Arlene, 63–64
Great American Experiment, 78
Great Depression, Keynesian economics and, 95–97
"GREEN RUN," 71
Greyson, Bruce, 127, 155, 157, 158
on near-death experiences, 151, 152–153
on primitive cultures, 150
Griffin, G. Edward, 174
Growing up, 187
Guerilla warfare, 112
"Guerrilla Skepticism" group, 138

H

Haddad, Tareq, resignation from *Newsweek,* 49–50
Hallucinations, dying brain as cause of, 150–155
Hammond, D. Corydon, 61
Hansas, John, 113, 114
Hare, Robert, 33–34
Hate training, 63
Hawkins, David, 160, 173, 185–186
on distinction of perception versus essence, xx
Hayek, F. A., 85, 88, 94, 174, 197
Hazlitt, Henry, 88, 197
Heine, Heinrich, 54
Heisenberg, Werner, 168
Henry, Richard Conn, 167
Herbener, Jeffrey, 98–99
Hinduism, 136
Hobbes, Thomas, 6–7, 10
Hofstadter, Douglas, 141
Hollywood, 50–51
Holocaust Memorial Museum, 66
Homesteading, 80–81
Hoover, Herbert, on Communist threat, 96–97
Hoover, J. Edgar, 42
Hoover New Deal, 97
Ho'oponopono, 186

Hoppe, Hans-Hermann, 11–12, 108
Human action
defined, 169
economics and, 169
source of, 170
Humanity
elevating level of consciousness in, 165–169
radical, 123
Human psychology, 29
Human-rights violations, 82–83
Humans, innate dark side of, 6
Humility, radical, 123
Huxley, Aldous, 44–45
Hylan, John Francis, 42
Hyman, Ray, 141
Hypno-programming, 65

I
The Idea of the World (Kastrup), 134
Ignorance, 187
recognizing extent of, xviii
Illuminati secret society, formation of, in Europe, 41
Individualism, 172–176
Individualistic collectivism, 174
Infinite intelligence, 163–164
Inflation, 88
Inner mechanics of power structure, 43–44
Innovation, competition in encouraging, 93
Innovative solutions, 106–107
Inouye, Daniel K., visions of government of, 43
In-Q-Tel, 51
Insanity, defined, 25
Intel, design of first microprocessor at, 134
Intellectual leaders, role of, in society, 56
Intelligence, infinite, 163–164
Intermission memories, 160
International anarchy, 9, 188
International Peace Project in the Middle East (IPPME), 166
Invasions of privacy, 18–19
Involuntary servitude, 17–18
Ireland
England's challenges in conquering, 111–112
voluntaryism in, 23
Ishii, Shirō, 58
Islam, mystical, 136

J
Jacksonian movement, 77–78
Jahn, Robert, 141
Jeffersonian movement, 77–78
Jenner, William E., 42
Jensen, Gilbert, 63
Jews, sending to concentration camps, xii
Johnson, Boris, 4
Johnson, Ron, 54
Jones, Candy, case study of, 61–65
Josephson, Brian, 140
Journalism, death of, 50
Journal of Nervous and Mental Disease, 148
Judaism, mystical, 136
Jury duty, as function for society, 17

K
Kabbalah, 136
Kahneman, Daniel, 23
Karma, 160, 192, 200, 202
Kastrup, Bernardo, 128, 129, 134, 203
Kelly, Ed, 140
Kennedy, John F., xvi
assassination of, 39
Kennedy, Robert F., xvi
murder of, 65
Kennedy, Robert F., Jr., 54
Keyhole, 51
Keynesian economics, 200
and the Great Depression, 95–97
Keynes, John Maynard, 96
Kinzer, Stephen, 57–58, 60
Knowledge, focus on, 184
Krauss, Lawrence, 140

Kundalini, 185

L

Laissez-faire capitalism, 88
Laws, existence of, without a State, 112–114
Less brain, more consciousness pattern, 127–128
Letting Go: The Pathway of Surrender (Hawkins), 185–186
Leviathan, 7
Levy, Paul, 145
Liberated mindset, promotion of, xx
Libertarianism, 200
 influence in early America, 76–79
 spiritual, 176, 203
 voluntaryism as form of, 76–77
Liberty
 erosion of, xii
 negation of, 189
 path to true, 183–194
 promotion of, 164
Liberty Defined (Paul), 24
Life After Death (Moody), 148
Life review, 155–159, 200–201
Lines of development, 201
Locke, John, 10, 80
Lommel, Pim van, 151
Long, Jeffrey, 149, 155
Lorimer, David, 156
Love, unconditional, 136
The Lucifer Effect (Zimbardo), 30
Lying, xviii–xix

M

Mack, John, 144–145
Mafia, 8
Maharishi Effect, 166, 167, 192, 201
Mahasaya, Sri Lahiri, 192
Mainstream media, 44–50
Malia, Martin, 86
Malice, Michael, xix
Malleability, mechanism and manifestation of, 192
Man, Economy, and State (Rothbard), 169
Manipulative capacity, 45–46
Manson, Charles, 65
March, William, 34
Marx, Karl, 83
Materialism, 95
 scientific, 124, 125
Maturation, 187
Media
 bias in the, 48–49
 mainstream, 44–50
 social, 51–55
Meditation, 134, 166
 transcendental, 166
Mediumship, 132, 201
Memories, intermission, 160
Memory implantation, 65
Menger, Carl, 88, 89, 197
Metaparadigm, metaphysical, 124–130
Metaphysical evil, 144–146
Metaphysical evolution, 26
Metaphysical level, enslavement on a, xi–xii
Metaphysical metaparadigm, 124–130
Metaphysics, relation to politics and economics, 121–180
Microsoft, efforts to curb extremism, 53
Milgram, Stanley, 31
Military emergencies, as problem for voluntarist society, 110–112
Military-industrial complex, 42–43
Mind control, 37–71, 142–144
 brainwashing in, 25, 37
 Candy Jones case study and, 61–65
 conspiracy theories and, 38–40
 defined, 201
 depopulation in, 68–71
 education in, 55–57
 false-flag operations in, 65–68
 government-sponsored programs in, 57–65
 Hollywood in, 50–51

mainstream media in, 44–50
secret influence in, 40–44
social media and technology companies in, 51–55
State reliance on, 25
universality of reports on, 61
Mind impacting matter, 131, 165, 167
Mind-matter interactions, 204
Mind-to-mind communication, 131, 205–206
Mises Institute, 197
Mises, Ludwig von, 88, 90-91, 169, 189, 197
MK-ULTRA mind-control programming, 60, 65
Monetary economic policy, 201–202
Monetary policy, central banks and, 100–103
Monopoly, 98–100
State as a, 9–10
Moody, Raymond, 148
Moral conundrums, 15–17
Morality
embedded in reality, 147–161
exemption from, 199
inverting, 14–15
taxation and, 12–14
Mossbridge, Julia, 137
Multidimensional influences, 144
Murphy, Philip, xvi
Mussolini, Benito, 85
Mystical Islam, 136
Mystical Judaism, 136

N
Nadal, Rafael, 4–5
Nag Hammadi scriptures, 143, 144
Namibia, sterilization of HIV-positive women in, 70
The Nature of the Rulers, 144
Nazi Germany, 30
life in, xii, 15–16
Nazis, xii–xiii
endorsement of eugenics, 68
use of Hitler Youth program by, 55–56
Near-death experiences (NDEs), 132, 134, 147, 202
basics, 148–150
dying brain as cause of hallucinations in, 150–155
life review in, 155–159
patterns in, 127
reincarnation and, 161
spiritual evolution and, 159–161
Near-Death Experiences in Indigenous Religions (Shushan), 149
Nebel, John, 62, 64
Negative externalities, 116
Nelson, Peter, 116
The New Freedom (Wilson), 41–42
Newman, Jonathan, 92
News Corporation, 45
New Zealand, COVID-19 in, xvi
9/11, 19
Nonaggression principle, 79, 105, 202
Nonattachment, 185
Nonduality, 178, 202
Nondual voluntaryism, 176–178, 192, 202–203
applications of, 178–180
Nonlocal consciousness, 205
North Korea
brainwashing in, 37
life in, xii
North Star, 24

O
Obedience to authority, 31–32
Obedience to Authority (Milgram), 31–32
Occam's Razor, 133
O'Keefe, James, 54
O'Neill, Tom, 65
One Mind framework, 133, 146, 203
alignment of voluntaryism and, 147

comparison of physicalism and, 177
direct experiences of the, 134
encouragement of collective evolution, 172
essence of who we are and, 174
intelligence of the broader consciousness and, 168
psychokinesis science within the, 167
referencing of, 176
State actions and regulations and, 171–172
statism as incompatible with, 147
true nature and, 185
Operation Artichoke, 58–60
Operation Bluebird, 58–59
Operation Mongoose, 67
Operation Northwoods, 67–68
Operation Paperclip, 57–58, 67, 201
Organization as stage in genocidal situations, 69
Organized crime, government as, 3–26
O'Rourke, P. J., 97
Oswald, Lee Harvey, 39

P

Paradigm shifts, 137
Paranormal, scientific evidence for the, 130–131
Parker, Adrian, 140
Parnia, Sam, 154
Passover, 83
Past lives, 132
Patriot Act of 2001, 18–19
Paul, Ron, xvii, 89, 96, 100, 102, 189–190
farewell address to Congress, 21
on freedom and safety, 19
on sacrificing for imaginary safety, xvi
PayPal, efforts to curb extremism, 53
Pelosi, Nancy, 45
People in authority, lying by, xvi
Perception versus essence, xx
Persecution, as stage in genocidal situations, 69
Peyton, Bettina, 154
Psychic phenomena, claims on, 139–142
Physicalism, 124, 133–136, 137, 178, 203. *See also* Scientific materialism
alternative to, 128, 129
comparison with One Mind framework and, 177
humanity and, 187
philosophical arguments that challenge, 133
worldview in, 125
Physical level, enslavement on a, xii
Physical reality, 166
Pinker, Steven, 140
Planck, Max, 128
Plato, 148
Polarization as stage in genocidal situations, 69
Police services
in protecting the poor, 109–110
in providing safety, 108–109
Political belief systems, rigidity of, xviii
Political Left, 13, 79, 205
Political monopolies, assumptions on, 10
Political Right, 13, 79, 205
Politics, 164
relationship of metaphysics to economics and, 121–180
Poor, police services in protecting, 109–110
Power
decentralization of, 191
nature of, 77
Power structure, inner mechanics of, 43–44
Precognition, 131, 203
Presidential elections

of 2016, 29
of 2020, 29, 47
Press, manipulative capacity of, 45–46
Princeton Engineering Anomalies Research Lab (PEAR), 141
Poisoner in Chief (Kinzer), 57–58
Privacy, invasions of, 18–19
Private property, 80–81
as central of voluntaryism, 80–81
control of, 82
sanctioned aggression against, 180
unique attributes of, 164
Private-property rights, 105, 204
Privatization, broader implications of, 116–117
The Privatization of Roads and Highways (Block), 115
Privatizing government functions, 105–118
Problem-Reaction-Solution, 65–66
Productivity, superiority in, 171
Project Veritas, 46, 52, 54
Proof of Heaven (Alexander), 148
Proofs of a Conspiracy (Robison), 41
Propaganda, triumphs of, 44
Psychedelic trips, 134
Psychic virus, 145
Psychokinesis, 131, 204
science of, 165, 167
Psychological imprisonment, xi–xii
Psychology, 27–35
human, 29
obedience to authority and, 31–32
psychopathy and, 32–35
Stanford Prison experiment and, 29–31
Psychopathy, 32–35, 204
Public domain, 10
Public interest, diversion from conspiracy theories, 39–40
Public sector, 105

Q

Quantum entanglement, 133, 204
Quantum mechanics, 133
Quantum physics, 133, 136, 204
Quantum theory, 168
Quigley, Carroll, 43

R

Radiation experiments, 71
Radical humility, 123
Radin, Dean, 124–125, 131, 133
Raschke, Carl, xix
Reality
morality embedded in, 147–161
nature of, xi, 121–146
physical, 166
Real Magic (Radin), 131
Reed, Thomas B., 24
Reichstag, burning of the, 66
Reincarnation, 161, 204
life review and research on, 159
near-death experience journey and, 161
Remote viewing, 130, 132, 204–205
Resonance, 135–136
Resonant Mind: Life Review in the Near-Death Experience (Lorimer), 156
Responsibility, abdication of, 30–31
Ritual Abuse in the Twenty-First Century: Psychological, Forensic, Social, and Political Considerations, 145
Roads, care of, 114–115
The Road to Serfdom (Hayek), 85
Robinson, James, 143
Robison, John, 41
Rockwell, Lew, 85, 191, 199
Rose, Larken, 8, 12, 14, 15, 19, 27–28, 32, 78, 107, 199
flawed thinking and, 27–28
Rosenblum, Bruce, 142
Ross, Colin A., 70–71
Rothbard, Murray, 88–89
as advocate of the free market,

170
on Britain's conquest of West Africa, 112
capitalism and, 96, 97
on communism, 83–84
on compulsory jury service, 17
on conscription, 17
on conspiracy theory, 39–40
on defining the State, 20–21
on development of legal systems, 112
on England's challenges in conquering Ireland, 111–112
on exhaustion of copper ore, 117
on the Federal Reserve, 100–101
on framing of the socialistic perspective, 82
on free market, 108–109, 110
on homesteading of nonland property, 80–81
on human action, 169
on human-rights violations, 82–83
on individual needs, 175–176
on innovative solutions, 106–107
on limited government, 77–78
on market economy, 94–95
modern ecology and, 116
monopolies and, 99, 100
on morality, 16
ostracization in the Middle Ages, 113
on public opinion, 56–57
rule of the State and, 9–10
on the State, 20, 205
superiority in productivity and, 171
on trying liberty in the modern world, 194
on variety in human beings, 171
on voluntaryism, 23, 206
Rousseau, Jean-Jacques, 10
Russ, Raymond, 167

S

Safety
erosion of liberty under guise of providing, xii
police services in providing, 108–109
Sagan, Carl, xix
Salerno, Joseph, 97
Sanger, Larry, 54–55, 138
Saunders, Patricia Anne, 166, 201
Saved by the Light (Brinkley), 155–156
Schopenhauer, Arthur, on truth, 38
Schrödinger, Erwin, 129, 203
Science, suppressed, 137–142
Scientific evidence for the paranormal, 130–131
Scientific materialism, 124, 125. *See also* Physicalism
Sears, J. P., 38
Secret influence, 40–44
conspiracy and, 40
Select Committee to Study Government Operations with Respect of Intelligence Activities, 50
Self-defense, aggression in, 79
The Self Does Not Die (Rivas et al), 127, 154, 206
Selfless service, focus on, 184
Servitude, involuntary, 17–18
Sheldrake, Rupert, 137–138
Shushan, Gregory, 149, 155
Sirhan, Sirhan, 65
Six Sigma statistical results, 130–131, 165, 206
Skepticism about the State, 77
Skeptics Society, 138
Slavery, escaping from, 75–76
Snowden, Edward, 18
Social control, 4
Socialism, 81–84, 205
Socialistic perspective, framing of,

82
Social media, technology companies and, 51–55
Society
governing of, 7–8
ideal involvement of State in, 177
Soviet Union
land ownership in, 117
life under Stalin in, xii
Spiegel, Herbert, 64
Spira, Rupert, 187
Spiritual bypass, 186
Spiritual economic theory, 169–172
Spiritual evolution, 159–161, 169, 192, 202, 205
political stance for, 165
Spiritual growth, inhibiting, 186
Spirituality
statism as incompatible with, 168
voluntaryism and, 169
Spiritual libertarianism, 176, 203
Spiritually transformative experiences, 136
Spivack, Barry, 166, 201
Spontaneous awakenings, 134
Spooky action at a distance, 133
Stanford Prison Experiment, 29–31
Stanton, Gregory, on genocidal situations, 68–69
State, 6–10, 205
actions and regulations of, 171
aggression in, 14–15
anarchy and, 9
authority of, as illegitimate, 8
care of roads and, 114–115
as centralized, monopolistic power structure, 40
creation of arbitrary standard of morality, 16–17
critiques of, 27
as danger to own people, 75
defining the, 20–21, 164–165
elimination of anarchy and, 9
exemption from morality, 14
functions of, 176–177
fundamental mode of operation of, 9
governing of society in, 7–8
as hub for insidiousness, 35
ideal involvement in society, 177
intervention in the economy, 171, 198–199
as a monopoly, 9–10
planning in, 91–92
regulation of corporate behavior, 115–118
reliance on mind control, 25
sanctioned aggression against private property, 180
skepticism about the, 77
statism in, 7
on unilateral decision-making authority, 18
voluntaryism and, 22
Statism, 7–8, 190, 205
as coercive, 188
democracy and, 175
humanity and, 187
as incompatible with spirituality, 168
as incompatible with the One Mind perspective, 147
as problematic manner of structuring society, 121
voluntaryism and, 169
Sterilization, 70
Stevenson, Ian, 132
Stockholm syndrome, 75
Sufism, 136
Superiority in productivity, 171
Supreme Court, 29
Sydney, Australia, enforcement of COVID lockdown in, xv
Symbolization, as stage in genocidal situations, 68–69

T

Taxation, and morality, 12–14
Technology companies, social media

and, 51–55
TEDx talks, 138
Telepathy, 131, 205–206
Thomas, Clarence, on censorship, 54
Thompson, Edmund R., 141
Thornton, Mark, 102
The Tibetan Book of the Dead, 148
Tragedy and Hope: A History of the World in Our Time (Quigley), 43
Tragedy of the commons, 117
Transcendental meditation, 166
Trudeau, Justin, xv
Truman, Harry, 58
Trump, Donald
in presidential election of 2020, 47
suspension of from Facebook, Twitter, and YouTube, 54
Turing, Alan, 141, 144
Tuskegee Experiment, 70–71
Twitter
article on Biden, Joe's son, 53–54
efforts to curb extremism, 53
on shadow banning, 52

U

Unconditional love, 136, 160, 163, 202, 205
United Kingdom
Freedom Day in, 4
handling of COVID-19 in, 4
United Nations, 191
United States
Constitution and Bill of Rights in, xvi
influence of libertarianism in, 76–79
Upside down liberty, as mistaken belief, xi
Utts, Jessica, 131, 139

V

Vaccination
COVID-19, 5, 52
importance of mass, 5
Vaccine hesitancy, 52
Veridical out-of-body experiences, 151-154, 206
Viacom, 45
Victoria, Australia, COVID-19 checkpoints in, xv
Vietnam War, guerilla warfare during, 112
Voluntaryism, 21–26, 79–80, 190, 200, 206. *See also* Nondual voluntaryism
alignment with One Mind worldview, 147
applications of nondual, 178–180
as form of libertarianism, 76–77
free market economy and, 88
military emergencies as problem for, 110–112
nonaggression principle and, 105
private property as central to, 80–81
as relative improvement, 121
spiritual evolution and, 165
spirituality and, 169
State and, 22
State-sponsored safety net in, 86–87
von Mises, Ludwig, 88, 90, 91–92, 169, 189

W

Waking up, 183–184
Water Capitalism: The Case for Privatizing Oceans, Rivers, Lakes, and Aquifers (Block and Nelson), 116–117
Weaponization of crisis, xv–xvi
Webb, Whitney, on life in Chile, xiv–xv
Weiss, Bari, 49
Welfare Harms Its Ostensible Beneficiaries (Franklin), 87
Welfare state, 86–88

West Africa, Britain's conquest of, 112
wetiko, 145
Where Is My Mind?, 122
Wikipedia, restriction of information by, 54–55
Wilbur, Ken, 183
Wilson, Woodrow, 41–42
Wisdom, focus on, 184
Without Conscience: The Disturbing World of the Psychopaths Among Us (Hare), 33
Wolf, Naomi, 54
Woods, Tom, xvii, 10, 22, 99, 107
Woollacott, Marjorie, 154
World Economic Forum, 191
World Health Organization, 55, 191
Worldviews
  challenging, xi–xx
  developing new, xviii
Wrap-up smear, 45
Wuhan Institute of Virology, leak of COVID-19 from, 38

X

Xi, President (of China), xiii

Y

Yogi, Maharishi Mahesh, 166
YouTube, 54
  efforts to curb extremism, 53

Z

Zimbardo, Philip, 29–31
Zuckerberg, Mark, 52

ABOUT THE AUTHOR

Mark Gober is an international speaker and the author of *An End to Upside Down Thinking* (2018), which was awarded the IPPY best science book of 2019. He is also the author of *An End to Upside Down Living* (2020) and is the host of the podcast *Where Is My Mind?* (2019). Additionally, he serves on the Board of the Institute of Noetic Sciences and the School of Wholeness and Enlightenment. Previously, Gober was a partner at Sherpa Technology Group in Silicon Valley and worked as an investment banking analyst in New York. He has been named one of *IAM*'s *Strategy 300: The World's Leading Intellectual Property Strategists.*

Gober graduated *magna cum laude* from Princeton University, where he wrote an award-winning thesis on Daniel Kahneman's Nobel Prize–winning "Prospect Theory" and was elected a captain of Princeton's Division I tennis team.

Made in the USA
Columbia, SC
20 February 2022